Modernities in Asian Perspective

Edited by

Kausik Bandyopadhyay

Setu Prakashani

Modernities in Asian Perspective, Ed. Kausik Bandyopadhyay
Cover page design : Dilip Ghosh, First edition : April, 2010

ISBN : 978-93-80677-02-6

Rupees : Four hundred fortyfive only

Published by

Archana Das & Subrata Das
on behalf of Setu Prakashani,
12/A Shankar Ghosh Lane, Kol-6, India.
Ph.: 033-2219 0704 / 09433074548,
setuprakashani@yahoo.co.in
Printed by Imprinta
243/2B, A.P.C. Road
Kolkata - 700 006

List of Contributors

KAUSIK BANDYOPADHYAY is Reader in History at West Bengal State University, Barasat, West Bengal.

RAKHEE BHATTACHARYA is an economist by profession and presently a Fellow at the Maulana Abul Kalam Azad Institute of Asian Studies, Kolkata.

SANJUKTA DAS GUPTA is Reader at the Department of History, University of Calcutta. She has been a Visiting Fellow at Uppsala University, Sweden and at University of Rome, La Sapienza.

SHARMISHTHA GOOPTU is a film scholar. She is a Founding Trustee of the South Asia Research Foundation and Joint Editor of *South Asian History & Culture* (Routledge).

BRIAN A. HATCHER is McFee Professor of Religion and Chair of the Department of Religion at Illinois Wesleyan University.

BINODA KUMAR MISHRA is Fellow at the Maulana Abul Kalam Azad Institute of Asian Studies, Kolkata.

PRIYA SINGH is Fellow at Maulana Abul Kalam Azad Institute of Asian Studies, Kolkata.

ANITA SENGUPTA is Fellow at the Maulana Abul Kalam Azad Institute of Asian Studies, Kolkata.

The tendency in modern civilization is to make the world uniform... Let the mind be universal. The individual should not be sacrificed.

Rabindranath Tagore

Acknowledgements

This volume dates back to a suggestion made by Professor Hari Vasudevan, Director of Maulana Abul Kalam Azad Institute of Asian Studies, Kolkata, in late 2007 to undertake parallel thematic studies in tandem with the project I was then pursuing as a Fellow at the Institute. I met Professor Brian Hatcher, one of the contributors to this volume, around the same time for the first time, and was struck by his idea of multiple modernities in the historical context of colonial Bengal, which, interestingly enough, resembled some of my naïve ideas on the plurality and heterogeneity of modernity, particularly as a cultural construct. I discussed the matter further in greater detail with two of my most affectionate colleagues - Anita Sengupta and Suchandana Chatterjee, who provided me necessary inspiration and support to go ahead with the idea of compiling a volume on the theme. To put it simply, without Anita and Suchandana, this book would never have been conceived, let alone compiled. Rakhee Bhattacharya, as always, has been a source of immense inspiration all through. I also thank the contributors to this volume, who spent their valuable time to offer some excellent pieces of thought in their writings. A special thanks to Riddhisankar Ray for his insightful comment on the title of the book.

Subrata Das of Setu Prakashani, a very good friend for quite some time now, has taken keen interest in publishing the work, and it goes to his credit that the book has come out so smoothly and nicely despite inordinate delays on my part in editing and submitting the final manuscript. Finally, while the ideas and views expressed in the volume are solely those of the authors, I stand solely responsible as the editor for any typographical errors or stylistic lapses in compiling the work.

Kolkata
March 2010

KAUSIK BANDYOPADHYAY

Contents

Prologue

Kausik Bandyopadhyay

> Modernity is easy to inhabit but difficult to define.
>
> Dipesh Chakrabarty[1]

The notion of modernity is prone to various problematic articulations. In the Asian world, given standards of attaining modernity are often implicated with a conventional paradigm of Western challenge and Eastern response in a colonial, semi-colonial or even post-colonial setting by erecting a simple dualism between modernity and tradition. In this model of understanding modernity, emphasis has mostly been put on the theoretical dichotomy between passive acceptance and active borrowing and the agencies of selection and rejection. Yet an assumed autonomy of the borrower suggests that respondent society always tries to create something distinctively modern, yet recognizably different from the Western. However, this holistic appreciation of modernity at times overlooks the heterogeneity, ambivalence and complexity in the process of growth of modern societies in different Asian countries. The transition of modernity from colonial to postcolonial systems has also varied representations and reflections in political philosophy, social thought, indigenous knowledge/education, popular culture or economic development, that raise questions about the received notions of a singular concept of *modernity*. It is therefore relevant to examine whether we can really talk of *modernities* rather than *modernity* in the Asian context.

In the recent past, modernity as a concept and phenomenon has been critically examined.[2] There is an overarching tendency to evaluate modernity as a concept, leading to a multitude of interpretations about what modernity represented. There has also been a critical approach towards modernity as a Western attribute. In critiques of modernity, the stereotypes of science and scientific reasoning were questioned and there has been an attempt to portray modernity as an indigenous tradition in Asia. Whether it is possible to envisage a variant of Eastern modernity that was distinct from its Western counterpart is open to question. Sometimes, it is impossible to dissect the invisible relationship between colonial hegemony and control on the one hand and nationalist appropriation on the other. Such ideas are no longer muted, and researches in the wider field of economics, sociology, history and politics portray the multitude of sensibilities and sensitivities about modernity as a postcolonial expression in Asia. On the other hand, some scholars prefer to talk about *modernity at large*.[3] Thus most of the scholarly responses revolve around contesting the idea that modernity has any necessary, ideal-typical form.[4]

In more recent times, scholars have reckoned with the aspect of 'multiple' or 'alternative' modernities[5], and have addressed the ambiguities and dialectics of modernity. K.N. Panikkar, for instance, has dealt with 'the idea of resistance to colonialism as a source of alternative modernity' in the context of colonial India.[6] In his opinion, 'the intellectual and cultural engagements which strove to transgress the limits of colonial modernity and to construct an alternative were ways of challenging and resisting colonial domination.'[7] In fact, the disenchantment with the liberal credentials of the colonial government which led to the search for alternatives, both in the political and cultural realms, demanded the notion of an alternative modernity to be 'distinct from colonial modernity, seeking to construct a state of subjectivity different from the colonial and traditional'.[8] While the alternative modernity was conceived essentially as a condition beyond colonialism,[9] its formation, argues Panikkar, 'was a weak and superficial process, unable to evolve an independent ideological foundation'.[10] As a result, it created 'cultural heterogeneity', and not 'acculturation' through a creative dialogue between Western culture and traditional knowledge. However, Panikkar's idea that 'cultural resistance to colonialism was mainly articulated in the efforts to evolve an alternative modernity by the intelligentsia' is only partially correct as the Indian public slowly but surely came to become a part of this process of cultural resistance, discerned more clearly in the fields ranging from tribal protest to popular cultural forms like cinema or sport.[11] As one goes beyond colonial history and steps into the realm of postcolonial nation/state building, one finds multiple attempts to establish the credibility of alternative modernities, particularly in the decolonized States of Asia in political, social, cultural and economic spheres,[12] nullifying at times the very viability of Western paradigm of modernity in such countries.[13]

In such context, *Modernities in Asian Perspective* wishes to address and interrogate the varied articulation of modernities in colonial and postcolonial Asian societies from an interdisciplinary perspective.[14] The volume unfolds with Binoda K. Mishra's essay 'Modernity on Trial: nationhood and nationalism in South Asia'. Mishra challenges the viability of one of the most fundamental and unique characteristics of modern society, i.e. nationality/nationalism with nation as its manifested institution in the South Asian context. The nation-building experiences in South Asia force one to question the conceptual validity of modern nation-state. Drawing on the nation-building experiences in South Asia he forcefully argues that the concepts of modernity, nationality and nationhood are primarily constructs grounded in ideas deeply rooted in the historical experiences of Western Europe and North America and are largely incompatible with South Asian endogenous concepts of modernity, nationality and nationhood. As he tries to show, the postcolonial experiences of political instability and socio-ethnic conflict in South Asian states reiterate the perpetual dichotomy of identities, thereby pointing to the non-viability of a unitary notion of modernity in the Western sense of the term in South Asia.

It has been argued that there have remained certain universal markers of modernity. Of these the two most crucial are complexly relational, yet at times contradictory - the parallel and complementary establishment of free markets and democracy, particularly in the wider perspective of a developmental discourse. Anita Sengupta situates her essay in the context of such relational complexities between market reform and political change during periods of transition for the new state, viz. Uzbekistan. As she points out, a study of the simultaneous implementation of what is identified as 'modern' in the political and in the economic spheres, i.e, the establishment of liberal democratic society and market relations, often leads to a problematic, rather anomalous scenario, where, in fact, there is often opposition between the transformation to a 'modern' liberal democracy and civil society on the one hand and the necessity of rapid economic development and transition to market relations on the other. The road to become 'modern' for a new state thus involves independent interpretation of modernity by each emerging state, which, in its attempt to reconcile with the dichotomy between continuity/tradition and change/modern, actually proposes alternative models of modernity. Sengupta's essay attempts to offer a critical understanding of one such alternative model of a 'modern' state, independent Uzbekistan, through the writings of President Islam Abduganievich Karimov. First, it deals with Karimov's writings that belong to an era when the developmental dynamics of the 'new' state rather than terrorism held centre stage. Reflecting upon Karimov's interpretation of the nature of the modern Uzbek state, Sengupta addresses the nature of an alternative model of state put forward by him. Gradually, however, her focus shifts from the construction of a new state based on the principles of democracy and market reform to the discourse on a 'nation under threat' with geopolitics and terrorism holding the centre stage.

The search for alternative discourses of modernity finds eloquent expression in Priya Singh's attempt to situate the Zionist discourse of modernization in Israel in the political context of ideological collision between the modernizing roles of Zionism vis-à-vis the Palestinians. For its proponents, argues the author, Zionism, the national movement aimed at the creation of the State of Israel and the Zionist ideology, the philosophy underlying the process of nation building, constituted a project of modernization and development for the benefit of the Palestinians. For its detractors, on the other hand, the Zionist project was aimed at the disenfranchisement of the Palestinians. The essay, by delving deep into the modernizing claims of the Zionists and the counterclaims of its opponents from within (the post-Zionists) and without (the Palestinians), suggests that the tensions and contradictions inherent in the so-called 'modern' Zionist discourse necessitated the construction and development of a 'postmodern' post-Zionist discourse.

Sanjukta Dasgupta's essay, which interrogates the biased representation of identity in colonial India, is a critique of the project of colonial modernity. The author's case study of the tribal group Hos of Chota Nagpur indicates the tendency of colonial narratives to subsume them as 'natives' and subjects who committed crimes. British perceptions of these tribals as a 'backward primitive' or 'a savage race' who resisted the local collaborators of the Raj or scourged the belt with their depredations were clearly lopsided and a misrepresentation of their identity. Dasgupta's essay is reflective of the genre of writings that critically examine the standardized tenets of modernity, articulated by British colonial rule in India. She is intensely critical about the working of the colonial mind. The essay projects colonial anthropology as a methodology of research and reflects on the colonial methods of governing unruly subjects. In between the colonial perceptions of the tribal subjects and the tribals' perceptions about themselves and their rulers, what has mostly gone unnoticed is the tribals' desire to reform their customary laws and practices. Reformism among the Chotanagpur tribals, as reflected in the discussion of the four socio-religious movements in the chapter, is a major corrective to the conventional contours of scholarship which either tends to highlight the encounter patterns or gets warped in the extremely sensitive discourse about 'Hinduised identities'. More importantly, the essay investigates the multiple dynamics of indigenous responses to colonial anthropology and seeks to locate the *agency* of the silent majority in the making of their own destinies, thereby questioning the very uniformity of a hegemonized project of colonial modernity imposed from above.

Brian Hatcher, in his chapter, introduces 'Sastric Modernity' as a heuristic category for thinking about the experience of modernity in colonial Bengal from 1820 to 1870. His aim is both to draw attention to the complex genealogy of modernity in the South Asian context and to situate the particulars of nineteenth-century Sanskrit intellectual practice within such a genealogy. In other words, the essay explores the possibility of viewing Sanskrit intellectual practice in colonial Bengal as one mode of emergent South Asian modernity. By examining literature created by Sanskrit *pandits* in connection with the mid-nineteenth century widow marriage movement, this essay demonstrates that such scholars worked with the resources of the sastric tradition to accomplish (or to contest) an Enlightenment-based project of social reform. The goal, according to the author, is to find a way to conceptualize Sanskrit intellectual practice in the colony as modern without reducing it thereby to a mere response to European epistemologies, oriental categories, or colonial governmentality. A close examination of the tracts created in the context of the widow marriage movement reveals them to be quintessential artifacts of a mode of colonial modernity in which Sanskrit knowledge was deployed in colonial India.

Sharmistha Gooptu traces the emergence of film-going as an important leisure activity in Bengal in the 1920s and early 1930s. This, according to her, not only helped consolidate a nascent film industry and generate cultural contestation around the new medium, but more significantly produced a film culture, integrated by a film-going public, an aspiring group of entrepreneurs and a new class of critics/commentators. Gooptu's essay examines this early film culture and the emergence of a discourse on cinema as the 'modern' popular. In an effort to unravel the mixed baggage of Bengal's early film culture, the author argues that, 'by the end of the 1920s and early 1930s, the range of signifiers of the early cinema had been sifted through by a Bengali discourse, to produce "bad" and "good" prototypes, the latter being linked to a Bengali bourgeois interest in the "modern" art form.'[15] She draws attention to the 'Bengali' prototype of 'good' and 'serious' cinema, which was informed by the bourgeois literary ideal of novelistic realism and an elitist self-consciousness of 'world standards' and pitted against the theatrical mode of early Indian films and corporate structures underlying the stage-cinema complex, setting up the model for a modernist project.

Kausik Bandyopadhyay's essay studies the domain of cultural imperialism and interrogates the stereotypes of representation in the field of sport in colonial India. The author challenges the stereotypical and naïve Eurocentric interpretation of the introduction, adoption and consolidation of modern sports like football in India in terms of a linear project of colonial modernity and argues that many amongst the Indian practitioners of such sports were keen to appropriate that modernity to serve entirely different purposes, thereby creating space for an alternative modernity in their *own* terms. Thus, 'while the overt imperial mission of games ethic in introducing the Indians to modern Western sports was wrought with the embedded notion of cultural imperialism, the Indian appreciation of that imperial purpose in adopting and adapting a particular sport (football in this case) ranged from emulation to appropriation, resistance and even subversion for nationalist purposes. In other words, one standard of Western modernity - namely sport - was appropriated to surpass and discredit that very West.'[16] However, Bandyopadhyay warns against understanding the formulation of cultural nationalism around modern sports in a colonial setting in linear terms. Accordingly, its origin, growth, character and impact need to be analyzed in the context of changing balance of intended imperial designs and their unintended consequences via appropriation. Using soccer as a lens, the chapter thus attempts to understand and explore the contestations of imperialism and nationalism in the relational perspectives of modernity and culture in colonial India.

Modernity can also be conceived as a discontinuity from the past unto the present, as Rakhee Bhattacharya argues in her essay 'Modernity: The abiding metaphor of India', a transition that takes place along a continuum of ever-changing historical and socio-political-economic ideas and ethos in the life of a nation or a society. While attempting to identify an index of modernity through some composite socio-economic indicators, one needs to look at the fundamental components like economic growth, urbanization, industrialization along with the social determinants like health, education, security etc. that help evolve the capability index of a society to transform the living for improvement. The world has undoubtedly witnessed several miraculous achievements in its economic front and human civilization can proudly claim that it is converging towards economic modernity that holds the promise of a better quality of life for the people. But has this modernity manifested itself in an egalitarian framework? Has not the concept of modern identity also created and contributed to multiple confusions across the globe? To examine these issues, the essay tries to unravel the crisis of modernity in the context of economic developments in India. India – one of the principal movers of Asian Economy – has almost magically transformed her economy and aspires to achieve much more, yet at the same time posing a number of interesting questions. Has this achievement spilled over to the improvised millions who languish in abject poverty, malnutrition, social discrimination, extreme deprivation and insecurity? Has so-called modernity improved the lot of women and underprivileged children in Indian society and brought any ray of hope for their dignity and rights? Can the challenges of modernity be met by targeting merely the 'numbers' or do the evils (mainly the second generation problems of health and cultural degeneration) that afflict the society need to be erased by some other coercive measures to make a meaningful break from a 'hope'-less past and to disperse the fruits of economic modernity among all the people across the country? Will the economic transformation also mean empowerment of the people who had no voice so far in a real sense? These are the questions that Bhattacharya's essay attempts to address and resolve.

The presence of different intellectual trajectories in *modernity* as a concept, theory or philosophy as well as a global experience compels us to study all the sites and dimensions embedded and represented in such a notion. As Appadurai and Breckenridge nicely put it, the global experience of modernity is 'as varied as magic, marriage, or madness'.[17] In fact, any interrogation of the historical meaning and viability of multiple modernities in colonial and postcolonial societies involves two simultaneous transitions – the more general transition from tradition to modernity and the more subtle one from modernity to postmodernity.[18] The essays in the volume endeavour to contribute to this wider perspective of understanding the reflexivity and radicality of the theory of *modernity* through a series of representations in polity, society, culture and economy, thereby addressing the contestations and alternatives ingrained in the very experience of *modernities*.

Acknowledgements

I thank Anita, Priya, my colleague Suchandana at Maulana Abul Kalam Azad Institute of Asian Studies, Kolkata, for helping me with their ideas and a number of important publications while I was working on this introductory essay.

Notes and References

1 Dipesh Chakrabarty, *Habitations of Modernity: Essays in the wake of Subaltern Studies*, Delhi: Permanent Black, 2002.

2 One classic example of study of recent trends of critical discussion on modernity in its myriad forms in the Indian context is Javeed Alam, *India: Living with Modernity*, Delhi: Oxford University Press, 1999.

3 See Arjun Appadurai, *Modernity at Large: Cultural Dimensions of Globalization*, Minneapolis: University of Minnesota Press, 1996.

4 Ibid., p. xx.

5 For a useful appreciation of the idea of alternative modernities, see D.P. Gaonkar, ed. *Alternative Modernities*, Durham: Duke Univ. Press, 2001. This work, underlining the globality and multiplicity of modernity, argues that modernity as a concept no longer has a 'Western governing center' to accompany it. The essays in that collection approach the dilemmas of modernity from transnational and transcultural perspectives. The idea of 'alternative modernities' holds that modernity always unfolds within specific cultures or civilizations and that different starting points of the transition to modernity lead to different outcomes. Without abandoning the Western discourse on the subject, the contributors to the volume propound that modernity is in truth a richly mulitiplicitous concept, and that the language and lessons of Western modernity must be submitted to comparative study of its global receptions. While the present work appreciates the historical viability of the notion of alternative modernities, it focuses more on the multiplicity of modernity through representations in the fields of polity, society, culture and economy. This very multiplicity, as the contributions in the present volume would suggest, makes out a case for the viability of a heterogeneous concept of *modernities* rather than a singular one of *modernity*.

6 See for details K.N. Panikkar, *Colonialism, Culture and Resistance*, New Delhi: Oxford University Press, 2007.

7 Ibid., p. 1.

8 Ibid., pp. 14-15.

9 This point finds ample illustration in Brian Hatcher's chapter on Sastric modernity in this book.

10 Ibid., p. 16.

11 Essays by Sanjukta Dasgupta, Sharmishtha Gooptu and Kausik Bandyopadhyay in the present volume bear testimony to this statement.

12 For such alternatives in political systems/thought in postcolonial Asia, see the chapters by Anita Sengupta and Priya Singh in this volume, while Rakhee Bhattacharya's essay gives us a fair idea of the economic manifestation of postcolonial modernist agenda.

13 Binoda K. Mishra's essay in this book offers a case study of South Asia on this premise.

14 These interrogations may be summarized as follows: How does one define the fundamental ambiguity of 'modernity'? Is it simply in terms of a set of institutions that are deemed modern or should it involve cultural imaginations that involve distinct forms of rationality, cosmology, beliefs, values and conceptualizations of time and space? How do societies deal with the continuities and discontinuities inherent in the process? Does modernity have a universal emancipatory essence like attaining maturity and freedom from dependence on others? How far Western modernities have impinged upon the Third World through a worldwide march of global capital? Is it really possible to envisage a kind of Eastern modernities appropriate for the postcolonial societies that might probably be different from their Western counterparts? How far are the modernities in Asia implicated with inbuilt and mostly invisible relations of power and hegemony (especially gender, class and racial discrimination), scientism, societal rationalization, cultural simulation, disciplinary regime, governmentality, industrialization, consumerism and globalization? Is modernity inherently globalizing? Finally, do modernities still have potentially responsible ways to interact with civil society and community?

15 See Sharmishtha Gooptu's essay in this book.

16 See Kausik Bandyopadhyay's essay in the book.

17 Arjun Appadurai and Carol A. Breckenridge, 'Public Modernity in India', in *Consuming Modernity: public culture in contemporary India,* edited by Carol A. Breckenridge, Delhi: Oxford University Press, 1996, p. 1.

18 For an insightful discussion on these transitions, see Gerald Delanty, *Modernity and Postmodernity: Knowledge, Power and the Self,* London: Sage, 2000.

Modernity on trial
nationhood and nationalism in South Asia

Binoda K. Mishra

'Modernity' is one of the most ambiguous words in social science lexicon. The term is often used as if there exists a common understanding of its meaning. The present era is termed as the modern era underlining the assumption that every existing object, idea or institution is either modern or striving to acquire modern characteristics. One such idea is nationality/nationalism with the nation as its manifestation. Nation-building experiences in South Asia force one to question the conceptual validity of the of the modern nation-state. Such experiences show that the contemporary idea of modernity, nationality and nationhood are primarily constructs grounded in ideas that are deeply rooted in the historical experiences of Western Europe and North America. These are largely incompatible with South Asian socio-cultural and political space. This chapter explores how the concept of a 'modern nation-state' did not fit into the South Asian reality. In fact, the creation of 'modern' territorially demarcated and 'nationally' organized states resulted in communal politics in South Asia. The essay further interrogates whether the concept of nation-state is an appropriate one in the South Asian context or not.

Political modernity and the birth of the nation-state

An idea that emerged from the medieval crisis and assumed the status of objective truth is 'modernity'. It has assumed many forms, if not meanings, depending on its interpretations at various points in time by scholars and often in contrasting ways.[1] The factors responsible for the emergence of this idea include: 'the emergence of the autonomous and rational subject; the differentiation of cultural spheres; the rise of liberal and democratic states; the turn to psychologism; and the dominance of secularism, nationalism, capitalism, industrialism, urbanism, consumerism, and scientism.'[2] It relegated all ideas that fall out of its explanatory purview, to the past as ancient or traditional or pre-modern. Like a campaign, it penetrated into all walks of human existence and manifested itself in all of them. The essence of the idea is fundamental and appealed instantly to the large section of the society due to its emphasis on human beings. Modernity replaced God from the centre of all explanations and began interpreting every idea or institution in terms of its utility to human beings. Modern ideas got manifested in all human institutions that demanded and in some cases commanded universal appeal. But what essentially is modernity? The term 'modernity' has no specific definition, which goes on to show the inherent fluidity of the concept. However, it is most often used to denote the socio-economic and political condition of a particular historical period.

In general, the modern era is believed to have begun with the process of industrialisation in Europe during the nineteenth century. It is not absolute as there are some schools that take modernity back to *Descartes* and others that refer to the twentieth century as the *only* modern period. The chief characteristic of modern era that distinguishes it from the traditional era is its emphasis on scientific enquiry as opposed to unquestioned belief in dictated explanations. One can also argue that modernity was a political invention for outshining others in the competition among states. During the sixteenth century, Europe witnessed fierce interstate competition among major powers. Of the major powers, France and Italy were culturally much superior to Great Britain which was experiencing a cultural decline. But Great Britain, due to her scientific advancements of that time, projected herself as a modern state and relegated the importance of France and Italy to the background as ancients. Thus started the divide between the modern and the ancient. Modernity was characterized by scientific temper and ancient by richness of culture. It is important to note that power and prestige started getting associated with modernity. This association of power and prestige with modernity became the motivating factor for all to crave for the modern status.

With time, like any other concept, modernity became rigid and tried to eliminate the fluidity and with it the scope for scientific enquiry, which was the hallmark of modernity. It assumed the features of a faith and anything that did not conform to the ideas of modernity was branded as un-utilitarian and thus redundant. Almost like a paradigm, modernity went on prescribing forms for the various institutions that man is member of or is regulated by. The campaign credited itself with success and went on to declare the arrival of a 'universal civilization'.[3] In political realms, it suggested that nation and nationalism are essential features of any civilized political system. Political systems that did not have the spirit of nationalism or were not based on the concept of nationhood defined by homogeneity were unviable nation-states.

As the concept of modernity, owing to different interpretations, cannot be dated precisely, the birth of modern state is also hard to date. It is not possible to map the appearance of modern state in a timescale but its emergence can be explained in terms of certain specific features that some political systems assumed. The features that characterize modern state are: shared power; constitutionally or legally defined individual rights to participate in the government; wide representation; secular state power; and well defined national boundary.[4] Again the appearance of modern state cannot be assumed to be the beginning of the era of 'modern nation-state system'. One of the most controversial issues in social sciences remains the origin of nations and nationalism. There are both traditional and modern definitions of nation and nationalism. According to Schleiermacher, nation is 'a natural division of the human race, endowed by God with its own character.' And it is God who directly assigns to each nationality its definite task on the earth and inspires it with a definite spirit in order to glorify Himself through each one in a peculiar manner.[5] The sacred character of nation and nationalism is also supported by scholars like Herder who call for its preservation on the ground that 'nation is as natural as a plant, as a family, only with more branches.'[6] On the other hand we have a host of scholars like Ernest Gellner, E. J. Hobsbawm, Anthony D. Smith, Ernest Renan and others who consider it a modern phenomenon. The consensual definition of nationalism as a modern phenomenon suggests that it is a functional prerequisite and/or a product of industrialization and capitalism.[7] There are two basic models that explain the rise of nation-state. One is the Western European model, i.e. from state-to-nation and the other is the nation-to-state model, supposed to explain the rise of nation-state in Eastern Europe and Asia.[8] It is important to remember that the development of nation and nation-state is not simultaneous. States existed as primary political units of individuals along with various other group identities in history. The merger took place in the late eighteenth century in Western Europe through the process of modernization either as a prerequisite of or a response to industrialization.

Modern state involving the above-mentioned characteristics first appeared in England. This sixteenth century phenomenon was an evolutionary process of transforming the crown's estate into a 'free state' under the sovereign authority of the people of England. Thus the emergence of modern state was a reflection of the growing nationalism.[9] The emergence of modern states in other parts of the world did not follow the same process as it did in Great Britain, but in essence, state formation in its modern form was based on the principle of nationalism. Thus one would have no problem in agreeing with Ernst Gellner's formulation that modernisation leads to nationalism and nationalism engenders nations.[10] There is a near consensus about the emergence of nationalism. It is a modern movement and ideology that emerged in the later half of the eighteenth century.[11] According to Gellner, nations did not create nationalism rather it is the spirit of nationalism that created nations. Nationalism, in his view was a requirement of the industrial society. It is the duty of the polity to sustain the spirit of nationalism in industrial societies in order to maintain cohesion of the society, which by nature is fluid and mobile.[12] The creation of the modern nation-state system had certain implied assumptions: 1) the nation-state thus created is independent of the society it functions within or with; 2) the nation-state is an objective in itself and the subjects have no moral rights to question its composition and will try to protect its solidarity under all circumstances. All traditional political values will modernize themselves according to the requirements of the nation-state; 3) political territory acts as a binding force among the subjects and promotes the sense of nationalism that absorbs all other identities of the subjects turning them into a homogenous group (nationals).

Nationalism and the development of modern nation-state in South Asia

If nationalism is a product of industrialization and modernity, then South Asia is not supposed to have the concept of nationalism since the region neither has experienced industrialization nor has it undergone the transformation of modernity in a true sense until recently. The region is atypical in a sense that there seems to be acceptance of both modern and traditional forms of values and institutions. Both value systems and forms of institutions coexist side by side though not always in harmony. Historically, political systems in South Asia have always been territorial states without any reference to nationalities and nationalism. The concepts of nation and nationalism are of recent origin to the region and like every other concept are heavily loaded with modern/Western characteristics. In the absence of suitable socio-economic base, the Western/modern political concepts have created a conflict that seems unending now. The introduction of the nation-state system and modern democratic forms of government have given rise to a tussle for acceptance between the traditional institutions of authority and the modern ones which are supposed to replace the traditional ones. The blame can be squarely put on the introduction of the concept of modern nation-state because before the advent of the colonizers, the Indian subcontinent's political systems were highly decentralized, and mostly secular and the central authority enjoyed nominal sovereignty. The idea of state was purely secular and did not have any communal characteristic whatsoever. This was an evolved system in which, in the words of Ayesha Jalal, the 'central sovereign authority was symbolically acknowledged, frequently challenged but only rarely rejected.'[13] The introduction of the concept of nation-state demanded that some homogeneity has to be evolved among the population that intend to form a nation. The introduction of this rigid form of nation-state, created the first friction in the Indian subcontinent that later became a South Asian phenomenon. So much so that the thousands of years' old secular credential of the subcontinent was sacrificed at the altar of homogenous nation-state. The Partition of India at the cost of the death and displacement of millions was aimed at creating viable nations in the lines of nation-state of the West. Suffice here to say that the creation of modern nation state does not necessarily entail the end to the inherent contradictions of the society, perhaps this has never happened in the West even. But modern nation state has demanded submission of the minority values to that of the majority and in the event where such submission was not forthcoming, brutal means have been applied in the name of discipline of the nation. Of the two so-called viable nation- states created through Partition, namely India and Pakistan, one adopted secularism with the hope of evolving an accommodative political system whereas the other followed its unavoidable path of building a nation-state on the base of religious homogeneity. The experiences of both the states tell us that neither have succeeded in building a modern nation-state particularly in the Western sense of the term.

The history of nation building in South Asia is a story of adaptation to alien values by prudent manipulation of political elites. In the name of modernization, South Asians were asked to relinquish their traditional values and opt for values that were purely Western and projected as rational and the only way to better socio-political future. In the process, for political expediency, the colonial masters dissected the composite society into compartments, thus unwittingly preparing grounds for debasing the concept of composite nationhood that was endogenous to the Indian subcontinent.[14] The dissection began as early as 1822 with the idea of divide and rule adopted by the colonial masters. Lt. Col. Coke, Commandant of Moradabad, wrote: 'Our endeavour should be to uphold in full force the (for us fortunate) separation which exists between the different religions and races, not to endeavour to amalgamate them. *Divide et Impera* should be the principle of Indian government.'[15] In a systematic manner the British managed to evolve nationalist feelings on religious lines in the subcontinent. The landmarks of this endeavour include the partition of Bengal in 1905; introduction of communal suffrage in 1909, introduction of separate electorates in 1919; and the final act of partition of the subcontinent on religious lines in 1947. The partition of the subcontinent failed to create viable homogenous nation-states.

On the other hand, it created permanent fissures having potentials to put the subcontinent on the path of fission. Important here to note that there were resistances to the efforts of introduction of modern nation-state in the subcontinent and the resistance was from within the two major religious communities of the subcontinent, i.e. Hindus and Muslims. Rabindranath Tagore and Muhammad Iqbal, the two leading poets and philosophers of late colonial India criticized the introduction of the notion of modern nation-state as the root cause of conflict in the subcontinent and opposed the concept of homogeneous nationalism as they were rightly apprehensive of its suitability for the socio-political consciousness of the people of South Asia. While Tagore, having seen the perilous effects of nationalism in other parts of the world, denounced nationalism as a destructive force, having the potential to destroy the Indian civilization, Iqbal blamed the Western notion of nationalism for creating modern conflict in Indian subcontinent by making religion relative rather than universal and territorially specific and unsuited to the temperament of other nations.

However, in a manner of predestination, the South Asian subcontinent was divided on religious grounds. The two infant nations set out to build nation-states that would be viable as modern states and united as nations. The attempt was desperate but there seems to be irreconcilable problems that had posed and are posing threats both to the viability of the state and the unity of the nation. The national leadership in India hoped to capitalise on the nationalist fever that swept the country during the independence movement. The Pakistani leadership hoped to ride on the religious nationalism that they had made the base for statehood and won, to create a strong and united nation. But both the nations are still struggling to build their desired nation-states, and the primary threat has come from the question of 'ethnicity' that has been haunting both India and Pakistan. The problems India and Pakistan face along with other South Asian nations are: multiplicity of nationalities; overlapping geographical boundaries among nationalities; and failure to articulate a common nationality.

Multiplicity of nationalities

John Stuart Mill once observed that representative government was not possible until the nationalities question had been solved.[16] After creating one religious nation out of the South Asian subcontinent it was hoped that the process of nation building would be smooth with both India and Pakistan adopting representative forms of government. The independence movement was called the 'nationality' movement to underscore the national unity of the Indian state. Similar eulogy was used in Pakistan for evolving an Islamic nation. But no sooner than the division had been effected, the seemingly benign fissures in the social spheres started widening and a web of nationalities appeared not only in the multi-cultural, multi-lingual and multi-ethnic India but also in the so-called homogeneous Pakistan. The Pakistan nation-state, within a period of 25 years, proved to be a non-viable state and more importantly a non-viable nation. The religious nationalism that was supposed to be the cohesive force for the Pakistani nationhood, was challenged by another form of nationalism namely, linguistic nationalism. The Bengali-speaking majority of East Pakistan asserted their 'Bengali' linguistic nationalism. Interestingly, the linguistic nationalism, though shared borders across the Islamic community, did not really accept the Bengali speaking Hindu population either of India or of Eastern Pakistan. The new nation that emerged setting the precedence of secession of nations from nation-states was called Bangladesh, meaning a nation of Bengalis or Bengali speaking population. It did not show any interest to take within its fold the numerous Indian Bengalis. Thus, in a theoretical sense, one can call it an assertion of sub-nationality within the larger nationality of South Asian Islamic nationhood.

India also saw the rise of linguistic nationalism. The Indian leadership were alarmed at the prospect of the linguistic nationalism escalating into crisis proportions to threaten the unity of the Indian union. But, the problem was managed, before it could actually reach crisis proportions, by linguistic reorganization of states in 1956. But the essential lesson is the acknowledgement of the aspiration of Indian population to create linguistic nationalities (be it) within the Indian statehood. The conclusion from the linguistic movements and subsequent reorganization of states on linguistic lines can be that the population of India could not come to terms with the overarching Indian nationality.

The weakness of Indian nationality is also evident from the fact that it is fiercely challenged by geographical, ethnic, and religious nationalities. The demands of regional autonomy to the extent of secession are being raised by linguistically organized states and ethnically composed north-eastern states not to speak of the religious Sikh nationalism putting constant pressure on the political sovereignty and national unity of India from time to time. This constant challenge to the nationhood of India exposes the fact that there is no congruity between the political and national identity that, according to Ernest Gellner, is the fundamental criterion for the evolution of the spirit of nationalism.[17] India being the most heterogeneous in terms of ethnic configurations faces pressing challenges from these forces. It is not to argue that these ethnic identities are always well articulated. But the mere fact that these identities often pose themselves as binaries in relation to the political nationalism of India proves that there are nationalities based on primordial identities that prefer to be recognized outside the Indian national identity.

These ethno (primordial)-nationalist movements are not unique to India, rather a feature of all the South Asian countries and some of such movements often cross-demarcate state boundaries and rarely but do create inter-state conflicts. The cases of India and Pakistan fighting over Kashmir and Bangladesh are cases in point. Ethnic conflicts internal to the political systems of South Asian states, apart from India, include: the Mohajir movement, the Sindh, Pukhtun and the Baloch problems in Pakistan; the Chakma problem in Bangladesh; the severely violent Tamil separatism in Sri Lanka. There may be differences in their objectives but the fundamental thing that underlines these movements is their challenge to the sovereignty of the political system they were supposed to merge into. In case of India, it is sufficient to mention that only the northeastern part of the country is housing 36 major or minor ethnic nationalist movements.

Added to this, among others, the rise of Hindu nationalism is the evidence of increasing weakness of Indian political nationalism. Bhutan, the other kingdom of South Asian subcontinent, also suffers from pressures of exclusive ethno-nationalism of Drupka community, which tries to 'turn Bhutan into a mono-ethnic polity.'[18] Nepal, though has not been a witness to ethnic conflicts as such, the provision for ethnic representation in the constituent assembly in the recently held election points towards the sensitivity of the population towards their ethnic identity vis-à-vis the national Nepalese identity. Most groups in Nepal including the Newars, Tamangs, Magars, Gurung, Sherpa, Limbu, Rai and Tharu, do not accept the labels 'ethnic groups' or 'minorities'. They prefer to be called 'nations' and believe they fulfil all the criteria of nationhood: language, religion, culture, territory and a history of independent statehood, which would be achieved again if rights to secession were granted.

The growing number and intensity of ethno-nationalist assertions and conflicts with the state-system in South Asia exposes the lack of accommodative ability of the political structures called nation-states. The problem persists not only because there are multiple nationalities in South Asian societies, but also because of the incongruity between the social and the geographical connotations of these identities.

Overlapping geographical boundaries among nationalities

There is no unanimity over the definition of ethnic group or ethnic community but the working definition of the ethnic group is important for our analysis of nationalism since the definition provides the possible bases for the formation of ethno-nationalism. Ethnic group is defined as:

> Either a large or small group of people, in either backward or advanced societies, who are united by a common inherited culture (including language, music, food, dress and customs and practices), racial similarity, common religion, and the belief in common history and ancestry and who exhibit a strong psychological sentiment of belonging to the group.[19]

Defined this way, 'ethnic communities can be of two types: *homeland societies* and *diaspora communities*'.[20] Given the long history of inland migration within South Asia, none of the above-mentioned criteria could remain in a geographically compact area, thereby making most of the ethnic groups or communities diasporic within the region. Exceptions to this are Maldives, to some extent the Tamils of Sri Lanka and the ethnic communities of the northeastern region of India who share fairly compact geographical locations. Such amalgamations of various kinds of identities make it difficult for identifying nationalities and take a measure of their potentials to pose threat to the politically constructed national identity of the political systems in the region. One can argue that had there been congruous geographical connotations to each of the bases of ethnic identity formation in South Asia, the present political systems would have failed long ago or would not have been created at the first place. From this perspective this amalgamation seems to have created a conducive social environment for the evolution of a nation as defined by Ernest Barker. To him:

> A nation is a body of men, inhabiting a definite territory, who normally are drawn from different races, but possess a common stock of thoughts and feelings acquired and transmitted during the course of a common history; who on the whole and in the main, thought more in the past than in the present, include in that common stock a common religious belief; who generally and as a rule use a common language as the vehicle of their thoughts and feelings; and who, besides common thoughts and feelings, also cherish a common will, and accordingly form or tend to form, a separate state for the expression and realization of that will.[21]

In a sense, 90 percent of the states in the world are multi-ethnic by virtue of the fact that they contain minorities in excess of 5 percent of their total population. Not all of these states are experiencing national assertions within their political boundaries. Some plausible explanations for harmonious coexistence of multiple ethnicities in multi-ethnic states are: inland diasporic nature of the nationalities; overwhelming presence of the majority ethnic community; and proper assimilation of ethnic communities into the constructed national identity of the political system.[22] Problems of ethno-nationalities challenging the political nationalities appear in societies wherein the political system, the state, fails to articulate a national identity that either accommodates the various nationalities or makes it preferable for the population vis-à-vis the exclusivist communitarian identities.

Failure of articulation of common political nationality

Since most of the nation-states are artificial creations, it is incumbent upon the political system to arrange for constant reinforcement of the spirit of political nationalism among the ethno-nationalities that constitute, or are made part of, the political system. The methods adopted by nation-states to reinvigorate the spirit of nationalism vary with the social geography of the states, the nature of the natural nationalities and the nature of the government in charge. As implied in Brendan O'Leary's analysis, maintaining national solidarity is a matter of political expediency for the regime in charge of the state. The two approaches, according to O'Leary, the regimes adopt are, to eliminate the differences among nationalities or to manage the differences. The techniques adopted include both negative and positive aspects. Negatively, differences are eliminated by means of genocide and ethnic expulsion, as seen in the case of Germany during the Nazi regime and the positive methods include territorial elimination in the form of secession, decolonization, or partition.[23] Central regimes or states try to manage differences among nationalities either through control strategies or through arbitration and federalization.[24] Irrespective of the methods, the objective of the nation-state and the regime in control is articulation of a concept of nationalism that stands outside each of the other primordial identities and into which all the primordial nationalities will either get assimilated spontaneously or can be forced to get assimilated.

In South Asia all methods mentioned above have been adopted in some degrees at some point of the process of nation building. The partition of Indian subcontinent and the further partition of Pakistan, the systematic assault on the Chakmas in Bangldesh, the federal features in Indian constitution, attempts of imposing Sinhalese ethnic hegemony in Sri Lanka, the recent resolve to turn Nepal into a federation, the expulsion of Nepalese from Bhutan are testimonies to all possible methods being adopted to create homogeneous (mono-ethnic) nation-states out of the multi-ethnic states. Needless to say, all of these methods have proved to be inadequate. Ethnic cleansing is not practicable in most of the South Asian countries owing to their democratic structures and long tradition of 'inter-communal'[25] comity. Owing to the multiplicity of bases of identity and their geographical overlapping, federalism on the basis of natural nationalities is not workable. Moreover, for the same reason, the identity formation keeps changing in most parts of South Asia making the question of nationality fluid for the regimes in charge to effectively control potentially threatening natural nationalities. Though secession has been adopted quite successfully for the creation of nation-state, it has not been entirely successful in the South Asian region for the absence of congruity between natural nationalities and geographical requirements.

The amalgamated nature of natural nationalities and the tradition of inter-communal comity present the regimes in charge with arguably the best opportunity to construct 'political national identities'. But on the contrary, South Asian states periodically suffer from assertions of natural nationalities. The question is why the political systems have failed to articulate an inclusive national identity to which the citizens would willingly refer prior to referring to their natural nationalities? Often this is answered in a nihilist fashion by blaming the colonial masters for creating permanent fissures in the otherwise coherent socio-political fabric of the region. It becomes imperative to look at the ways the South Asian states have tried to articulate a political national identity and/or the way they try and manage the questions of natural nationalities in the process of consolidating the concept of nation-state. The various strategies adopted by the South Asian states are marked by two sets of approaches namely, structural and distributive.[26] While the structural approach does not address the ethnic questions specifically, the distributive approach is aimed at complementing the structural strategies to facilitate integration of natural nationalities into the constructed political national identity.

In India, the distributive approach included strategies such as improvised secularism, and patronizing protectionism. The classical concept of secularism that implies a division of jurisprudence between the temporal and spiritual spheres was modified to allow the regime in charge to create provisions for the minor religious nationalities to protect their identities. The objective of this improvisation is to reassure the religious minorities that the protection of their natural nationalities is guaranteed within the larger political nationality. Similar methods are adopted to lure nationalities of other connotations. Provisions for patronized education, special and economic provisions for backward social categories, and ensuring adequate political representation are such strategies the Indian political system adopts for consolidating the political national identity.

Pakistan, on her part, had the task easy as the nation was created on the basis of Muslim identity. But it was her cultural diversity that required reformulating the national identity in such a fashion that would encapsulate the cultural diversities. In the initial period after independence, Pakistan debated between two strategies: 1) Creation of an Islamic nation based on Islam that would accommodate the other nationalities according to the provisions prescribed by Quran and Shariat; 2) Promotion of Pakistani nationality that would accommodate nationalities of all connotations and take care of the cultural diversities. However, Pakistan has not been able to evolve a consensus around the nature of Islamization and often such strategies have evoked violent reactions. The best option for Pakistan was to manage the cultural diversities through proper federalization but its periodic lapses into dictatorship and its natural requirement of concentration of power have turned the attempts of federalization into unacceptable form of centralization causing more pressure of (sub)nationalistic assertions on the political sovereignty of Pakistan. Bangladesh, on the other hand, used Islam as a tool of national identity formation though it stopped short of using it the way Pakistan has been trying, but nevertheless Bangladesh's shift from the Indian-model secular practices towards religious nationalism certainly created more problems than its positive uniting impact. The non-Muslim population of Bangladesh, the Hindus and the Buddhist Chakmas are dissatisfied. While the Hindus adopt constitutional and political methods to get their grievances redressed, the Chakmas have turned violent, and the problem is far from over for Bangladesh.

Sri Lanka is a case of strategy of concealed majoritarian domination. The regime in charge adopted constitutional methods to ensure minority representation but the distributive mechanism was strategized to ensure marginalization of ethnic minorities. The positive strategies the regime in charge in Sri Lanka adopted include secularism and ethnic electoral federalism. But such strategies have been trumped by the discriminatory distributive strategies and the dynamics of competitive electoral politics that ensures the dominance of the Sinhalese over the ethnic Tamils. The regime in charge in Nepal saw the best bet in articulating a political nationalism that included the principal identity of most of the natural nationalities, i.e. Hinduism and those who were left out of this identity were allowed to practise their own identities within the political identity of Napali nationality. Single language - language of Khas (Nepali) - was adopted as the official language to project a concrete image of Nepali nationality. Nepal, though has not witnessed large-scale ethnic cleavage, has felt the pressure of natural nationalities standing against the attempt of the regime in charge to submerge their nationalities within the overarching Nepali Nationality. Fresh attempts are being made to develop a nationality of the new Republic of Nepal. Provision of ethnic representation and plans of creating a federation are steps in that regard. Bhutan seems to have managed the problem of nationalities better than other South Asian states. There are two primary nationalities populating Bhutan: the ethnic Bhutanese and the ethnic Nepalis. There have been apprehensions of the Nepalis trying to replace the ethnic Bhutanese from the position of majority and power. Such apprehensions are arrested by imposing restrictions on the movement of the ethnic Nepali population. The regime in charge in Bhutan has embarked on a strategy of inclusion by adopting a method of proportional representation, absorption of Nepalis in official positions and encouraging social alliances between the two ethnic communities. The nearly homogeneous Maldives has had no problem of nationality but regionalism is emerging as a bane for Maldives. After the withdrawal of the British from the

Addu atoll, there seemed to be problem of geographical nationalism but the regime in charge in Maldives has adopted the strategy of development to lure the population of Addu atoll to the national mainstream of Maldives.

This synoptic description of the attempts of promoting political nationality within South Asian countries by their regimes in charge underlines the fact that the process of nation-building is in transition and there are both optimistic and pessimistic allusions about these states succeeding in constructing nation-states. The present forms of nationalistic assertions the South Asian states are experiencing is a transition of what Gellner calls from the 'low cultures'[27] into the 'high cultures'. This is essentially a part of the project of modernization that the Western societies experienced long back in history. But the essential difference in the two processes is that in the case of the West the transformation ended with the consolidation of nation-states, while in case of South Asia, it has led to instability of the political states and a perpetual fight between the primordial low cultures and the state and among the low cultures themselves. As discussed earlier, in South Asia, the idea of nation (state) was composite and purely political that allows autonomous existence to other identities (low cultures). The current project of modernization and nationalization is more of an attempt to remove the compositeness with homogeneity. This generates the most important question - is the concept of nation-state inappropriate for South Asia? Or to put it differently, is it modernity with nationalism [with its emphasis on homogeneity] as its political offshoot that is preventing the articulation of nationality or national identity that is congruent to the nationalist aspirations of the population forming the political units in the region?[28]

By any analysis, the spirit of nationalism was an evolution in Western societies. In contrast, in developing societies like South Asia, the first upsurge of nationalism was more of an advent through emulation than an evolution. The leaders of the freedom movements in South Asia had a notion of nationalism that was firmly grounded on the territorial connotation of nationalism and the statist ideals inherited form the colonial masters, the West.[29] The political units of South Asia qualify as nations only if we take Anthony Giddens' definition of a nation. He defines nation as a 'collectivity existing within a clearly defined territory, which is subject to a unitary administration, reflexively monitored both by the internal state apparatus and those of other states.'[30] He further suggests that nationalism is a psychological phenomenon, which is evident from 'the affiliation of individuals to a set of symbols and beliefs emphasizing commonality among the members of a political order'.[31]

South Asia as a socio-political space did not and does not have the requisite socio-economic infrastructure to build and hold the Western defined political superstructure. Does that make South Asia an ancient or traditional state?[32] There was only a hope that if some Western nations such as the United States of America and Switzerland, which were not homogeneous but could manage to evolve as successful nation-states, political units in South Asia will also evolve into nation-states. The hope was grounded on two historical facts: 1) 'prior to the British conquest, relations between the regional peoples and the sovereign power had never been regulated wholly by religion', 2) 'a web of economic and social linkages had survived periods of imperial consolidation, crisis and collapse, to bind the subcontinent into a loosely layered framework of interdependence.'[33] One can argue that the post-colonial nation-states in South Asia have survived for more than half a century (with one secession only), thus providing sufficient evidence of the concept of civic nationalism functioning. The counter argument to this is that mere survival of political units defined by a boundary does not prove the consolidation and success of nation-state. The essential measure of the strength of a nation-state lies in the functioning of the essential feature of modern nation-state system, i.e. 'representative form of government' or democracy. A cursory look at the functioning of the democracies of South Asia would reveal that all of them are under stress from the assertions of ethnic nationalism. One of the factors primarily responsible for this friction is the imposition (if it can be said) or adoption of the Western defined modern nation-state and again Western defined democratic form of governance. This introduction or adoption was more an optimism than based on any logical understanding of the history of political culture in the region. The optimism can be loosely connected to the kind of optimism expressed by Lord Macaulay during his introduction of English as the medium of education in colonial India. In his words, the introduction of English language would create 'a class of persons, Indian in blood and colour, but English in taste, in opinion, in morals and intellect' and would make them quit their primordial religious identities in favour of modern secular identity.[34]

Nationalism, as conceptualized by various scholars, is of two kinds, namely, civic and ethnic. The nationalism that works as the base of the modern nation-states is a civic one, which is supposed to transcend the traditional orderly principles of a given society and bind them together in a spirit of nationalism, 'based on shared principles of justice and democracy.'[35] The South Asian nation-states, created through the process of decolonization, were hoped to emerge as nation-states based on such civic principles accommodating the interests of numerous ethnic nationalities. Shared sense of history and cultural practices were expected to act as cohesive forces for the emergence of the spirit of civic nationalism resulting in the consolidation of nation-state systems approximating the European nation-states.

The optimism has proved to be futile though the introduction of English language has achieved partial success by changing the orientation of a section of South Asian population, mainly the elite. However, unlike West European states, South Asia was not culturally or economically prepared for the establishment of modern nation-state system. The elites in South Asia had the dual task of establishing a state and a nation simultaneously since cohesive nationalism did not precede state formation. The unwanted but inevitable spin off of the dual effort was relative frustration among the elites both traditional and modern. The modern elite were frustrated since the nation-state could not achieve the level of development experienced by matured nation-states of the West while the traditional elites were frustrated by the loss of their power, position and identity to a newly formed incomprehensible identity. The problem is compounded by the use or abuse of the concept of nationalism by the elites in the name of national protection for political purposes not connected with the definition of nationhood.[36] As a result South Asia commonly experiences a confusion of civic and ethnic nationalisms. The confusion has taken conflict proportions. While the civic notion of nationalism is trying to succeed, the ethnic notion of nationalism is trying its best to ensure the failure of civic nationalism.

There are arguments to defend the Western conception of nation and nationalism in the face of their failure to account for the inability of the political systems in articulating a national identity congruent to their territories and acceptable to all the citizens belonging to various other categories of groups. It is argued that the political systems of South Asia are 'illegitimate states.'[37] Guibernau argues that states that accommodate more than one nationalities within their territory are illegitimate states that try to homogenize either by eliminating the identity of the minorities or by creating coextensive nation-states.[38] The assertive manifestations of natural nationalities in South Asia are explained as an inevitable failure of the political systems in their unnatural attempts to create a nation out of nationalities. The natural nationalities, it is argued, are developing counter strategies (nationalistic movements or sub-national assertions) against the homogenizing attempts of the states.[39]

The alleged failure of South Asian political systems in articulating an all-inclusive nationalism is not due to their illegitimacy or artificiality, but because of the attempt to develop nation-states in the region in the line of Western Europe on the basis of homogeneity. The emergence of nation-states in the West provided data support to the formulation that nation-states are essentially homogeneous and that multi-community societies are not suitable for nationhood. But such argument is incomplete as they are based on the assertive quality of nationality or identity and ignore the adaptive and integrative nature of identity. State being an artificial creation, can certainly be maintained by creating and recreating civic virtues. The power of nationalism does not rest in inventing historical commonality to arouse emotional communal feelings, rather it rests in getting associated with demonstrated success as a unit and if that unity is represented by geographical territory, then it creates a successful nation-state.

The people of South Asia during the colonial times had only

one basis to get united into one nation and that was the 'will' to belong to one nation. This 'will' prevailed over all other criteria of group formation. But the important question is: is the will lost? Or have the people willed to form primordial nationalities? The answer lies in the failure of the political units in getting the constructed nationality endorsed through the daily plebiscite.[40] The nation building project in most of the South Asian societies have a two-way action front: a) to articulate the concept of nationalism in the modern sense of the term; b) to preserve the distinctive feature of the endogenous culture vis-à-vis the cultural colonization of Western form of modernity. In both fronts it faces severe challenges. If homogeneity is a pre-requisite of nationalism, in South Asia, it lacks geographical support to add territoriality so essential for the formation of nation-state. On the second front, the nationalist movements lack the power of resistance owing to the fractures already created by percolation of Western cultural values into South Asian society during the period of colonization and sustained by the forces of globalization. Nationalism that created nation-states in the West is not as universal as it is made out to be. Its success had depended upon its being imported from other places and rightly modified in the light of indigenous traditions. In South Asia, the idea of nation and nationalism was imported from the West through the colonial masters but the post-colonial leadership have failed to modify it in the light of the rich tradition of the region resulting in *the problem.* The reason for non-modification of the original idea of nationalism by mixing up local traditions is the assumption that the local traditions are not modern and are against the modern idea of nation and nationalism. The South Asian experience of nation building exposes the weakness of the concept of nationalism. It raises the central question; is nationalism an essential feature that every state must possess? The failure of articulation of political nationalism congruent to the political boundaries of South Asian political units proves that it is not always possible to build states on homogeneity of any kinds, not even cultural as suggested by Gellner. The civic nationalism that inspired the Americans and the French to build nations or nation-states seems to be not working in South Asia calling for improvisations or modifications to the concept of nationalism.

Conclusion

If one accepts Tamir's argument that 'Nationalism is not the pathology of modern age but an answer to its malaise',[41] then the process of nation building in South Asia can be described as a process of first making the society ill and then provide the remedy. This process was thought necessary for the fact that the age-old socio-political patterns of South Asia did not conform to the standards set by modernity and anything not conforming to modern definitions is unviable and thus must be modernized. The urge to West-determined modernity and its iniquitous effects have produced three major conflicts in South Asia – struggle to create composite nation-state, conflict over power-sharing and conflict over resource-sharing. All these three problems have to be overcome if the present political units of South Asia are to evolve as nation-states in the Western/modern sense of the term. In other words, the South Asian states have to demonstrate their power (material success) among the community of states. This, given the irreversible path of nation-building followed by the South Asian states, is the only means by which the power of constructed political nationalism can make the citizens realize that membership of the states they belong to provides them 'a powerful means of defining and locating individual selves in the world through the prism of the collective personality.'[42] In the absence of this demonstrated success, the spirit of nationalism that was at the base of the freedom movements of the South Asian states has got aligned with primordial identities, thus, creating pressures on the South Asian nation-states. It is the failure of the political nation-states in South Asia in living up to their promises – economic, cultural, and political – that has created the scope of primordial nationalisms to stand up against the political system and undermine the sovereign and national character of the nation-states in the making. In an urgency to attain the materialistic achievements matching their Western counterparts, the postcolonial states of South Asia neglected the traditional base of South Asian society and thus failed to modernize it indigenously. In the words of Partha Chatterjee, the misery of the postcolonial South Asia is not in their inability to think out new forms of modern community but in their surrender to the old forms of modern state.[43] Such surrender has taken away the liberty and scope to think about national community and national state together congruously.[44] Devoted communist Eric J. Hobsbawm may remain optimistic about the withering away of the concept of nationalism along with the nation-states,[45] but the fact is nationalism once created is immensely difficult to eradicate[46] as evident from the South Asian experience. Now it is the task of a South Asian variant of modernity to come up with a concept of nationalism that allows primordial identities to associate with each other to create viable composite nation-states. In the words of Richard Devetak, 'the project of history is not to be understood as fixed or bounded in any way. Rather, it signifies an open question around which conflicting responses will revolve. The meaning and idea of the project of modernity are not to be determined or foreclosed in advance, but are to be constantly worked out anew.'[47] Modernity, therefore, in order to live up to its claim of universality, has to succeed in reconstructing the concepts of nationhood and nationalism.

Notes and References

1 Michael Salar, 'Modernity and Enchantment: A Historiographic Review', *The American Historical Review* 111, no. 3, online version, www.historycooperative.org.

2 Ibid.

3 V. S. Naipaul, 'Our Universal Civilization', The 1990 Wriston Lecture, The Manhattan Institute, New York Review Books, 30 November 1990, p. 29, cited in Samuel P. Huntington, *The Clash of Civilizations and the Remaking of World Order*, New Delhi: Penguin Books, 1997, p. 56.

4 Stuart Hall, 'The State in Question', in *The Idea of Modern State*, edited by George McLennan, David Held, Stuart Hall and Milton Keynes, Philadelphia: Open University Press, 1984, pp. 9-10.

5 Elie Kedourie, *Nationalism*, London: Hutchinson University Library, 1986, p. 58, cited in Montserrat Guibernau, *Nationalisms: The Nation-State and Nationalism in the Twentieth Century*, Cambridge: Polity Press, 1996, p. 49.

6 Johann Gottfried Herder, *On Social and Political Culture*, translated and edited by F.M. Barnard, Cambridge: Cambridge University Press, 1969, p. 324, cited in Guibernau, Nationalisms, p. 49.

7 Liah Greenfield, 'Nationalism and Modernity', *Social Research* 63, no. 1 (1996), p. 8.

8 Anthony D. Smith, *Nationalism and Modernism*, London: Routledge, 1998, p. 74.

9 Greenfield, 'Nationalism and Modernity', p.24.

10 Ernest Gellner, *Thought and Change*, London: Weidenfeld and Nicolson, 1964, Chapter 7.

11 Smith, *Nationalism and Modernism*, p. 1.

12 Ernest Gellner, *Nations and Nationalism*, Oxford: Basil Blackwell, 1983 p. 24-9.

13 Ayesha Jalal, 'South Asia', *Encyclopaedia of Nationalism*, Academic Press, 2000, p. 7.

14 If nationhood has to have a territory then the concept of nationhood in Indian subcontinent is composite in nature. In his book *The Nation and its Fragments: Colonial and Postcolonial Histories* (Delhi: Oxford University Press, 1994), Partha Chatterjee has discussed various components of nationhood under the construct of 'fragments' though his categorization is not exhaustive and many more components can be identified that constitute a nation in the subcontinent. The notion of nation in the Indian subcontinent certainly transcends the identity of each of such components and fragments.

15 'Genesis of communal violence in India', http://www.panjab.org.uk/english/genesis.html

16 John Stuart Mill, 'Considerations on Representative Government', in *Three Essays*, Oxford: Oxford University Press, 1975, Chapter 16, cited in *The Nation-State in Question*, edited by T.V. Paul, G. John Ikenberry and John A. Hall, Princeton: Princeton University Press, 2003, p. 3.

17 Gellner, *Nations and Nationalism*, p. 1.

18 Shibashis Chatterjee, 'Ethnic Conflicts in South Asia: A Constructivist Reading', *South Asian Survey* 12, no. 1 (2005), p. 83.

19 Rajat Ganguly and Ray Taras, *Understanding Ethnic Conflict: The International Dimension*, New York: Addison Wesley Longman, 1998, p. 9.

20 Urmila Phanis and Rajat Ganguly, *Ethnicity and Nation-Building in South Asia* (Revised Edn), New Delhi: Sage Publications, 2001, p. 19.

21 Ernest Barker, *National Character and the Factors in its Formation*, London: Methuen, 1927, p. 17, quoted in Phanis and Ganguly, *Ethnicity and Nation-Building in South Asia*, pp. 19-20.

22 In most cases, particularly in Asia and Africa, state-building preceded nation-building making the national identity of the state not as natural as ethnic nationalities.

23 Brendan O'Leary, 'Introduction' and 'The Elements of Right-Sizing and Right Peopling of State', in *Right-Sizing the State: The Politics of Moving Borders*, edited by Brendan O'Leary, I. S. Lustick and T. Callaghy, Oxford: Oxford University Press, 2001.

24 Ibid.

25 The term 'communal' here is used to refer to groupings that could be formed on various identities.

26 Phanis and Ganguly, *Ethnicity and Nation-Building in South Asia*, p. 146.

27 'Low culture' here refers to the culture of the agroliterate societies. Gellner identifies nationalism with 'high culture' prevalent in industrialized societies from the 'wild' or low culture that characterizes the agroliterate societies. See Gellner, *Nations and Nationalism*, pp. 50-2.

28 In line with the endogenous conception of nationhood in South Asia, nationalist aspiration means preserving the primordial identities within a composite political unit.

29 Smith, *Nationalism and Modernism*, p. 73.

30 Anthony Giddens, *The Nation-State and Violence*, Cambridge: Polity Press, 1985, p. 116.

31 Ibid.

32 There cannot be a single answer to what could have been better suited political structures for South Asia. A probable alternative could have been the creation of accommodative political structures that provided a space for the traditional institutions to operate and act as agents of modernization.

33 Jalal, 'South Asia', p. 2.

34 Donald Eugine Smith, *India as a Secular State*, Princeton: Princeton University Press, 1963, pp. 337-39.

35 Habermas defined nationalism in terms of constitutional patriotism. See, William Kymlilka, *Multicultural Citizenship*, Oxford: Oxford University Press, 1995, p. 238.

36 George Schöpflin, 'Nationalism and Ethnicity in Europe', in *Nationalism and Nationalities in the New Europe*, edited by Charles A. Kupchan, Ithaca: Cornell University Press, 1995, p. 49.

37 Guibernau, *Nationalisms*, pp. 59-62.

38 Ibid., p. 61.

39 Ibid.

40 As Ernest Renan argues, '[a] nation's existence is a daily plebiscite'. Ernst Renan, 'What is a Nation?', translation of Renan's Lecture delivered at Soborne, 11 March 1882, available at www.cooper.edu.

41 Yael Tamir, 'The Enigma of Nationalism', *World Politics* 47, no. 3 (1995), p. 432.

42 Anthony D. Smith, *National Identity*, Las Vegas: University of Nevada Press, 1991, p. 17.

43 Partha Chatterjee, *The Nation and its Fragments: Colonial and Postcolonial Histories*, Delhi: Oxford University Press, 1994, p. 11.

44 Ibid.

45 Eric J. Hobsbawm, *Nations and Nationalism since 1780: Programme, Myth and Reality* (2nd Edn.), Cambridge: Cambridge University Press, 1992, p. 192.

46 Anthony D. Smith, 'A Europe of Nations or Nation of Europe', *Journal of Peace Research* 30, no. 2 (1993), p. 131.

47 Cited in Albert J. Paolini, *Navigating Modernity: Postcolonialism, Identity and International Relations*, Boulder, London: Lynne ReinnerPublishers, 1999, p. 170.

'Modernity' and the Uzbek State : the writings of President Islam A. Karimov

Anita Sengupta

> Modern is what some of us think we are, others of us wish desperately to be, yet others despair of being, or regret, or oppose, or fear, or, now, desire somehow to transcend.[1]

Modernity as process

Modernity has been defined as a process, a sequence of occurrences that transforms a traditional form of life, stable and self contained into a venturous one, adaptive and continuously changing.[2] As a concept, it emerged in the post colonial world, clinically dividing it between advanced societies that had been modernized and backward ones that had not. The challenge was to close the gap and turn the second into the first through a process of development. The spread of the concept of 'developmentalism' was intense in most 'new' states, which were seen to be emerging from a general condition of negativity towards that of a developed world. In the process, social advance was assumed to be fixed, linear and universal. However, as Clifford Geertz notes:

> ...in practice, the matter was less simple. (That) the road was less smooth and unidirectional, was a surprise only to enthusiasts – theorists of national liberation, peasant revolution, or economic takeoff into endless growth. What was surprising and disorganizing as well, was that modernity turned out to be less a fixed destination than a vast and inconsistent field of warring possibilities, possibilities neither simultaneously reachable nor systematically connected, neither well defined nor unequivocally attractive. 'Becoming modern' was not just closing gaps or negotiating stages, mimicking the West or growing rational. It was laying oneself open to the imaginings of the age and then struggling to realize them. Finding a course, not following one.[3]

While Geertz had been commenting in the context of the emergence of postcolonial states in Asia and Africa in the 1950's, 'finding the course' remains the most significant aspect of the elusive search for modernity for most emerging states even today. Every 'new' state finds itself in a curious position where the necessity for transformation is evident, but where there is very little that is actually clear about the path to be taken. There have, however, remained certain universal markers of modernity. The parallel and complementary establishment of free markets and democracy has remained one of the elusive goals that classical liberalism identifies as critical, arguing that markets and politics are linked in a fabric of closely related and necessary institutions. Empirical observation, however, does not support such conclusions. Some countries succeed in economic reform but not in political reform. Some succeed in political change but fail to make progress in economic development. The specificity of the relationship between market reform and political change thus requires examination.

During periods of transition the implementation of the two critical markers of modernity often becomes problematic for the new state. Particularly problematic is the simultaneous implementation of what is identified as 'modern' in the political and in the economic spheres, i.e, the establishment of liberal democratic society and market relations. In fact, there is often opposition between the transformation to a 'modern' liberal democracy and civil society and the necessity of rapid economic development and transition to market relations. The path to modernity is thus interpreted by each emerging state independently. Also, while transition to a 'modern' state is projected as the desired goal in every case it would be simplistic to measure the transformation to modernity in linear terms. In any case the dichotomy between the 'traditional' and the 'modern' is shaped by a set of circumstances that are historically circumscribed. While defining themselves as 'modern', newly emerging states, more often than not, retain elements of the 'traditional'. In actuality, during periods of transition, coming to terms with continuity and change is one of the major challenges that states are faced with. How each state reconciles itself to this dilemma determines how successful its project of state building will be. In the course of this reconciliation, alternative models of modernity have been proposed by emerging states.

This essay is an attempt at understanding one such alternative model of a 'modern' state, independent Uzbekistan, through the writings of President Islam Abduganievich Karimov. The independent Uzbek state emerged in 1991 in the wake of the disintegration of the Soviet Union. Along with the other states that made an appearance at that time, Uzbekistan also faced the problem of defining itself in a 'new' form. Yet this new form could not ignore its past particularly since it was assumed that a search for its own traditions and history that had been suppressed in the recent past was one of the principal reasons for its emergence. An attempt at this reconciliation is clearly evident in the writings of President Karimov. An ethnic Uzbek, born in Samarkand in 1938, Islam A. Karimov was appointed as first secretary of the Communist Party of Kashka Darya oblast in 1986. In June 1989 he became first secretary of the central committee of the Communist Party of UzSSR and on 24 March 1990, the Supreme Soviet of the UzSSR elected him as the President. With the demise of the Soviet Union in 1990, Karimov became the head of the Peoples' Democratic Party of Uzbekistan. On 31 August 1991, independence of the Republic of Uzbekistan was declared. In the first nation-wide election for President, Karimov was elected President on 29 December 1991. On 26 March 1995, in a national plebiscite his period of office was extended to 2000. On 9 January 2000, Karimov was reelected for a further five years to end in 2005. However, on 27 January 2002, in another national plebiscite Uzbek voters extended the presidential terms from five to seven years. He was reelected as President in the December 2007 Uzbek Presidential elections.

During his tenure as President, Karimov has written extensively on the need to develop a democratic state, a free market economy and a civil society that supports the political values of a liberal 'modern' society. Yet interwoven through all of this is an emphasis on the specific Uzbek characteristic that these will assume. What has remained central to the writings of Karimov is the interrelatedness of the political and economic spheres as they intersect the sphere of civil society. The declaration of Uzbekistan's independence meant that there was need to develop a model of political, economic and social development for Uzbekistan. This model had to take note of the values of 'liberal' societies but could not also ignore the Soviet legacy. As such there appeared the need to reconcile private interest with public good while developing the model for the 'new' Uzbek state. While a distinction between the public and the private is the marker of a modern state, a dynamic boundary was developed between the two in the Uzbek case. The challenge was to peacefully effect the transition to a unique 'modern' state where 'deideologization of the economy' and 'supremacy of laws' would be the definitive criteria. In the course of appreciating the politics of a new born Uzbek state, as elucidated in the writings of Karimov, the developmental dynamics through which the post-Second World War states were formed and came into being is once again encountered. While a focus on building the foundations of a 'new' state and society dominated the discourse till the mid 1990's it changed dramatically following the attempt on the life of the President in February 1999. Thereafter the developmental dynamics of the new state took a backseat as 'threats' to the security of the state and a discourse on danger replaced the earlier emphasis on the need to develop a democratic state with a market economy. This new discursive construction of danger assumed centre stage in the creation and maintenance of the identity of the 'new' state. Here particular attention is paid to the geopolitical position of the state that becomes critical particularly in the post 9/11 context.

This chapter is an attempt at understanding the nature of the new state through the writings of President Karimov. In his capacity as President, Karimov has published numerous books that are generally collections of speeches and are widely distributed. Central to his writings is the contention that the state of Uzbekistan is the fulfillment of the historic destiny of the Uzbek people. The first two sections principally deal with writings that belong to an era when the developmental dynamics of the 'new' state rather than terrorism held centre stage. What is the nature of the modern Uzbek state that President Karimov is talking about? Was there a claim that the new Uzbek state is at all a 'modern' state? If not what is the alternative model of state that is then put forward? [4] The last section deals with an era when the discourse on a 'nation under threat' is predominant and geopolitics holds centre stage.

'An ancient dream has come true'[5]: the 'new' Uzbek state

> The inalienable right of the Uzbek people to self-determination was realized on August 31, 1991 with the proclamation of independence of the Republic of Uzbekistan. An ancient dream has come true: Uzbekistan has peacefully, through parliamentary means acquired genuine statehood. This is the most significant event in the centuries long history of the nation.[6]

On 31 August 1991, the Uzbek Parliament declared independence. The 1st of September 1991 is thus celebrated as Uzbek Independence day – the day when the *Uzbekskoi Sovietskoi Sotsiliastichiskoi Respublika* that had appeared in 1924 was just as suddenly transformed into the *Uzbekskoi Respublikasi*. President Karimov's writings in the immediate post-independence period are marked by euphoria about the emergence of a 'new' state and the fact that the Uzbek people are now the masters of their own destiny. Karimov's first book, *Uzbekistan, The Road of Independence and Progress*, summarizes its content as a desire to 'examine the fundamentals of political and economic relations in the light of present day realities; the goal to build a genuinely independent democratic state'. It goes on to note that Uzbekistan's domestic policy is aimed at creating a socially-oriented free market economy, while at the same time strengthening the spiritual and moral values of the nation.[7]

What is significant is the emphasis that the revival of spiritual values should be combined with the more pragmatic consideration that the region has a tradition of multiple faiths. This has been emphasized by President Karimov in these words:

> Spiritual revival should also embrace the attitude of human beings towards the land and its richness. On the area, where agriculture during centuries has been based on irrigation, a careful treatment of land and water is not less important moral imperative than a careful attitude towards objects of

> civilization. Soil, air, water and fire, (the Sun) have been traditionally worshipped in Central Asia, they were given respect by all religions of our ancestors, from Zoroastrianism to Islam.[8]

In the writings of President Karimov there is clear indication that the new Uzbek state would look towards devising an alternative theoretical paradigm to guide public policy formulation. It is significant that the new state, though based on 'liberal' norms, is not individualistic in essence. The significance of the collective is the first aspect of the new state that President Karimov stresses upon. In the search for its own model of building a new society, therefore, he emphasizes 'historically, a collective identity is inherent to the people of Uzbekistan and is rooted in the traditionally communal way of life'.[9] This has remained significant in defining the emerging state. However, the primacy of the collective has not been defined in terms of identification of private and public good thereby rendering irrelevant the need for civil society. In fact, there is commitment to the building of a viable civil society through the development of a market economy and adherence to the rule of law. In his words:

> We have begun the building of a democratic, lawful and secular society with an open market economy and a strong system of social protection.[10]

This model of the 'new' Uzbek state is thus different from that projected as the norm in a large number of writings on political transition in the region. Here, political transition in the region has been projected as a transformation from 'partially communized societies' to 'new political orders'.[11] This would imply a ritualized appeal to democratic norms evident in the frequency of consultative exercises, which legitimize political elites in varying degrees. The assumption is that the major tasks of economic development and nation building are best served in this process. Paradoxically this fails to take into account the tensions between economic modernization and political freedom that exists in the phase of transition.

Recognizing this, Karimov stresses that there are no universal models of social and economic development equally acceptable to each country and no ready made formulas or models of statehood.[12] In keeping with this while addressing the 48th Session of the United Nations General Assembly, he spelled out five basic principles of reform:

> First we have proclaimed the priority of economy over politics, deideologization of both domestic and economic relations.
>
> Second, we consider that the state needs to play the role of the main reformer and initiator of democratic transformation in the Republic during the transition period.
>
> Third, preservation of law and order and supremacy of Law.
>
> Fourth, of exceptional importance to us is a strong social policy protecting the interests of the citizens, especially the most needy stratum and all those who need government support.
>
> And finally, transition to free market relations will have to be carried out gradually on an evolutionary basis.[13]

He goes on to talk about the need to shape new and free thinking about ideological indoctrination, which would reveal the entire diversity of the forms and ways of transition of each country to a qualitatively new condition. What emerges as significant here is the fact that there seems to be recognition of the fact that even these will, in fact, be subject to change.

According to President Karimov, the state that was being built would have to be based on the mentality of the people characterized by spiritual and cultural values, education, culture and justice. He points to 'the philosophy of the Orient and enlightened Islam' as the origin of these values. The wisdom of his ancestors and progressive world experience would combine to build Uzbek statehood and society. There is also recognition in his writings that there is an Islamic structure, which today needs to be examined in order to assess its role in the formation of a new Uzbek state. Karimov stresses:

> the revival of the spiritual-religious foundation of the society, of Islam (ic) culture that has accumulated centuries old experience of the moral consolidation of our people, all this is an important step on the path to self-identification, and restitution of the historical memory and cultural-historical integrity. Old mosques are constructed and new ones are

built, educational centres are expanded; religious literature is published.[14]

However, in Uzbekistan, as in all the post-Soviet constitutions the secular nature of the state is emphasized, as is the principle of separation of the Church and the State. Yet as a break from the recent past, the new constitution recognizes:

> Freedom of conscience is guaranteed to all. Everyone shall have the right to profess or not to profess any religion. Any compulsory imposition of religion shall be impermissible.[15]

Karimov also addresses the question of the role that the state would play in the process of transition:

> And now the time has come to comprehend and to make a decision as to what state we are building. What should it be like? What is its role in the formation of new democratic society?[16]

While there has been general agreement on the necessity of post-communist governments to undertake domestic structural reforms and liberalization, two contrasting approaches have defined the role that the state would play in the process. The first is the 'open competition' approach and the second is the 'guiding state approach'.[17] The open competition approach argues that the best structural reforms are those that most rapidly and effectively free fundamental economic forces to play their natural roles in economy. The guiding state approach differed in maintaining that incremental reform measures are viewed as most likely to lead to rational industrial and agricultural restructuring than would an allocation of resources that were structured by forces operating in the existing imperfect markets. It argues in favour of a phased and gradual introduction of reform oriented measures, emphasizing government guidance throughout the process. While variations of the two have been adopted by states, in his writings Karimov clearly recognizes the primary role of the state in the formation of a new society, a role that extends to the economic sphere.

Underlying the writings of President Karimov is a belief that a strong economic base is a necessary condition for democracy to exist and flourish in state and society. Karimov argues that economic reforms have been guided by the inevitable influence of the dynamics of market economies throughout the world.[18] Consequently there is encouragement for a movement towards a market economy though with the warning that the transition will be difficult. He also emphasizes, '...building a market economy is not an end in itself. The final objective of all reforms be they economic, democratic or political is the creation of decent conditions of life for man'.[19] It therefore becomes crucial that the transition be a stage by stage policy of economic reform. What is also emphasized as crucial is that while the state guides the transformation of economy, it must also secure the social protection of the people. The presence of the state will therefore continue to be felt as it regulates market activity to minimize social dislocation. Therefore Karimov emphasizes that

> We need our own principally new model of building a socially oriented free market economy taking into account the peculiarities of the Republic and being in harmony with the past, present and future development of Uzbekistan.[20]

President Karimov's writings clearly indicate that transition to modernity cannot be examined as an unproblematic implementation of a set of policies involving 'economic liberalization' and 'marketization' along with 'democratization' enabling the creation of a market economy and a liberal polity. Such an explanation of change reduces the complexity of the transition and fails to underscore the need to examine the diversity of forms of transition.[21] The fundamental reorganization of material life, the transformations of geopolitical relations and the major discursive shifts in the way that policies are to be framed and implemented require a more rigorous study of the specificity of the situations, and also call for a complex model of transition. The diversity of historical experiences of these states is also a compelling factor in the determination of the trajectory of transition.

Similarly, the political economy of transition itself has to be critically examined. Here, the national mode of regulation and accumulation, the historical and geographic specificity of the path taken for transition, the role of different institutional actors and social relations have to be taken into account. This will show how 'legacies' become a central component in the understanding of the possibilities and limits to transition. While the 'national road to transition' is the central focus of the examination, the emergence of regionally differentiated transitions also needs to be taken into account. All these involve a study of the complex system of adjustments of various issues and the intersections of political and economic arguments in the wake of globalization.

'Conditions for market reform'[22]: reorganizing the economy

A simultaneous requirement of restructuring of economy to meet market requirements and maintenance of democracy was faced by the Uzbek state in the period of transition. The line to be followed here is indicated by these words of President Karimov:

> Independent Uzbekistan is traveling along the road chosen by the nation along the road of open and free market relations and along the road of building a just society and a strong law governed democratic state.[23]

and that

> The final objective is the construction of a strong democratic law governed state and secular society with a stable socially oriented market economy.[24]

Most analysts would argue that it is difficult to do both and maintain the initial popularity of the government. Each state deals with this in different ways particularly as it is also faced with the 'growing expectations' that a regime change promises. By 1995, the initial objective of 'construction of a strong democratic law governed state' was outpaced by that of 'a stable socially oriented market economy and open foreign policy' and Karimov, in his writings, identifies 'strategic objectives of the state' as being almost entirely dominated by economic concerns and the removal of state interference in the economy. He also clearly points to the fact that economy should prevail over politics.

For the fledgling state the crucial problem as also the dominating rhetoric in the immediate post-independence days, was an accent on building a viable state that ensured the rights and freedoms of citizens and established a genuine democracy. Along with this was a concern for the establishment of a 'national statehood.' In the decade following independence, the 'national question' has assumed an entirely new character. While the emphasis, in the immediate post-independence days, was on political transformation and on the transition to a new society free from ideological constraints, the new emphasis is on economic development and only secondarily on the preservation of cultural heritage. The change in the focus of the official position is clearly evident from the difference in the overriding concerns of the two books written in the gap of three years by Karimov.

In 1995, Karimov wrote *Uzbekistan, Along the Road of Deepening Economic Reform.*[25] The first part of what is called the 'manual' on 'results and lessons of the first stage of economic reform' deals with the problems of shaping a new strategy, ways of implementation of economic reform and establishment of legal foundation of market relations. It also focuses on privatization of state property, formation of multi-structured economy and the course of reform in agriculture and the establishment of agrarian relations of a new type. The second part on 'tasks and priorities of the second stage of economic reform' deals with the basic tasks in the sphere of economic advancement of Uzbekistan. These include deepening of the privatization process and introduction of a competitive environment ensuring macro-economic stability, consolidation of national currency, carrying out deep structural transformations, and shaping a democratic state with strong social guarantees. The principal objective of the second part is to identify directions of activities of prior significance in this sphere.

Economic concerns dominated the affairs of the state in Uzbekistan since it was assumed that economic development would play a crucial role in the new state.[26] An interesting example of this is a book entitled *Independent Uzbekistan Today,* published in 1993 from Tashkent where the first section, describing the land and its people and the social system, is entitled 'Prerequisites for Business' and then the subsequent sections, 'The Overview of Economy', 'Business in Uzbekistan' and 'Fundamentals of Economic Legislation'.[27] It seems reasonable to argue from this rather one-sided vision of independent Uzbekistan that reorganization of the economy is a major challenge of the state. Karimov's preoccupation with economic issues is equally revealing. He is reported to have pointed out that independence was important primarily to bring Uzbekistan out of the then existing economic situation. This is reflected in the subject matter for the laws of the new state which deal overwhelmingly with economic issues like the setting up of *Fonds*, registration of companies, investments, taxes, economic sanctions, grants for citizens, banks, exports, economic reforms, foreign investments.[28]

The reorganization of economy has assumed central place in the Uzbek situation:

> strengthening of the integrative process among the states, formation of common political-economic space, transformation to unified international norms, rules and standards, on the one hand and downfall of the command economic and administrative system on the other.[29]

The new social and economic policy would however not only move towards integration in the world community, but would also *promote the social programme* in the country. This policy would take note of the *unique way of life* of the various cultures and civilizations in Uzbekistan and would consist of a variety of forms and methods.[30] The necessity of developing the basis of one's own model of development is recognized; a model which would be based on market relations but would also take into account the national historical heritage, foundations of life, traditions and mentality of the people. Karimov points to this when he says:

> We have selected an approach of rejecting egalitarianism in the system of social protection of the population and finding our own path corresponding to moral values, way of life and frame of mind of the nation which took shape throughout millennia in the East.[31]

There is clear recognition of the fact that there can be no universal model of economic development, which can be followed. The Uzbek model would have to take note of concrete historical, socio-economical, national-psychological and demographic aspects. This is being interpreted to mean an emphasis on stabilization.

This would mean that while on the one hand there would be an effort to move out of the administered economic structures of the Soviet system, this it would not do without taking into account the requirements of society. What is interesting is that in the course of this transition it is clearly recognized that while ensuring the macro economic stabilization of the society for market oriented reforms in order to ensure economic growth, is the foremost task, this is crucial for ensuring the *welfare of the society*.[32] There is also stress on the fact that social assistance reaches those for whom it is meant. Also development is projected on the basis of the gains of the last seven decades, which has transformed Uzbekistan into a 'developed' society as far as social indicators are concerned. The emphasis here is on the transformation without *shock therapy*.[33]

This is particularly evident in the case of monetary policy where quick transformation was postponed in favour of *stabilization with parity*. In fact in all this a *gradualist* policy is evident that makes place for the old within the new structures. The *Uzbek model of development* then goes on to point out that 'privatization is not the ultimate goal'. It is the means for ensuring competition of economic motivation, and more importantly, the fact that each man must 'improve his own position without hampering the position of others'.[34] The Decrees and Resolutions of the Republic of Uzbekistan further stress the 'social orientation (of the policies) should be reflected in every act under consideration'. The problems of protection of family with children during the reorganization are addressed. Karimov identifies the final objective of the economic policy as the construction of a strong democratic law-governed state and secular society with a *stable socially oriented market economy* and open foreign policy.[35] This is also reflected in the fact that it is still the state that has primary responsibility in implementation of programmes relating to land reclamation, irrigation, raising soil fertility etc. Since Uzbek economy is primarily dependent on the cultivation of cotton, it is important that the state has a definite agricultural policy.[36]

This would mean that while there would be complete *deideologization* of the economy, the state would still be required to play the role of the chief reformer during the complicated transitional period. As Karimov points out,

> ...economy should prevail over politics and constitute its own content, to be more precise, the economy and problems of its further development form the core of the current policy.[37]

The first step was directed towards the establishment of a legal foundation for a new economic system, formation and consolidation of statehood and elimination of old stereotyped thinking. Yet there is emphasis on the fact that

> We have made a simple choice—to consistently advance towards market economy stage-by-stage —evolutionary, not by great leaps or by revolutionary destruction....Popular saying has it never destroy the old house before you build a new one, It is unforgivable to neglect what could be used in the interest of economic reform during transition to market relations and make this process more efficient and less painful.[38]

This examination of the 'reorganization' of economy now underway points to the fact that for a correct understanding of this phase of transition, a more nuanced reading of the form the economy will assume is crucial. A unilinear trajectory of transition to market economy may not reflect the complex local cultural forms that Uzbek economy has assumed in recent times.

By the middle of the 1990's it was assumed that the tasks of building the 'new' state was complete. This was also the period when there was recognition of the fact that the states could survive in a post-Soviet era and the realization that given this stability there was the possibility that its natural resources, like oil and natural gas, could be exploited. Geo-economics assumed an important position in the mind of the outside powers and this was reflected in the state discourse that focused both on the advantages and the disadvantages of strategic location. Geopolitics became a persistent theme in President Karimov's writings and as the regime was challenged a counter discourse that portrayed a 'nation under threat' became evident.

'Conditions of stability and guarantees for progress[39]': geopolitics of a 'nation under threat'

Geopolitics is a persistent feature of the present process of constructing political space in Uzbekistan and this is reflected in a large number of Karimov's writings. In situating Uzbekistan there is first and foremost an emphasis on projecting it as the pivotal state in the region and as the geopolitical basis of Central Asia. It is evident that Uzbekistan is seen as a major regional power with a large population within the state and influential minorities in the neighbouring ones. In fact the theme of a transcendent nationhood is an abiding feature in a large corpus of literature in Uzbekistan today. Speaking at the 48th session of the United Nations General Assembly in September 1993, President Islam Karimov described his state as follows:

> Uzbekistan with its twenty-two million strong population makes up both the geographical and political basis of Central Asia. One of the most ancient world civilizations has emerged in this region. This land was a crossroad of the Great Silk Road. The history of my people goes back deep into the past and is more than three thousand years old. Once prospering empires and kingdoms in the territory of ancient Turan, Transoxiana and Turkistan have left a bright impact on the development of world culture. [40]

It is emphasized that the population of Uzbekistan is 22 million, which makes it the most populated country to the south of Russia.[41] It is also significant that 75% of the population is Uzbek. To this may be added the large Uzbek minorities in the neighbouring countries, amounting to some 2.5 million. This gives the Uzbeks around half the total population of Central Asia. Uzbekistan also has the capacity to exercise influence in the neighbouring states with leaders of ethnic Uzbek origin holding leadership positions. There is then an attempt to equate this contemporary reality with an ancient civilizational basis. Turan, Transoxiana and Turkistan are all identified as part of this ancient Uzbek civilizational past. This theme of an ancient past for the Uzbeks that Karimov emphasizes finds echoes in a large number of writings, which have been published in post-Soviet Uzbekistan. These remain interesting in terms of examining how the story of the Uzbek past is now being told.[42] While on the one hand the antiquity of the state is stressed, on the other there is an attempt to situate the state within the geopolitical imperatives of the twenty-first century:

> Today Uzbekistan represents not only an area with huge

> natural and raw material resources, but also an immense market and a place to invest capital. Our country possesses the enormous intellectual, spiritual and cultural potential. All these in combination with a unique geographical location cannot but cause a great geopolitical and geostrategic interest, particularly when a new political and economic order in the world is actively being formed.[43]

This emphasizes the fact that Uzbekistan is self-sufficient in energy, the world's second largest producer of cotton and the fourth largest producer of gold. It achieved self- sufficiency in food in 1996. There is then an attempt to stress that Uzbekistan is the strategic centre of a geopolitical area that is at the core of the energy-providing region in Eurasia. There is emphasis on the fact that in the modern world no country can exist in isolation but must enter into definite geographical and political systems. It is pointed out that the geographical location of Uzbekistan between the Amu Darya and the Syr Darya has provided a favourable geostrategic situation from the point of view of establishing international links. Through the territory of Uzbekistan the Great Silk Road passed connecting the East and the West. The trade routes converged here. The intensive process of external contacts and mutual enrichment of various cultures took place here. Also today routes from Europe and the Middle East to the Asia Pacific region cross here.

> Uzbekistan is actually located in the strategic centre of the semi ring comprising the richest oil and gas deposits of the Persian Gulf, Caspian Sea and Tarim Basin, i.e. in the centre of energy resource fields that in the circumstances of the overall energy deficit are called upon to play a key role in the future of Eurasia and finally the whole world.
>
> More than that we are a part of the region where exist uncoinciding interests of Russia, China, India and other eastern and western states. Actually being located on the conjunctions these potentially very powerful Eurasian centre of forces still in the process of formation and which undoubtedly will determine that these are the countries where the image of the 21st century, our territory, the territory of the whole region will also remain an object of interests for such powerful countries of the Islamic world as Turkey, Pakistan, Iran and Saudi Arabia.[44]

In fact, Karimov notes that the importance of Uzbekistan and other Central Asian Republics in the modern geopolitical system is so noticeable that the events occurring here will attract the attention of the world's largest powers and various geopolitical formations. He goes on to note that the Uzbek state takes note of this interest in forming its geopolicy and when it seeks to obtain for itself political, economic and strategic advantages.

In terms of situating Uzbekistan within a larger region, Karimov clearly indicates that the twenty" - "first century will be a century of globalization in international relations. Under these conditions the process of integration, growing participation of sovereign states in international institutions and organizations should be regarded not only as a historical necessity but also as a powerful factor of sustainability and stability both in separate regions and the entire planet. In terms of situating the state within this global arena, Karimov delineates various levels of integration. In terms of integration within the world community he emphasizes Uzbekistan's integration within the United Nations Organization and such international financial and economic organizations as International Monetary Fund, the World Bank, International Financial Corporation, European Bank for Reconstruction and Development. The second level of integration is in terms of expansion of relationship with various regional organizations. Here emphasis is placed on the European Union, OSCE, NATO, ECO, OIC, Non-Aligned Movement and others. Here, he emphasizes the significant role of the European Union. What is more interesting however is the emphasis that Uzbekistan is an Asian country. As he writes, 'we should not forget that Uzbekistan is situated in Asia.'[45]

Another level of cooperation is with other international organizations primarily from the Asian region. Here, particular attention is to be paid to deepening of relations with other Turkic language speaking nations. Karimov notes that Uzbekistan is keen to build up relations on both a bilateral and multilateral basis. He begins with the significance of Uzbekistan's relations with the United States. He also emphasizes bilateral relations with European states like Germany, Great Britain, France,

Belgium, Portugal, Austria, Greece, and the Czech Republic, Slovakia, Romania and a number of others. Similarly relations are being built with the countries of the east and the southeast like Japan, South Korea, China, Vietnam, Malaysia, India and Indonesia. Karimov stresses that relations that are shaped between countries of the former Soviet Union occupy a special place in the solution of regional stability issues, development of integration processes on the regional level.

The discourse on the Commonwealth of Independent States(CIS) and the official Uzbek attitude towards the organization deserves particular attention and is being cited in some detail. Karimov begins by noting that there exists vast opportunities for mutual cooperation between the CIS on the basis of equitable bilateral and multilateral partnerships. The basis of such cooperation is not just territorial proximity and economic contacts but also deep historical roots, cultural and spiritual linkages and the common fate shared by the nations during a long historical period. Karimov argues that the post Soviet states are not against integration however; this would not be acceptable at the cost of their independence. Karimov emphasizes that the CIS would be viewed in terms of integration of genuinely independent sovereign states. Karimov questions the formation of certain Communities and Unions within the CIS and argues that joining these is unacceptable to Uzbekistan. The reason is made clear. Uzbekistan does not wish to be a party to 'any reanimation of the old empire system'.[46] Karimov criticizes the creation of supra-state structures within the CIS. He argues,

> In setting up within the Commonwealth supra-state structures vested with the right to make direct action decisions, which are mandatory for all bodies and organizations passing by the relevant legitimate bodies of each individual member state, it would be very difficult to call these states sovereign and independent. [47]

He argues against joining any of these Unions, which have a predominantly geopolitical character. However, he does emphasize the necessity of Central Asian integration.

In more recent writings Karimov has suggested two ideas about the development of the CIS. According to the first, which he supports, the future development of the CIS is possible by implementing the EU model where he proposes the creation of zones of free trade as initial steps. After that there would be an opportunity to go for the next more prospective and long term stage about the creation of a common economic zone. The second, which he does not, is to keep it in its present 'shapeless' state.[48] This is a change from his earlier stance where he seemed to be opposed to any integration, which could affect the sovereignty of the state.

The importance of the social construction of danger is evident from a comparison of two books written by the President within a gap of a few years. His 1992 book *Uzbekistan: The Road of Independence and Progress* that was republished in India in 1993 is a celebration of independence and a patriotic statement of hope for the future. His 1997 book *Uzbekistan on the Threshold of the Twenty First Century* is subtitled *Threats to Security, Conditions of Stability and Guarantees for Progress*. Threat to security is at the heart of the Presidential analysis. Part one is entitled 'Threats to Security' and lists in detail a range of problems that Uzbekistan would face including drugs and arms trafficking, religious extremism, terrorism, nuclear weapon manufacture, ecological dangers, regional conflicts and 'great power chauvinism'. The late 1990's thus witnessed a shift in Karimov's sense of the geopolitical identity of Uzbekistan, from a self confident polity at peace with itself and its neighbours to a besieged island of civilization in a sea of anarchy that threatened to submerge it.[49]

The portrayal of 'a nation under threat' is reflected in Presidential writings, media reports and even in popular culture.[50] One representative example is a part of the speech delivered by President Karimov on the occasion of the First Session of *Oliy Majlis* of the Republic of Uzbekistan:

> Today our region is attracting attention of different extremist forces and centers that strive to undertake the expansion of religious extremism and international terrorism, to divert the states of the region from the democratic and secular path of development with a due rule of law. The drugs and arms trafficking represent a credible threat not only on the region, but also on the entire world. The current developments in

> the region and in the world urge us to create a system of security that would be able to guarantee in real terms the non-violability of our borders, territorial integrity of the country, stability and sustainable development of Uzbekistan. It is important that people comprehend the inseparable link between ensuring the public order, their personal safety and increasing their own watchfulness and an active participation in what is happening around them. It is necessary to promote the involvement of the population in eliminating extremism in all its manifestations, securing peace and stability in our common home.[51]

The first channel that inculcated a sense of danger was Presidential writings themselves. The importance of the social construction of danger is highlighted by the fact that President Karimov's book *Uzbekistan on the Threshold of the Twenty-First Century* is subtitled *Threats to Security, Conditions of Stability and Guarantees for Progress*. The same geopolitical visions were conveyed through the national news media (*Halk Sozi*), which presented opposite images of a happy and prosperous Uzbekistan in contrast to consistent images of neighbouring states as spaces of chaos. There is also the suggestion that the chaos in the neighbourhood is threatening to engulf Uzbekistan. The image of a 'nation under threat' is also reflected in popular music which is often an important site in struggles to control utilize and define space. In fact music plays an important part as a medium for shaping identities. Here, both the power of national music in generating collective feeling and also music as a site for identifying cultural differentials by creating a sphere where identities are affirmed, challenged and reconstructed, will be briefly examined.

Since 1991 the Uzbek language music industry has been reoriented in line with the 'ideology of national independence'. In fact it has been argued that Uzbek popular music plays a major role in nation-building since independence. The notion of a nation under danger is portrayed clearly in the music of the group *Setora*. The video of one of their best known songs *Sen Borsan* (You're There) is a poignant depiction of the tragic end of a love affair between a young woman, a university student and her partner, a soldier. The video opens by cycling between scenes of a wicked looking man restraining frightened children, three young women in mourning, a military funeral, the handsome soldier on drill and rose tinted images of the lovers. This confusing medley is explained as the plot unfolds. The lover is part of a unit that moves in on an empty warehouse where a helpless woman and children have been kidnapped by a stereotypical 'Islamic terrorist' with a malicious smile, bearded and sporting a Palestinian headscarf. The haunting music provides an atmospheric accompaniment to rising tension as rotating camera angles follow the soldiers as they close in on the terrorists who are callously beating their captives. These scenes are intermingled with further images of the happy young couple. The captives are eventually released and the terrorists are overcome but the hero dies in the firefight, apparently to avoid hitting a girl held by a knife to her throat as a human shield. The video concludes with the girls singing besides the grave of the soldier remembering his handsome smile and the lost days of love.

On 13 May 2005, the city of Andijan staged the most determined challenge to the government of the President. As Nick Megoran notes, it was a serious challenge to the legitimacy of Karimov's rule both in the immediate nature of the armed attacks on state representatives and the occupation of public space but also to the extent that subsequent reports risked damaging his position and reputation. [52] The Andijan incident proved to be somewhat of a watershed that was followed by an upsurge of condemnation of the Uzbek government's actions. Once again the necessity to justify transformation to modernity assumed centre stage. In the aftermath of the incident a booklet was published from Tashkent that summarized the statements and responses of President Karimov to the local and international press about the Andijan events of 12-13 May 2005. Entitled, *The Uzbek People Will Never Depend on Others,* the booklet seeks to provide an explanation of the Government's actions during the incident and show that this incident had nothing in common with the 'revolutions' that had led to changes in governments in Georgia, Ukraine and Kyrgyzstan. In common with most writings of the post-1997 period this also portrays the image of a 'nation under threat'.

> During the first years of our independence we thought we were free and we had something different: we became members of the UN so now we would move towards democracy and everything ahead would be perfect. We freed ourselves from the Soviet communist ideology. But what filled the vacuum left behind? Different radical religious groups, some not always peaceful, started to make their presence felt in the region. Everywhere they proposed building mosques and they did so until we started opening our eyes. Something similar has been happening to our neighbours; for instance Kazakhstan has at the moment 1500 mosques of which 500 are not officially registered. Sometimes these groups offered loans or sometimes they showed their readiness to build these mosques for free.
>
> I want to reiterate again, using the ideological vacuum left after the collapse of communism, Hisb-ut-Tahrir put down its deep roots in the countries of Central Asia and in Uzbekistan, in particular in the Ferghana Valley. In the city of Tashkent you can find evidence of this sect .[53]

Despite this it reiterates that Uzbekistan is a constitutional state that follows the path of secular democracy:

> We have chosen the path of democracy, a secular way of life and are moving towards the standards, which have been achieved by developed countries. Indeed we are not inventing anything new and would like to build the same type of society, which now exists in France, Netherlands, Belgium, Italy, Spain and the United States itself. We want to create a similar system like that found in Japan or in South Korea. Democracy is unique everywhere, its main principles are clear – it is an authority of the people, it is a will of the people, it has free and transparent elections which is an indispensable part of democracy. It has a civil society, which in the end, represents the highest level of democracy.[54]

In his most recent book, the emphasis is once again on social development. It is titled *Progress of the Country and Better Living Standards of the People as the Ultimate Objectives of all Democratic Innovations and Economic Reforms*. The emphasis here is on social responsibility of the individual as a necessary element for the creation of a prosperous life and a free civil society.

'The path we have chosen'[55]

The emphasis in Karimov's early writings was on the construction of a new state based on the principles of genuine democracy. In the economic sphere the emphasis was on building a stable and dynamic economy and the gradual formation of a socially oriented market economy. While defining the priorities in the programme there was appreciation of the fact that it was impossible to solve all problems at once.

There is, thus, the important recognition that each state is 'unique' and the result of distinct culture of the people. As he argues,

> The state we are building now must be based on the mentality of our people characterized by spiritual and cultural values, education, culture and justice. These features for the most part have been formed under the influence of the philosophy of the Orient and enlightened Islam to the promotion thereof the Uzbek people made an invaluable and universally recognized contribution.
>
> It is with due regard to this philosophy that absorbed and incorporated the wisdom of such of our great ancestors as Khoja Akmad Yassavi, Bakhouddin Nakshbandi, Imam-al-Bukhari, Imam-al-Termezi, AmirTimur, Ulugbeg, Alisher Navoi, Bobur as well as with regard to the progressive world experience that we should build our statehood, our society.[56]

In the course of his writings, he stresses this 'unique' path of development by underlining the existence of unique national pathways to development. He sees nation states as each having their own individual routes towards some eventual form of national democracy. He rejects the idea that models of social change are transferable from one place to another. Therefore, he emphasizes the 'importance of the recognition of local traditions, the one based on the *mahallah* for instance. During his speech at the first session of the *Oliy Majlis* on 23 February 1995, President Karimov made the point that while the aim was to build a state based on democracy, it should harmonize with the basic moral principles of the Uzbek society. He went on to point out that while there does exist universally recognized principles of democratic society, enshrined in all democratic constitutions, in most situations this does not lead to harmony. The specific features of democratization in the Orient are its 'consistency and gradualness'.

> The Orient on the contrary presupposes that democracy is based on the ideas of collectivism, paternalism and priority of public opinion. The democratic process is developing influences by such features of our people as law obedience, priority of moral and spiritual principles in political relations....It is necessary to take this into account when trying to determine the system of social management. And we do take it into account. I mean the institution of mahallah. We all know that from time immemorial the mahallah was that place where all issues were and are still solved, khashars are conducted, national traditional ceremonies and other functions are held. It is this place where the public opinion on politics and economy is formed ....Mahallah must become a reliable supporter and an efficient instrument of implementation of reforms in our society.[57]

An understanding of these features becomes critical both in appreciating the forms that modernity assumes and the specific form that the Uzbek state assumed in the post-independent period.

NOTES AND REFERENCES

1 Clifford Geertz, *After the Fact, Two Countries, Four Decades, One Anthropologist*, Cambridge, Massachusetts, London, England: Harvard University Press, 1996.

2 Ibid.

3 Ibid.

4 Uzbekistan's road to modernity, defined in terms of transition to a 'liberal democratic society', has been examined in a number of recent writings. Most of these have critically examined the official position on the transformation to modernity in the writings of President Karimov and the laws of the new state particularly with regard to individual freedom. See for an instance John R. Pottenger, 'Civil society, religious freedom, and Islam Karimov: Uzbekistan's struggle for a decent society', *Central Asian Survey* 23, no 1 (March 2004).

5 This phrase is taken from I.A. Karimov, *Uzbekistan: The Road of Independence and Progress*, Tashkent: 'Uzbekiston', 1992

6 Karimov, *Uzbekistan*: p 3.

7 Ibid.

8 Islam. A. Karimov, *Uzbekistan in the Threshold of the 21st Century, Threats to Security, Conditions of Stability and Guarantees for Progress*, Tashkent: Uzbekistan, 1997, p. 124.

9 Karimov, *Uzbekistan*, p. 10.

10 Cited from the Address of H.E. Mr Islam Karimov, President of the Republic of Uzbekistan at the 48th session of the United Nations General Assembly, Tashkent: Uzbekistan, 1993.

11 See John Anderson, 'Elections and political development in Central Asia', *The Journal of Communist Studies and Transition Politics* 13, no 4 (December 1997), pp. 28-53.

12. Address of H.E. Mr Islam Karimov, President of the Republic of Uzbekistan at the 48th session of the United Nations General Assembly. Similar ideas are present in his speech to the First Session of the Oliy Majlis in February 1995. See Islam A Karimov, *Basic Principles of Social, Political and Economic Development of Uzbekistan*, Tashkent: Uzbekiston 1995.

13 Address of H.E. Mr Islam Karimov, President of the Republic of Uzbekistan at the 48th session of the United Nations General Assembly.

14 Karimov, *Uzbekistan in the Threshold of the 21st Century*, p. 123.

15 *Konstitutsiya Respubliki Uzbekistan*, Tashkent: 'Uzbekiston', 1992, Statiya 31.

16 Karimov, *Basic Principles of Social, Political and Economic Development of Uzbekistan*.

17 For details see, Gregory Gleason, *Markets and Politics in Central Asia: Structural Reform and Political Change*, London and New York: Routledge, 2003.

18 Islam A Karimov, *Building the Future: Uzbekistan, Its Own Model for Transition to Market Economy*, Tashkent: 'Uzbekiston', 1993.

19 Ibid, p. 65.

20 Ibid., p. 6.

21 For an examination of transitions in Eastern Europe and Russia, see John Pickles and Adrian Smith, eds. *Theorising Transitions: The Political Economy of Post-Communist Transformations*, London and New York: Routledge, 1998.

22 Karimov, *Basic Principles of Social, Political and Economic Development of Uzbekistan*.

23 Islam A. Karimov, *Uzbekistan Along the Road of Deepening Economic Reform*, Tashkent: 'Uzbekiston', 1995, p. 3.

24 Karimov, *Uzbekistan*, p. 9.

25 Ibid.

26 There are large numbers of articles in journals on economic reforms. See for instance, A. Kh. Khikmatov and A.M. Shyepyelyev, 'Nyekotorye Aspyekte Osushyestvlyeniya Economichyeskoi Reformi v Uzbekistanye', *Obshyestvyenneye Nayuki v Uzbekistane*, nos. 3-4 (1997).

27 M.N. Akhundi, A.M. Kadirov and I.K. Faizullaev, eds. *Independent Uzbekistan Today*, Tashkent: 'Bainal Millai' External Economics Association, 1993.

28 See *Sobraniye Postanovlyenii Pravityelstvo Uzbyeksoi Sovietskoi Sotsialistichieskoi Respubliki*, Tashkent, 1990-1997.

29 G. Karimova, *Politico Ekonomichyeskoiye Reforme v Uzbekistane, Realii i Perspektivi*, Tashkent: 'Uzbekiston', 1995.

30 Ibid.

31 Karimov, *Uzbekistan along the Road of Deepening Economic Reform*, pp. 115-16.

32 *Respublika Uzbekistan: Ukazi i Postnovlyeniya, Vtoraya Kniga*, Tashkent: 'Uzbekiston', 1994.

33 Karimova, *Politico Aakonomichyeskoiye Reforme v Uzbekistane*.

34 See 'Uzbek Model of Development' in ibid, p. 22.

35 See for instance Karimov, *Uzbekistan; Basic Principles of Political and Economic Development of Uzbekistan; Nash Putch Nezavisimoi Gosudartsvyennosti i Progressa*, Tashkent: 'Uzbekiston', 1994.

36 See Karimov, *Uzbekistan*, pp. 52-66.

37 Ibid., p. 10.

38 Ibid., p. 11-12.

39 This phrase is taken from Karimov, *Uzbekistan in the Threshold of the 21st Century*.

40 Address by H.E. Mr Islom Karimov President of the Republic of Uzbekistan at the 48th Session of the United Nations General Assembly, p. 6.

41 Uzbekistan's current population exceeds 25 million.

42 Tahir Qahhar, 'Uzbek Literature,' (translated from Uzbek by William Dirks) *World Literature Today*, Summer 1996, p. 611.

43 Karimov, *Uzbekistan on the Threshold of the Twenty-First Century*, p. 7.

44 Ibid., p. 11.

45 Islam A. Karimov, *The Uzbek People Will Never Depend on Others*, Tashkent, 2005, p. 50.

46 Karimov, *Uzbekistan on the Threshold Of The Twenty-First Century*, p. 268.

47 Ibid., p. 269.

48 Karimov, *The Uzbek People Will Never Depend on Others*, pp. 28-29.

49 Nick Megoran, 'The Critical Geopolitics of Danger in Uzbekistan and Kyrgyzstan', *Environment and Planning D: Society and Spaces* 28, no. 3 (2005).

50 For a detailed discussion see ibid.

51 Address by H.E. Mr Islam Karimov at the First Session of Oliy Majlis of the Republic of Uzbekistan. As already noted, Karimov's book on *Uzbekistan on the Threshold of the Twenty-First Century*, is subtitled *Threats to Security, Conditions of Stability and Guarantees for Progress.*

52 Nick Megoran, 'Framing Andijon, narrating the nation: Islam Karimov's account of the events of 13 May 2005', *Central Asian Survey* 27, no 1 (2008).

53 Karimov, *The Uzbek People Will Never Depend on Others*, p. 18.

54 Ibid., p. 17.

55 The phrase is chosen from ibid.

56 Karimov, *Basic Principles of Social, Political and Economic Development of Uzbekistan*, p. 8.

57 Ibid.

Zionism : A modernizing discourse

Priya Singh

Introduction

According to Anthony Giddens, modernity is a simple term for modern society or industrial civilization. Portrayed in more detail, it is associated with (1) a certain set of attitudes towards the world, the idea of the world as open to transformation by human intervention; (2) a complex of economic institutions, especially industrial production and a market economy; (3) a certain range of political institutions, including the nation-state and mass democracy. Largely as a result of these characteristics, modernity is vastly more dynamic than any previous type of social order. It is a society—more technically, a complex of institutions, which unlike any preceding culture lives in the future rather than the past.[1]

The 'project of modernity,' as Jurgen Habermas has termed it, evolved as a distinctive discourse in the eighteenth century and this project of modernity prepared by eighteenth-century philosophers 'consisted of their efforts to develop objective science, universal morality and law, and autonomous art according to their inner logic', their aim being, according to Habermas in this context, 'the rational organization of everyday social life'.[2] Conceived of as a 'new order of things' or an 'awakening of new life', modernity involved movement into a new episteme; political, cultural, and scientific elites developed a universal positivistic and technocratic science, morality, law, and rationality that could grasp and control a world in which change, rather than tradition, had become ubiquitous, and the past had become a burden from which men needed to be freed.[3]

The ideology inherent in this project, whether liberal or Marxist, was that the appropriate application of these new tools would lead to an unlikely and previously unheard of progress and freedom for humankind. However, more than just calling for liberty, equality, and fraternity, which was the motto of the

French Revolution, modernity represented a new, accelerated mode of existence caused by the new modes of industrial production, circulation, and consumption that was the consequence of the development and eventual universalization of the capitalist market.

The notion of 'progress' was to be understood from the point of view of a teleological analysis of history (common to both liberals and Marxists) in which capitalist modernity was considered an advance in human civilization that by characterization began in Europe and would spread, one way or another, to the 'backward' regions. Moreover, thinkers such as Nietzsche, Adorno, Horkheimer, and Schumpeter pointed out that the logic underlying Enlightenment rationality and capitalism more specifically was one of 'creative destruction'.[4] This implies that the only way progress could be achieved was by destroying the traditions and rationality that governed the 'old' world. For most peoples, especially outside of the metropolitan countries, the creative destruction engendered by the growth of capitalist modernity signified imperial colonial domination and oppression by Europe, and the destruction of indigenous paradigms of modernity that accompanied this domination and oppression.

At the ideological level, the traditional Orientalist and Zionist historiography that developed alongside capitalist, imperialist modernity had as its starting point an ontological and epistemological duality between East and West, with the latter ushering in at the dawn of the 'modern' era a period of immense progress, and the East continuing a pattern of decline or stagnation that began, by many accounts, sometime around the tenth century.

As a consequence of this supposed stagnation attributed by Hegel and Marx to 'Oriental despotism' and the 'Asiatic mode of production' respectively, the Islamic world was thought to possess no internal motor for change; hence no change could occur until European penetration roused the East out of its long 'stupor'. Thus the histories written by the great Orientalist H.A.R.Gibb, and pro-Zionist Orientalists such as Bernard Lewis, Gustave von Grunebaum, and others were by definition teleological, with the West having progressed to a cultural, political, and economic level that the East had no choice but to accept and attempt to imitate. [5] There are many explanations offered for the evolution of the ideology of separate and autonomous development by Europeans. A crucial facet was the transformation from competitive capitalism to imperial capitalism, a transition necessitated by the fact that no matter how efficient European capitalism became, it still could not compete with the ability of the local producers to squeeze wages lower in order to keep prices competitive with Europe. Therefore the only way for European capitalism to conquer foreign markets was to wipe out the indigenous capitalist sector, which it did through a process of capitulations, commercial treaties, debt, and finally, military conquest and occupation.

In addition to this commercial and military imperialism, postcolonial writers such as Edward Said, Samir Amin,[6] and others have revealed the cultural component of European imperialism and colonialism, demonstrating how the 'point of departure for the conquest of the world' by Europe was the universalization of both the economic and ideological aspects of modernity. As Ella Shohat[7] explains, related to the imposition of European economic superiority was an appropriation of 'cultural and material' production which allowed Europeans to attribute the 'failures' of the Middle East to internal causes, rather than seeing them as the result of a process in which the underdevelopment of the Third World was intertwined with European 'progress'.

The question that arises is how does Zionism fit into this picture? The Zionist leadership felt that the mental and social chasm between them and the indigenous Arab population of Palestine was that between 'a nation living in the twentieth century and one living in the fifteenth century, some of them in the seventh century.'[8] In the initial period, they viewed the native population including native Jews as 'indolent and torpid', incapable of being productive partners in building up the country. As Ben-Gurion put it, 'We do not recognize their right to rule the country to the extent that it has not been built up by them and is still awaiting its cultivators.'[9] This statement is indicative of a 'modern', well-organized, and well-financed national movement, with a European-inspired paradigm of development and progress, looking down upon the indigenous agrarian, non-capitalist society with which it was competing for scarce land and natural resources.

Discourses of modernization and development in the Zionist ideology

As Michel Foucault demonstrated in *The Order of Things*, the development of the concept of 'the economy' as based on circulation and exchange of value- i.e., capitalism, is a central component of modern epistemology.[10] In their defence the Zionist leadership utilized many of the central components of modern economic discourse, particularly those surrounding 'modernization'. In fact, as Baruch Kimmerling[11] points out, reducing central political components of the conflict to 'economic' problems was an essential Zionist goal in the debate over Palestine, since doing so gave the Zionist leadership the opportunity to provide new formulas that would demonstrate the harmless, even beneficial, effects of their enterprise upon the Arabs.

Statements regarding the modernizing role of Zionism in Palestine can be traced back to the year 1899, two years after the convening of the first Zionist Congress which identified the establishment of a national home for Jews in Palestine as the main objective of the Zionist movement. Yousef al-Khalidi, then the mayor of Jerusalem, sent a letter to Herzl advising him to look for another place for their national home. In his response, Herzl, the founder of the Zionist movement, highlighted the benefits which the Palestinians would gain as a result of the fulfillment of the Zionist project:

> You see another difficulty, Excellency, in the existence of the non-Jewish population in Palestine. But who could think of sending them away? It is their well-being, their individual wealth which we will increase by bringing our own. Do you think that an Arab who owns land or a house in Palestine worth three or four thousand francs will be very angry to see the price of his land rise in a short time, to see it rise five and ten times in value perhaps in a few months? Moreover, that will necessarily happen with the arrival of the Jews. That is what the indigenous population must realize....[12]

The argument advanced by Herzl regarding the role of Zionism as a modernizing project that would be enormously beneficial for the Palestinians, was spelled out in his fiction of *Altneuland*, published in 1902:

> Those [Palestinians] who had nothing, stood to lose nothing, and could only gain. And they did gain: Opportunities to work, means of livelihood, prosperity. Nothing could have been more wretched than an Arab village at the end of the nineteenth century. The Peasants' clay hovels were unfit for stables. The children lay naked and neglected in the streets, and grew up like dumb beasts. Now every thing is different ... They benefited from the progressive measures of the New Society [Zionist Colonizing company] ... When the swamps were drained, the canals built... the natives were the first to be employed, and were paid well for their work. These people are better off than at any time in the past. They support themselves decently, their children are healthier and are being taught something. [13]

Herzl's writings on Palestine and his claims concerning the country, its inhabitants and the role of Zionism as a modernizing agent, have had a considerable influence on the Zionist mode of thought. Several Zionist political leaders, academics, writers and propagandists have ever since repeated his argument that Zionism is a modernizing force in relation to the Palestinians. For example, contending Zionist politicians such as Weizmann, Jabotinsky and Ben-Gurion articulated, in a like manner, the higher moral stand they ascribed to Zionism owing to its proclaimed role of a modernizing agent. Thus, after the establishment of the British Administration in Palestine, Weizmann arrived in Jaffa, and stated:

> ... (our objective) is to invigorate education and the sciences in Palestine through the establishment of public institution for the spread of knowledge and learning. What we ask for, is that we be given opportunity to attain these objectives to get together and work shoulder to shoulder for the sake of the development and prosperity of this country...[14]

In fact, from their first negotiations with the Arabs, Zionist leaders sought to emphasize the benefits of their colonization efforts. Chaim Weizmann, in his correspondence with Emir Feisal in 1918, explained how Zionist development would not be injurious to the indigenous population but rather would 'revive' Palestine's long-suffering and moribund economy without encroaching on the ownership rights of the Arab peasantry. The underlying theme of the Zionist response was that, far from hindering the development of the Arab economy in Palestine, Jewish colonization would be the primary impetus for such development.

In a similar vein Jabotinsky, the leader of the extremist Revisionist Party, expressed the morality and the worth of the Zionist colonization in his testimony to the Palestine Royal Commission in 1937:

> We maintain unanimously that the economic position of the Palestinian Arabs, under the Jewish colonization and owing to the Jewish colonization, has become the object of envy in all the surrounding Arab countries. [15]

Ben-Gurion went a step further with this initiative during the 1930s by trying to sell the notion of modernization to a leader of the Pan-Arab national movement by pledging Zionist support for a united Arab state in terms of economic and technological assistance in return for condoning the Zionist project in Palestine.[16]

The Zionists claimed that before Jewish colonization the land was sterile, barren, and vacant, and that the cultivation that did take place was 'primitive', utilizing traditional methods of cultivation that failed to bring out the productive potential of the land. As Moshe Smilansky stated in 1930, 'The only hope for future development and to return the land to its ancient level of fertility is the influx of new energy' – i.e., 'creative destruction'.[17] The Arabs, fitting the general stereotype of the East, were thought to lack such 'energy,' as 'the indolent spirit of the east seemed to diffuse its languorous influence throughout the country.' Joseph Weitz, one of the architects of Zionist land policy, wrote.

> Formerly uninhabited or sparsely settled areas are flourishing after the soil has been reclaimed. The settlements prove that it is within the power of man to restore to a country its natural assets which may have been lost through centuries of neglect...to transform the very nature of the land through reclamation and development. [18]

The late 1930s and 1940s witnessed intensification in the struggle for Palestine. The superiority of the Zionist claim over the Palestinians was described as stemming from the modern features of Zionism and the primitive nature of the Arab inhabitants of Palestine. The Palestinians were described as a primitive people, unable to develop a sense of nationhood. Leading Zionist figures strove to prove that the Palestinian rebellion of 1936-39 was not a manifestation of nationalist feelings. Various Zionist leaders such as Belinson, Tabenken and Katzenelson described the Palestinian Rebellion in terms drawn from European reality, such as Fascism, Nazism and Imperialism.[19] According to them, this attests to the inability of the Arabs of Palestine to develop a 'positive' national movement. Others spoke about a Pan-Arab movement with which the Arabs of Palestine could identify. All of them, however, adhered to the long-standing Zionist consensus according to which Jews were the only national group in Palestine. Moreover, according to the Zionists, the morality of the Zionist project derives from its ability to develop the country. Drawing on a tradition of Zionist myths on Palestine such as 'the making of the desert bloom' and a utilitarian argument for colonization, Ben-Gurion developed a 'worker-ist theory'. He argued that there is no moral principle according to which Jews could be prevented from developing the country. Their ability to develop the country gives them the right over it.[20] In 1932 Ben-Gurion wrote:

> We who came here over the past fifty years could not be absorbed in the economy existing, but were obliged to create new sources of livelihood. We did not settle in Arab villages or in the occupied towns, but founded new settlements and build new urban quarters and suburbs. We did not look for work in Arab vineyards and groves, nor in Arab shops and factories; we planted and erected our own. We came not as immigrants but as settlers, not to ancient Palestine, but to a new land we made ourselves.[21]

Equally important is a remark by a British, Sir Martin Conway, used by the American Zionist and Supreme Court Justice Felix Frankfurter in a significant *Foreign Affairs* article in 1931:

> We who love the simple Oriental life in its beautiful setting may be pardoned if we regard with a sigh its pulverization

> beneath the wheels of progress, Change is inevitable. It's a mere accident that the Jews should happen to be its agents...Palestine is inexorably part of the modern world. No cordon sanitaire can protect her against the penetration of the forces behind Western ideas and technology.[22]

Similarly, Smilansky argued, 'The fellah can thus be raised from the depths of his present misery and transformed into a prosperous modern farmer only with the aid of Jewish immigration and settlement.'[23]

It was soon realized by the Zionists that their discourse of modernization could gain ultimate credibility only by being promulgated by Palestinians, the alleged beneficiaries. Therefore, since the inception of Zionism, there has been a tireless pursuit of Palestinians who would recognize with gratitude the modernizing role of Zionism. Herzl acknowledged the need for such witnesses and in his fiction of *Altneuland,* he describes a contented Arab community living in the Jewish Commonwealth. Since 1948, methods of co-option became a core instrument of control, which the Israeli state used to subdue its Palestinian citizens. This included the granting of peripheral benefits to members of the traditional elite, and the awarding of jobs in the public sector (mainly in the state-run Arab educational system) to young and educated Palestinians.[24]

However, Zionist efforts to recruit Palestinian witnesses did not bear much fruit. The Palestinian resistance to the Zionist project since its formative stages also cast grave doubts on the credibility of the modernization discourse. Responding to this reality, the Zionists have argued that owing to their cultural backwardness, Palestinians were unable to comprehend the true progressive nature of Zionism. Therefore, as and when the Palestinians achieve modernity they will exhibit more rational and positive attitudes and it is only a matter of time until Zionism's moral stand will be recognized and condoned.[25]

Moreover, it was claimed that the Zionist-led modernization process should be viewed in the light of the antagonistic interests of the Palestinian classes. Modernization serves the interests of both Zionism and the Palestinian masses as through this process the Palestinian masses will increase their opportunities, improve their material well-being, set themselves free from the control of the land-owning classes and become acquainted with civilized values, while Zionism will be able to achieve its purpose more easily. According to this theory, the enemies of modernization, and consequently the common enemy of both Zionism and the Arab masses, are the Palestinian political elite and the Palestinian dominant classes (landowners, influential families, the political leadership, and leaders of trade-unions). As a consequence of that, observes G. Mansur, Zionism had presented Palestinian nationalism and the Palestinian labour movement as manifestations of hostility instigated by effendis (landowners), and not genuine mass movements.[26]

In due course of time, subsequent to the example set-up by Herzl who created the figure of Rashid, a European educated young man, educated Palestinian characters came to be portrayed in works of fiction as credible witnesses. A typical, although simplistic version of such a character, is the Palestinian teacher in the children's story *The Sons of the First Rain*, by E. Semoli. This is a fiction about Palestinian pupils, at the same time, citizens of Israel, who visited a Jewish school and were impressed by the school's high standards. An Arab, and not a Jewish teacher explained how this was achieved, signifying the connotations for the Arabs in Israel:

> I always say in my heart: God sent the Jews here to serve as an example for us. We shall observe them and do the same. The main thing is that we live in peace as good neighbours. Here you paid us a visit and also we came to see you at your school ... We have obtained through you better welfare. We have benefited from your capital, your energy and your good example. [27]

Even though Palestinian witnesses could not always be incorporated into the Zionist discourse of modernization yet, the claim that Zionism is ontologically a modernizing force was always maintained.

It has been observed by many Zionist scholars that the modernization discourse rests upon two main assumptions. Firstly, there is, by and large, a predetermined Arab personality, which can be conceptualized and presented. Secondly, there is a hierarchy of cultures: Arab culture versus a European culture and Zionism as a component of the Western civilization is superior to the native culture. To possess the role of a modernizing agent inevitably implies that those who are objects of modernization are inferior with regard to a variety of primarily positive qualities. They are backward, less enlightened, less cultured and somehow less human. Since the inception of Zionism, Palestinians have been described as backward, primitive, and occasionally they have been depicted as evil. Such descriptions have been mobilized to serve a variety of positions within the discourse of modernization.

The eminent Jewish writer and proponent of cultural Zionism Achad Ha'am who saw the 'historical rights of the Jews as outweighing the Arabs' residential rights in Palestine,'[28] described the Palestinians along these lines (in 1891):

> Arabs are wild men of the desert, an ignorant people who do not see and do not understand what is going on around them ... in time, when our people in Palestine shall have developed to such an extent that they will begin more or less to push aside the natives, the latter will not give way easily.[29]

Shami, a Hebrew novelist and essayist, presented a two-dimensional character of the Arab in an essay published in 1911:

> Within the Arab soul there are two centres of authority. In his daily life he is practical and clever, weighing every thing in the scale of cold logic and analyzing it minutely; and he is not easily fooled. However, the same Arab is a different person in his spiritual life; no people in the world has developed the power of imagination and fantasy, as has the Arab people. For them there is no distinction between fiction and an event that actually happened. Overstatement and exaggeration are second nature to them...[30]

Weizmann shared Shami's perception of the existence of two layers in the personality of the Palestinian. For him, however, these layers are situated according to a hierarchical order. The second layer, which is the negative one, reflects the 'true' nature of the Arab. In a letter addressed to Balfour, he makes this distinction:

> The Arabs who are superficially clever and quick witted, worship one thing and one thing only-power and success ...

> The British Authorities ... knowing as they do the treacherous nature of the Arab, they have to watch carefully and constantly...[31]

Amos Oz, in some of his writings, conveys the view that the Palestinian is not only primitive and evil, but he epitomizes evil itself. Oz, as the 'national writer' of Israel, was able to deconstruct the complexity of images and feelings, which are associated with the 'Palestinian' among Israelis, and was able to articulate them in a creative manner.

The Zionist discourse of modernization is Eurocentric. The superiority of the Zionists over the natives is partly explained by their European culture. In his main political pamphlet *The Jewish State*, Herzl described the Zionist endeavour as follows: 'We should there form a part of a wall of defence for Europe in Asia, an outpost of civilization against barbarism.'[32]

It has been contended that the self-image of Israel as a Western society has been bolstered despite the existence of a considerable Jewish population who do not adhere to Western values (in the case of Oriental and Orthodox-religious Jews). This has been achieved through a two-dimensional perspective. Firstly, the belief that Oriental Jews, with the help of state-sponsored programmes, will catch up, and that the acculturation process will gradually bring them to internalize an Israeli version of Westernization (a mixture of Western values, nationalist attitudes and some religious beliefs). Secondly, the Israel, which is presented, is the Israel of the affluent classes of Ashkenazi (European-American) origin. These include businessmen, managers, academics, top military and diplomatic personnel, and professionals. As a result, Israel has retained the image of a Western society.

As far as the Palestinian citizens of Israel are concerned, the modernization argument has been put forward in a different manner. It is argued that they are ambivalent towards the Western model. Since they are not part of the Jewish collective, it is not possible to incorporate them into the Israeli version of modernization. Moreover, they are described as being unable to present any viable alternative to Westernization. The Arab civilization to which they belong is degenerate and has been unable to regenerate itself. Articulating this notion, Avineri writes:

> Arab society is a truly baroque society, where manners and style, facade and imagination are all the outgrowth of an overripe culture. Such a society may have greater difficulties in coming to terms with the modern world than a purely tribal 'primitive' society of the African variety. [33]

In keeping with this category of interpretation, Israeli politicians, administrators and academics frequently refer to the 'cultural backwardness' of the Palestinians in Israel as the source of their underdevelopment.[34]

In 1976, Koenig, then the Commissioner of the Northern district of Israel, a district with a high concentration of Palestinians, submitted a memorandum to the prime minister outlining the policies that the state should pursue toward its Palestinian citizens. Koenig drew on the 'common knowledge' of the Arab personality and Arab culture when he wrote:

> The Jewish democratic and open society, which swallowed the Arab population remaining in the country after the establishment of the state, failed to absorb it as far as its way of thinking, its manners and its vulnerability are concerned ... At the same time, however, time and again they [Israeli officials] made proclamations about equality, integration and so forth ... though the actions were contradictory. This policy did not take into consideration the superficial and Levantinistic Arab character whose imagination tends to exceed rationality. [35]

The emergence of alternative discourses

The modernization discourse has been central to the Zionist movement since its inception at the end of the nineteenth century. However, political developments, which took place in the period between the mid-1930s and the early 1950s, led to the demise of this discourse. Since the mid-1930s, and especially since the eruption of the Palestinian revolt of 1936-39, the Zionist leadership felt that the time had arrived to declare openly that the objective of Zionism was to be the establishment of a Jewish state in Palestine. As to the Palestinian population, their existence was presented as a political problem, which needed to be dealt with accordingly. The Zionist Congress, which was convened in Zurich, 1937, officially approved the idea of transfer of Palestinians.[36] The Holocaust and the suffering of Jews during the Second World War was used by the Zionist movement to highlight the urgent need to create a safe haven for Jews in Palestine.

In 1947 the United Nations adopted the partition resolution according to which, two states were supposed to be established in Palestine, a Jewish and an Arab state. The history of the decisive years of 1947 and 1948 is still highly contentious. However, in recent years, new scholarship has revealed that the primary claims of Zionist historiography are unfounded.[37] Simha Flapan details and traces the origins of the myths, which surrounded the establishment of Israel.[38] Two points relating to this debate are of significance. Firstly, the Zionist leadership colluded with Emir Abdullah of Trans-Jordan to prevent the establishment of an Arab Palestinian state. Secondly, the exodus of Palestinians, who became refugees, was mainly the result of acts of expulsion.[39] The expulsion of Palestinians during the 1948 war and the obdurate refusal of the Israeli state to allow their return not only contradict the modernization discourse, but also the basic principles of morality.[40]

The 1948 war signalled the official demise of the modernization discourse. After the war, a minority of 156,000 Palestinians out of 900,000, who lived in the area upon which Israel was established, remained to become citizens of the Jewish state. Prominent figures in Israel expressed their disappointment that a minority of Palestinians stayed back in Israel, and that some of them inquired about the feasibility of their expulsion.[41] However, when it became clear that the results of the war were permanent including the existence of a Palestinian minority in Israel, the modernization discourse was revived. The central theme of the post-1948 discourse of modernization is that the state and the Jewish community act as agents of modernization and they assist the 'Arab' minority in progressing from a situation of backwardness to modernity.

The first alternative discourse highlighted the fact that the fulfillment of Zionism, as it had been taking place, led to the disenfranchisement and not modernization of Palestinians, and consequently to a bitter struggle with them. According to this viewpoint, since the beginning of the Zionist colonization in Palestine, a continuous struggle has erupted as a result of Jewish acquisition of lands cultivated by Palestinians. Mandel, in his work on Zionism before World War I, reported on clashes that had already occurred between the first Jewish colonies and adjacent Palestinian villages during the 1880s.[42]

However, those who developed this line of thought were not ready to advocate publicly either of the two logical conclusions: the abandonment of the Zionist project, or the disenfranchisement of Palestinians. According to Epstein one answer was that an alternative strategy of colonization would lay down the foundation for a long-term Jewish-Palestinian cooperation and brotherhood. Another answer was that the recognition of a transitory period of conflict but harmonious relations based on Zionist-led modernization will characterize the long-term prospect.[43] This discourse reflects a revisionist interpretation of modernization discourse. There was, on the one hand, an acknowledgment of the difficulties involved in the Zionist project; however, on the other, the answers, which were offered, were drawn from within the general framework of modernization.

The second alternative discourse to that of modernization proceeds from the premise that the Zionist project leads to the disenfranchisement of Palestinians. However, by contrast to the previous one, it did not look for solutions, which attend to the interests of both parties. According to its main argument, there is an inherent conflict between Zionism and the Arab inhabitants of Palestine over the country. What the Zionist leadership should do is to devise ways and to implement plans to get rid of the Palestinians. Paradoxically, most of those who developed the discourse of transferring Palestinians were those who articulated the modernization discourse. Already in 1895, two years before the convening of the First Zionist Congress, Herzl developed a two-part plan of transferring the Palestinians:

> We shall try to spirit the penniless population across the border by procuring employment for it in the transit countries, while denying it any employment in our country ...Both the

process of expropriation and the removal of the poor must be carried out discreetly and circumspectly. As to the rich:

> Let the owners of immovable property believe that they are cheating us, selling things for more than they are worth. But we are not going to sell them anything back. [44]

Nur Masalha has illustrated that almost all Zionist leaders, including prominent figures, advocated the idea of transfer and even accepted the solution offered by way of the creation of a bi-national state to the question of Palestine.[45]

From the Zionist to the Post-Zionist discourse

The Zionist discourse of modernization has found its most systematic articulation in social science literature. Even prior to the establishment of Israel, Zionist social scientists had highlighted the modernizing role of Zionism vis-à-vis the Palestinians. In fairly recent times, Yehoshua Porath stressed upon the role of Jewish agriculture in modernizing its Palestinian counterpart during the Mandate period.[46] He argued that the money received from the sale of Arab land to Jews was invested in the profitable branch of citriculture. However, it has been pointed out that Porath failed to produce substantial evidence concerning the existence of a direct correlation between the sale of land by Palestinians and the amount of investment, which they made in developing orange groves. In addition, he failed to validate his assumption that medium or even small levels of accumulation were beyond the capacity of Palestinian middle and upper classes, and that the only source for plausible investment was the sale of lands. Tamar Gozansky introduced another conceptualization through which the modernization discourse was offered.[47] Her principal argument was that Zionist colonization was indispensable for the development of capitalism in Palestine. This view has been countered and it has been argued that as a prosperous province of the Ottoman Empire, Palestine had experienced a steady incorporation in the World Capitalist System since the 1830s, about half a century before the beginning of the Zionist colonization.

Alongside the discourse of modernization a 'dualist thesis' emerged. Its key argument was that the Zionist colonization did not lead to the constitution of an upper class of European (Jewish) settlers. Rather the Jewish community created an autonomous economy, which had only insignificant links with the Palestinian sector. This discourse was developed to distinguish Zionist colonization from other settler movements, which took place during the same period. This 'dualist' discourse has been criticized as it reflects a 'self-centered' narrative, which creates a strong impression that the Jewish community had developed in a socio-economic and political vacuum.[48]

Modernization has been the dominant paradigm for analyzing the relations between the Jewish majority and the Palestinian minority in Israel. The Parsonian evolutionary theory was adopted by most Israeli social scientists as the appropriate framework for analyzing the 'ethnic relations in Israel'. The existential conditions of the Palestinian minority in Israel have been explained in terms of the well-known polarity of Modernity-Traditionalism in which the Palestinians are described as a traditional (backward) community, which is being led to modernity by the State and the Jewish sector.[49] This transformation has been presented through indices of equating present with past averages, which always prove that a change for the better has taken place. In this way, the modernization in various facets of Arabs' lives has been described: education, health, employment, the infrastructure, and so on.

To demonstrate a linear progress from backwardness to modernity, this research evolves through three stages. Firstly, it begins by describing the helpless conditions of the Arab minority when the state was established. Secondly, it reviews at length state policies of modernizing the Arab minority and the role of the Jewish majority as a modernizing agent. At this stage, statistics, which compare past with present averages are supplied. The results always 'reveal' that a change for the better has taken place. Thirdly, scant attention is given to the gaps, which continue to exist between Jews and Arabs. These gaps are usually attributed to the different stages of development of the two communities when the state was established, as well as to the cultural backwardness of the Arabs. Despite its simplicity, this framework has been helpful in two essential ways: it enables these researchers to present their case in a systematic way, and it allows them to deal with thorny subjects from a convenient position.[50]

According to the framework just described, the state is characterized as an agent of modernization, which acts for the benefit of all its citizens. Thus, the nature and function of the state is reduced to its public policy dimension. However, its critics point out that when dealing with the specific case of Israel, such a definition is misleading, since the official and legal definition of Israel is the state of the Jewish people.[51] The Zionist movement to realize Zionist goals created the state, and on many occasions these goals were achieved by disenfranchising Palestinians as individuals or as a national minority.

The role of the state in Zionist and Israeli political discourse is also of fundamental importance to our discussion. Both conceptually and structurally, the state is one of the basic components of the modern social, political, and economic order and in the case of Israel, *mamlachtiut*, or statism, was the ideological expression of this dynamic. The term was coined by Ben-Gurion, who felt that the new institutions of the *Yishuv* (the prestate Jewish community) and then the new Israeli state were the highest expression of Zionism, and that their relationship to the people was central to the development of the nation. In fact, the various international and local Zionist institutions, such as the World Zionist Organization, Zionist Executive, Histadrut, Jewish National Fund, and various political parties, all gave the impression of a 'state within a state' even before the creation of the Israeli state in 1948.

In 1953 Ben-Gurion succinctly described this epistemological transformation when he labelled Israeli society *am mamlakhti*- a 'statist nation'- as opposed to the earlier socialist conception of *am oved*, or 'working nation'. Thus the nation-state stood above society, representing the universal interests of the nation, and took on the appearance, common to most modern centralized states, of being autonomous and independent from the rest of society. This forced the country's leadership to identify itself with the 'state' rather than identifying its interests with those of the working class, the traditional base of the Labor Party. The state became the embodiment of the nation, while socialism, along with the socialist institutions, became the handmaiden of the state, as *mamlachtiut* policies sought.

Moreover, the Histadrut and other key state structures, such as the army and the schools, also served as the means through which Arabs were first excluded from the Jewish economy and polity in the pre-state period. After 1948, these vehicles incorporated non-Jews within a framework of institutionalized dualism that was pro-Jewish and anti-Arab. The centrality of the state also affected the development of the army, the Histadrut, and the absorption of the wave of Arab Jewish immigrants that began in the 1950s, providing the necessary technologies and methods of control to socialize them, not into a socialist ideology, but rather into a culture in which the primary categories were the inherently exclusivist 'nation' and 'state'. While it is taken for granted that Zionism was and is the nationalist movement of the Jewish people, what has not been sufficiently explored is how a nationalist movement and its various discourses were imbricated in the larger dynamic of capitalism: that is, how this 'imagined community' created an identity that defined itself as an essentially autonomous, unitary historical subject and that labelled as 'other' all who were not part of its self-identity (in this case both Palestinian Arabs and non-European Jews), and how the political and cultural technologies associated with capitalism played a crucial role in this dynamic. [52] As Edward Said has pointed out, both in his seminal *Orientalism* and the later *Culture and Imperialism*, the construction of these 'others' is a central dynamic of the interrelated processes of capitalism, imperialism, and nationalism. [53] In fact, if we look at the first two generations of Zionist/Israeli historiography, it is clear that scholars and official historians such as Arthur Ruppin, S. N. Eisenstaadt, and others either ignored the Arabs altogether or conceived of them from within an 'autonomous elite' paradigm in which the two peoples were seen as self-formed and independently developing. It was left to the post-Zionist writers to question this assumption.

Post-Zionism as a postmodernist critique of Zionist modernity

Fredric Jameson[54] has studied how the transformation from the modern to the postmodern world is centered on a 'mutation in the sphere of culture', in which culture becomes a product or commodity fully incorporated into the dynamics of the market, in the process destroying old allegiances and producing new kinds of people capable of functioning in the new socioeconomic world. At the same time, the new postmodern attitude is characterized by a loss of faith in the emancipatory promises of modern politics and economics. It has been posited that this transformation and the cultural and economic globalization that accompanies it poses a serious challenge to the centrality of the state in the formation of Jewish Israeli identity (particularly since the raison d'etre of the Zionist enterprise was the 'emancipation' of the world's Jews and the associated benefits it would bring to the indigenous population of Palestine). It was out of this crisis in Zionist ideology that the movement toward post-Zionism was born.

One of the prerequisites for post-Zionist discourse was the development of political economy as an alternative method of historical research. First of all, political-economic historians have understood the ideological nature of traditional European historiography and as a result, they have demonstrated how Orientalist history was inextricably linked to the imperialist project. Thus the efforts of more contemporary historiography have been aimed at 'decolonizing' Middle Eastern history. Moreover, political economy has demonstrated how Arab/Islamic societies possessed their own political economies, which were equally as 'rational' as those of the West and attuned to those societies' 'indigenous roots' for the development of capitalism, roots that Europe's imperial and colonial policies were specifically designed to destroy. Political-economic studies have revealed, for example, how the Ottoman governments and local rulers of the so-called period of 'decline' were in fact much more involved in the daily lives of their populations, often with the goal of protecting the peasantry, the very group whom the Europeans and Zionists claimed to be liberating through imperialism and colonialism.[55]

So far from being 'stagnant', the changing patterns of land ownership and economic development in late nineteenth-century Palestine not only indicate the dynamic nature of the situation, but moreover present the clearest example of how Islamic patterns are intimately woven into the fabric of communal society, thus contradicting the Orientalist 'stagnation' model that historically dominated Middle Eastern scholarship. As Ya'akov Firestone points out, the evolving land-owning patterns

> smoothed [the] adjustment to final absorption into the world market centered on Western capitalism, [and were] an adaptation to deal with poor public security, benefits of scale operation, equalize economic opportunities...[all of which is] only natural in economies like the Middle East, where production is subject to such uncertainties.[56]

While for the most part it was not until the mid-seventies at the earliest that so-called 'revisionist', or post-Zionist, analyzes of Palestinian society and its economy came to the fore, an extremely insightful early critique exists in the form of a 1925 article by Yitzhak Elazari-Volkani, titled 'The Transition from Primitive to Modern Agriculture in Palestine'. His analysis provides an alternative view to the traditional Zionist critique of Arab agriculture and attendant glorification of Zionist methods and ideology by illustrating how the profits extracted by Zionist intensive farming were in the end no greater than those extracted via the 'primitive' methods employed by the fellah. While the Zionists might have earned more gross income, 'having neither tradition nor science, [they] create[d] only defective farms, half modern intensive in expenditure and primitive in income.' Of course, this view is at odds with the general Zionist belief that European techniques were superior to native ways; many early Jewish colonists refused to use local tools because they saw the Palestinians as 'backward and decadent'.[57]

Postmodernism as a critical methodology has both discerned and influenced these advances, grounded as it is in the 'awareness of the value and significance of respecting difference and otherness.' While there are numerous debates about the ultimate meaning of the term, and about whether post modernity represents a radical departure from or just a heightened form of modernity, what concerns us here is the undebatable emphasis in all postmodernist critiques on 1) problematizing and deconstructing the effects of the universalizing tendencies of modernism discussed above; and 2) replacing these with a more circumspect, localized discourse that accepts the absence of an ultimate center or truth, and not only embraces the previously demonized 'others' but understands that one's identity, ambivalent though it may be, is intimately tied to them. 3) Finally, postmodern discourse seeks to break down the 'effects' of structure and boundary that in the modernist paradigm allowed us to think in terms of the duality of state and society, Jew and Arab.

On the face of it, there is a strong link between the development of post-Zionist and postmodern discourses in Israel, since, as Anita Shapira points out, post-Zionism was created in an associative context within the debate in the Israeli press on the issue of postmodernism.[58] Thus the main themes of traditional historiography that post Zionist historians attack involve the following areas: the uncritical use of terms such as *Eretz* Israel and *aliyah*; the tendency towards a teleological reading of Jewish history, in which all the events of the past two thousand years, even the Holocaust, are conceived of as inevitably leading to the creation of the State of Israel; and the use of physical and ideological boundaries to separate out progressively 'other' groups from the dominant Jewish-Zionist-Ashkenazi elite.

Given the tendency in traditional Zionist historiography to diminish the role of Palestinians in the formation of Zionist and Israeli identity and society, the most notable characteristic of the post-Zionist historians has been the reexamination of the myths of Israeli history from a more open and honest perspective, one that is willing to acknowledge the negative repercussions of Zionism and the creation of Israel on the indigenous inhabitants of the country, and that emphasizes the mutually formative relationship between Zionist/Israeli and Palestinian histories and identities. The pioneering studies of the 'Oriental problem' by writers like Smooha are part of this trend. [59]

The idea of history and identity as narrative is important in this respect, history as narrative is one of the soundest insights of postmodernism, for as Uri Ram (one of the foremost post-

Zionist figures) notes, developing on the historian Eric Hobsbawm's theme: 'In the act of constructing modern nationhood, cultural traditions and historical trajectories are invented.'[60] The challenge of the modern Jewish nationalist narrative was to weave the multifarious layers of memories and histories of a diverse group of cultures into a coherent story that could unite these people into a modern nation-state. The task of postmodernism and post-Zionism is to open up this narrative to those it formerly excluded. It is clear that methodologically, post-Zionism falls well within the parameters of postmodernism, since one of its central characteristics is an awareness and critique of the positivist ideology that has been central to traditional Zionist historiography. Moreover, post-Zionism uses discourse analysis to demonstrate how Zionist/Israeli history was socially constructed and linked to institutionalized configurations of power.

So at the experiential level, we see that a true post-Zionist discourse will create new relationships between community, state, and society, remould the spaces in which these groups and structures interact-and in the process reorder the space of Palestine/Israel, not just in terms of borders, but in terms of cities and neighborhoods. From this perspective, while many Israeli historians have embraced a postmodern or post-Zionist perspective, Israeli and Palestinian societies are still mired in a modernist worldview. A true post-Zionist discourse will therefore strive to create the conditions in which the many sectors of Israeli society - Ashkenazi, Sephardi, Arab, Ethiopian - could live together in a sense of community as yet unattained. From the perspective of postmodern geography, such a community would, as Edward Soja described it, reflect a new spatiality and historicity that are 'archetypes of vividness, simultaneity, and interconnection', rather than of myopia and exclusion. [61]

Conclusion

The critics of Zionism contend that modernization is neither an ideological presentation nor a credible narrative of Jewish-Palestinian relations but modernization has been a very powerful discourse in conveying the Zionist idea, and the history of the

Zionist project, to various groups, which comprise a significant audience of Zionist leaders, intellectuals and activists. The modernization discourse is established upon the premise of a longstanding tradition of Orientalism and through this discourse Zionists endeavour to establish at the intellectual and cultural levels a common identity with Europeans by presenting the Zionist project through vocabulary, ideas, images, and constructions drawn from European experience.[62] Moreover, the post-Zionists argue that the Zionists can always present the Zionist project (to themselves as well as to others) as moral and progressive, regardless of actual developments, since its primary motive is claimed to be moral. In this way, they separate the actual history from its representation. Behaviours and practices perceived as negative can always be interpreted as 'unintended results' or as a 'deviation', and so on, from an otherwise moral and progressive pathway. Furthermore, some Israeli-Jewish and Zionist intellectuals found that the sociological theory of modernization could 'provide a convenient shield behind which the analyst, who wishes to avoid unpleasant questions with regard to the Palestinians in Israel and in various periods Palestinians in general, can feel safe'.[63]

David Ben-Gurion understood the exclusionary basis of Israeli and Palestinian nationalism all too well, as a revealing 1918 comment illustrates:

> There is no solution to the Arab problem, no solution! There is a gulf and nothing can fill this gulf. It is only possible to resolve the conflict between Jewish and Arab interests through sophistry...We as a nation want this country to be ours, the Arabs, as a nation, want it to be theirs.[64]

Thus the emergence of Zionism as a European nationalist movement in a Middle Eastern country with a well-established indigenous population made the Israeli-Palestinian conflict inevitable, However important and even beneficial a movement to the Jewish people, Zionism in fact fell far short of its core ideals, the imperative to repair and transform the world. Indeed, the same tensions and contradictions within 'modernity' that led to our present 'postmodern condition' have necessitated the development of a post-Zionist discourse. But as with postmodernism, the jury is still out on whether post-Zionism can succeed in sustaining the fulfillment of both Palestinian and Israeli nationhood while at the same time working towards the creation of a postnational, and therefore truly postmodern, Israeli Palestinian identity.

Notes and References

1 See Anthony Giddens, *Conversations with Anthony Giddens, Making Sense of Modernity*, Stanford, California: Stanford University Press, 1998.

2 See Jurgen Habermas, *The Philosophical Discourse of Modernity*, Tr. by Frederick Lawrence, Cambridge, MA: The MIT Press, 1987. See also Jurgen Habermas, *Modernity – An Incomplete Project*. This essay was originally delivered as a talk in September 1980 when Habermas was awarded the Theodor W Adorno prize by the city of Frankfurt. It was subsequently delivered as a James Lecture of the New York Institute for the Humanities at New York University in March 1981 and published under the title 'Modernity Versus Postmodernity' in *New German Critique* 22 (Winter, 1981).

3 See Mark Levine, 'Is Post Zionism Post Modern?', *Response Magazine*, Summer/Fall, 1996.

4 Ibid. The notion of creative destruction is found in the writings of Mikhail Bakunin, Friedrich Nietzcshe, Adorno, Horkheimer and in Werner Sombart's *Krieg und Kapitalismus* (War and Capitalism) (1913, p. 207), where he wrote: 'again out of destruction a new spirit of creativity arises'. In *Capitalism, Socialism and Democracy*, the Austrian economist Joseph Schumpeter popularized and used the term to describe the process of transformation that accompanies radical innovation. In Schumpeter's vision of capitalism, innovative entry by entrepreneurs was the force that sustained long-term economic growth, even as it destroyed the value of established companies that enjoyed some degree of monopoly power.

5 Ibid.

6 Ibid. See also Edward Said, *Culture and Imperialism*, New York: Knopf, 1993.

7 Ibid.

8 See Simha Flapan, *Zionism and the Palestinians*, London: Croom and Helm, 1979, p. 132.

9 Cited in Yosef Gorny, *Zionism and the Arabs, 1882-1948*, Oxford: Clarendon Press, 1987, p. 140.

10 See Michel Foucault, *The Order of Things*, New York: Vintage Books, 1973.

11 See Baruch Kimmerling, *Zionism and Economy*, Cambridge, Massachusetts: Schenkman Publishing Company, 1983.

12 W. Khalidi, *From Haven to Conquest*, Beirut: The Institute of Palestine Studies, 1971, pp. 91-2.

13 Theodor Herzl, *Old-New Land (Altneuland)*, New York: Bloch Publishing Company, 1960, pp.123-4.

14 Khalidi, *From Haven to Conquest*, pp. 189-90.

15 Ibid., p. 321.

16 See S.Teveth, *Ben Gurion and the Palestinian Arabs: From Peace to War*, Oxford: Oxford University Press, 1985, pp. 142-4.

17 Levine, 'Is Post Zionism Post Modern?'.

18 Ibid.

19 See Gorny, *Zionism and the Arabs1882-1948*.

20 Teveth, *Ben Gurion and the Palestinian Arabs*, pp. 37-8.

21 See D. Ben Gurion, *Rebirth and Destiny of Israel*, London: Thomas Yoseloff Ltd, 1954, p. 42.

22 Cited in Felix Frankfurter, 'The Palestine Situation Restated', *Foreign Affairs* 9, no 3 (April 1931), pp. 409-34.

23 Levine, 'Is Post Zionism Post Modern?'.

24 See Ian Lustick, *Arabs in the Jewish State: Israel's Control of a National Minority*, Austin: University of Texas Press, 1980, Chapter 6.

25 See Teveth, *Ben Gurion and the Palestinian Arabs*.

26 See G. Mansur, *The Arab Worker Under the Palestinian Mandate*, Hong Kong: Commercial Press, 1937.

27 See El Asmar, *Through the Hebrew Looking Glass: Arab Stereotypes in Children's Literature*, London: Zed Books, 1986, p. 87.

28 See Y. Gorny, *Zionism and the Arabs1882-1948*.

29 See A. Elon, *Israelis: Founders and Sons*, New York: Rinehart and Winston, 1971, p. 172

30 See G. Shaked, 'The Arab in Israeli Fiction', *Ariel* 54 (1983), pp. 74-85.

31 See Edward Said, *The Question of Palestine*, New York: Times Books, 1980, p. 26.

32 See Arthur Hertzberg, *The Zionist Idea: A Reader*, New York: Atheneum, 1982. p. 227.

33 See Shlomo Avineri, 'Modernization and Arab Society: Some Reflections', in *Israel and Arabs in the Middle East*, edited by I. Howe and C. Gershman, New York: Bantam Books, 1972, p. 306.

34 See A. Haidar and E. Zureik, 'The Palestinian seen through the Israeli Cultural Paradigm', *The Journal of Palestine Studies* 16 (1987), pp. 68-86.

35 See 'The Koenig Report', *Journal of Palestine Studies* 6 (1976), pp. 191-200.

36 See Israel Shahak, 'A History of the Concept of Transfer in Zionism', *Journal of Palestine Studies* 18 (1989), pp. 22 –37.

37 See Simha Flapan, *The Birth of Israel: Myths and Realities*, New York: Pantheon Books, 1987; Benny Morris, *The Birth of the Palestinian Refugee Problem 1947-48*, Tel Aviv: Am-Oved, 1988; Ilan Pappe, *The Making of the Arab Israeli Conflict, 1947-51*, London: Tauris, 1988; Avi Shlaim, *Collusion Across the Jordan*, Oxford: Clarendon, 1988.

38 Flapan, *The Birth of Israel: Myths and Realities.*

39 See ibid. as also Shlaim, *Collusion Across the Jordan.*

40 See Flapan, *The Birth of Israel* and Morris, *The Birth of the Palestinian Refugee Problem 1947-48.*

41 See Tom Segev, *1949¯The First Israelis*, New York: Owl Books/Henry Holt and Company, 1998, p. 59.

42 See N. Mandel, *The Arabs and Zionism before World War 1*, Berkeley: University of California Press, 1976.

43 See Gorny, *Zionism and the Arabs: 1882-1948.*

44 Cited in Benny Morris, *Righteous Victims, A History of the Zionist-Arab Conflict, 1881-1999*, New York : Knopf, 2001, p. 21-22.

45 See Nur Masalha, *Expulsion of the Palestinians: The Concept of Transfer in Zionist Political Thought, 1882-1948*, Washington D.C: The Institute of Palestinian Studies, 1992.

46 See Y. Porath, *The Palestinian Arab National Movement 1929-1939: From Riots to Rebellion*, London: Frank Cass, 1977.

47 See Tamar Gozansky, *The Development of Capitalism in Palestine, 1988*, consulted on internet at http:\\www.books.google.com

48 See Baruch Kimmerling, 'Sociology, Ideology and Nation Building: the Palestinians and their meaning in Israeli Sociology', *American Sociological Review* 57 (1992), pp. 446-60.

49 See N. Eisenstadt, *Israeli Society*, London: Weidenfeld and Nicolson, 1969.

50 See Khalidi, *From Haven to Conquest*.

51 See N. Chomsky, *Peace in the Middle East*, Glasgow: Collins, 1975.

52 See Levine, 'Is Post Zionism Post Modern?'

53 See Edward Said's *Orientalism*, *New* York: Vintage Books, 1979, and *Culture and Imperialism*.

54 See Frederic Jameson, *Postmodernism or The Cultural Logic of Late Capitalism*, London: Verso, 1991.

55 Michael Shalev and Gershon Shafir emphasize on the study of political economy as the key to understanding Israel in the past and in the present, see for instance, Michael Shalev, *Labour and Political Economy of Israel*, Oxford: Oxford University Press, 1992 and Gershon Shafir, *Land, Labor and the Origins of the Israeli-Palestinian Conflict, 1882-1914*, California: University of California Press, 1996.

56 See Levine, 'Is Post Zionism Post Modern?', p. 6.

57 p. 5.

58 See Benny Morris, ed. *Making Israel*, Michigan: Univerisity of Michigan Press, 2007.

59 See Sammy Smooha, *Orientation and Politicization of the Arab Minority in Israel*, Haifa: University of Haifa, 1987. See also, Flapan, *Zionism and the Palestinians*.

60 See Levine, 'Is Post Zionism Post Modern?', p. 8

61 See Edward Soja, *Post Modern Geographies: The Reassertion of Space in Critical Social Theory*, London: Verso, 1989, p. 248.

62 See Said, *Orientalism* and *The Question of Palestine*.

63 See Scott Atiou, 'The Surrogate Colonigation of Palestine, 1917-1939', p. 10, available at www.jstor.org

64 See Teveth, *Ben Gurion and the Palestinian Arabs*., p. 36.

Encountering colonial modernity

British rule and the Hos of Singhbhum

Sanjukta Das Gupta

In recent years, the identification and categorization of 'tribes' in India has been attributed to the colonial initiative. Notions of modernity that informed colonial rule, it has been argued, led to the construction of 'natives', among whom the 'tribals', in particular, were increasingly viewed as 'natural' resources.[1] This, as also the need on the part British rulers to 'know' the subjects led to particular constructions of nature, natives and modernity in India. Yet colonial attitudes towards the indigenous communities in Chota Nagpur were not dictated solely through ideology; pragmatic consideration also played a major role in the manner in which the British rulers viewed the colonized *adivasis* of the region. This chapter seeks to examine two broad issues. In the first place, it traces the changing colonial notions of the 'tribal natives' of Singhbhum, a district in the Chota Nagpur Division of the erstwhile Bengal Presidency. It analyzes the gradual evolving of colonial policies in the region and the eventual formulation of the notion of the 'tribe' as a backward primitive. The second section investigates the dynamics of indigenous responses to colonial anthropology and seeks to locate the agency of the silent majority in the making of their own destinies. It therefore traces how the Hos accommodated themselves to such changes under colonial rule and, in the process, carved out for themselves a new identity. This is studied with reference to four social-religious movements among the Hos which greatly influenced the contours of the identity that Hos were attempting to create for themselves.

Colonial perceptions of the Hos

The British were first drawn to Western Singhbhum, a region inhabited almost exclusively by the Hos, by the recurring law and order problem there. Economic insecurity often forced the tribal people, who depended principally on subsistence agriculture, to raid the neighbouring settled peasant tracts. Although such uprisings did not threaten the political stability of the colonial empire, these were interpreted as a law and order problem and as an improper defiance of the state's legitimate authority. The tribal world, therefore, figured in official perceptions as the backdrop for the counter-insurgency measures of the colonial state. In the early nineteenth century, a period when British political authority began to impinge on the Chota Nagpur region, the Singhbhum rulers sought British assistance in quelling their turbulent subjects who increasingly displayed a tendency to repudiate their obligations to the ruling class. In Singhbhum, as in other parts of Chota Nagpur, the early nineteenth century British administration came to regard the local feudatory chiefs as the lawful rulers and the tribal population there as being subject to their authority. The former were considered to be local controllers with a long-standing anchorage in indigenous society. As in England, the 'respectable' inhabitants and men of property were recognized as the protectors of the locality. It was with the support of this group of local collaborators that the British intended to maintain a system of loose control over the tribal regions which then lay at the outskirts of the empire.

Since British intervention in Singhbhum in the early nineteenth century occurred at the request of the Singhbhum raja, the image of the tribal population that they formed at this initial point of contact was therefore entirely based on the prevailing notions that existed among the local Hinduised ruling groups. In fact, the term 'Kol' which early British military officers and administrators applied to much of the tribal population of Chota Nagpur was derived from the Hindus of the region. Whether the term was derived from the Sanskrit *kola* meaning pig[2], or from the word *horo* (meaning man in the Ho language), is difficult to decide, but it is certain that in popular usage, Kol was, and remains, a contemptuous epithet of abuse that the Hindu population of the region used for the tribals. Both Kol and its female equivalent Kui were resented by the Hos as offensive. As stated earlier, in the case of the Hos the term was further qualified and they were referred to as the Larka Kols rather than as Ho, a term by which the Singhbhum tribal would normally identify himself. The Larkas were perceived to be 'dreadful pests to the civilized part of Singboom'[3], who terrorized the adjacent country through their depredations. Thus British officialdom in the early nineteenth century portrayed the *adivasi* population as a 'savage race' whose 'atrocious crimes' challenged the legitimate political authority of the 'civilized' 'reputable castes'. The Ramgarh Magistrate described the Hos in 1817 as 'the lowest kind of Hindoos and in their manners and customs are little removed from savages'[4]. The Hos were also characterized as a fiercely exclusive community who would not permit the entry of any outsiders in their territory. Commenting on their famed propensity for exclusiveness Major Roughsedge, who led the British forces into Singhbhum in 1821, wrote, 'A traveller would as soon think of venturing into a tiger's den as of traversing any point of Larka Cole.'[5]

In was only in the wake of tribal rebellions, such as the Kol rebellion of 1831-32, that the British began to put in place a tribal policy in Singhbhum. The state no longer regarded the tribals as 'predatory raiders' and 'savages' prone to violence, but rather came to see them as a community grievously wronged by alien intruders and therefore goaded into violence. Enquiries into the recurring tribal rebellions convinced the Government of the distinctiveness of the tribal regions which made them particularly vulnerable to powerful adversaries and this changed perception was reflected in administrative innovation. The British Government reassessed their policy of befriending the indigenous ruling classes in Singhbhum and questions were raised about the utility of a political alliance with the discredited chiefs of the region who could barely keep their overmighty subjects in check. Such considerations finally prompted the British to assume direct control over the Ho of Singhbhum. Declaring their intention of extending *pax Britannica* over Singhbhum, it was decided in 1837 to separate the Ho villages of the region from the control of the indigenous rajas and to form with these the Government Estate of Kolhan, incorporated within the South West Frontier Agency, under the direct control and management of the British Government.[6] Later, under Act XX of 1854

Singhbhum became a non-regulation district under the jurisdiction of the Lieutenant Governor of Bengal.

The Larka Kols were now seen as isolates and from the 'savage' the British elevated the tribals to 'noble savage' living a life of Arcadian simplicity, unable to cope with exploitation of the non-tribal outsiders.[7] This myth served to justify the presence of the Raj and the role of the missionaries as the protectors of the 'wild' yet 'innocent' tribals against 'rapacious' outsiders and even from their own 'self-destructive' customs, the most significant of which related to witchcraft and witch-killing. While force was advocated to quell the outbursts against law and order, the British also claimed to provide for protection of the tribals from the exigencies of the outside world. Thus the twin features of the new government policy were paternalism and isolationism. The paternalist rule of district officers was designed to protect the tribals against the machinations and designs of the non-tribal population, projected by the British as the chief enemy of the tribals. As Ashis Nandy observed, the dominant imagery of nineteenth century British governance was that of an adult caring for and chastising an innocent yet wayward child.[8] In tribal India this paternalism was taken to extremes. For instance, Tickell, the first Assistant Political Agent of the Kolhan Government Estate (whose duty was to conduct the administration and enforce law and order in the country), was provided with a set of 'Instructions' by the Political Agent Wilkinson designed to assist him in the administration of the district. These instructions spelt out his duties: the administrative functions and social reforms he was expected to undertake and also provided him with a brief outline of the nature of the country and the customs of the people he was expected to govern. Above all, Tickell was exhorted to be at all times in direct touch with the tribals and to be meticulous in the discharge of his duties.[9]

The third influence on governmental policy was the need to extend among the Hos the 'civilizing' influence of British rule through a programme of reform which would make them less independent and more amenable to control. One of the first targets of the civilizing zeal of the new rulers was the practice of witch hunting. A hospital was set up, which was especially devoted to the care of the Hos who were believed to be the victims of witchcraft.[10] The relatives of all sick people, whose illness was supposed to be caused by witchcraft, were to be persuaded to take them to a government hospital. Cures from diseases would, it was hoped, overcome the belief in witchcraft. The Assistant Political Agent was also instructed to remove the person suspected of practicing witchcraft, together with his property, to another village where the same prejudice did not exist against him. Yet another aspect of the reformist measures was education for the Hos. It was felt necessary to establish a school in order to 'relieve a rising generation of Larka Coles from that gross ignorance', which, according to the British, was responsible for 'much of the foolish and vicious habits of the people and their consequent misery.'[11] Tickell was advised by the Bengal Government to get in touch with the Committee of Public Instruction with his proposals for setting up a school in Chaibasa.[12]

The principles of protectionism and paternalism were endorsed in the administrative changes that were introduced at a later period. The system of governance as laid down by Wilkinson's Rules was modified through Act XX of 1854, which made Singhbhum a non-regulation district[13] under the jurisdiction of the Lieutenant Governor of Bengal. Kolhan Government Estate was placed under the supervision and control of the Deputy Commissioner of Singhbhum. Above him was the Commissioner of Chota Nagpur. The Deputy Commissioner enjoyed the same jurisdiction and powers as that of the Assistant Political Agent. Further changes occurred after the mutiny of 1857, when a need was felt for establishing greater control over the Hos. The post of the Kolhan Superintendent was created and was placed under the supervision of the Deputy Commissioner whom he assisted in all administrative matters.

The mid-nineteenth century saw the emergence of anthropologically-inclined British administrators such as E.T. Dalton, the Commissioner of the Chota Nagpur Division. Unlike earlier British officials, they were not limited to narrow considerations of the need to maintain law and order. Dalton portrayed the Hos as, 'A people who till recently, had no notion what it was to pay rent to anyone, or even to give pecuniary support to their chiefs. They had their Mankis and Moondahs; but no one exercised any right arising from a title in the land except the cultivators.'[14] Thus a notion of total isolation came to be perpetrated. This was in fact one of the myths that was being popularized by the colonial administration since the annexation of Kolhan 1837. In the early nineteenth century the British had recognized the claims of the indigenous rulers over the Hos[15] and British records of the early nineteenth century, a period of general unrest and turbulence in Singhbhum, reveal that the apparatus of state power was very much in existence in the countryside, even though this may have lost much of its potency over the years.[16] Gradually, however, since the mid-nineteenth century, the assumption that the Hos had never been fully under the control of the ruling families of the region and were virtually a 'stateless' people found acceptance among the colonial authorities in their endeavour to legitimize their authority as the protectors and the guardians of the Hos.

Dalton believed that the endemic restiveness of the tribals of Chotanagpur was explainable partly in terms of the enforcement by the government of its laws and regulations, which had not taken into account the historical specificities of the local tribal society:

> The same law for all is a very high sounding and popular cry, and it is much favoured in the legislature of recent years; but I think in this craving for homogeneity, the heterogenous character of the component parts of the population of India should always be borne in mind.[17]

Nonetheless, the hegemonizing colonial will was very much present in Dalton, even if was not confined to the mere pursuit of governmental ends. Dalton had no doubt that the British rule as protectors of the Hos had proved to be beneficial for the Hos. Thus he wrote:

> they have been directly under our Government for about 37 years, and coming to us as unsophisticated savages, we have endeavoured to civilize without allowing them to be contaminated, and whilst they still retain those traits which favourably distinguish the aborigines of India from Asiatics

> of higher civilization, a manner free from servility, but never rude, a love or at least the practice, of truth, a feeling of self respect rendering them keenly sensitive under rebuke, they have become less suspicious, less revengeful, less blood thirsty, less contumacious, and in respects more amenable to the laws of the realm and the advice of their officers.[18]

It was also from the mid-nineteenth century that we find the increasing use of the term 'Ho' to designate the tribe rather than Kol or Larka Kol in both official and non-official accounts. The switchover to Ho was evident by the time of the Census operations. Since 1872, the Census came to be used as tool of social control to gather knowledge of the colonized which would thereby strengthen the Raj. The Census provided data on the questions of religion, ethnicity, the nature of demographic movements, emigration and immigration and the circumstances necessitating these shifts. Conceived originally as a statistical operation to quantify the subject population, the census also proposed a new classification of Indian society. The Census report of 1872, for instance, divided the indigenous population into five broad groups: aboriginal tribes, semi-Hinduized aboriginals, Hindus proper, persons enumerated by nationality only and Hindus not recognizing caste. The criteria adopted in this classification were those of racial origin and occupation. Race however was not just a biological category here, but also referred to religious groups. The Census represented the Hos as a homogenized community and portrayed them as belonging to the first category and largely professing animism with a small minority of Christians.

The Census data therefore tended to categorize different communities as specific 'tribes', with their own inherent specific attributes. Yet, simultaneously with the Census operations, official data was being collected for yet another purpose: standardization of revenue assessment through land settlement operations. Since the mid-nineteenth century down to the twentieth century, settlement operations took place throughout Chota Nagpur. In contrast to the Census reports, settlement reports were more concerned with differentiating classes of tenants rather than identifying tribes, about fixing revenue payment rather than with determining degrees of primitivism associated with tribes. Yet, the Hos, in contrast to the Santals and Oraons of the neighboring districts, were depicted as backward in their agrarian practices and thus settlement reports also served to popularize the notion of the backward and primitive *adivasi*.

In the colonial imagination, Hos figured as poor cultivators who seemed to lack any systematic knowledge of settled agriculture and were apparently involved with largely slash and burn techniques. Their agricultural practices came in for criticism by successive district administrative heads who compared them unfavourably to the methods of cultivation of the surrounding settled peasant tracts populated by the Hinduized peasantry. In the 1840s Tickell wrote in his *Memoir on the Hodesum* that, 'They are bad husbandsmen, and no agricultural works on a large scale, such as tanks and *bunds* to meet the exigency of a dry season, are met with in the country.'[19] In the mid-nineteenth century, Dunbar, in his ethnographic account of the Hos, observed that cultivation and agriculture were at low ebb in Kolhan. 'Scarcely anything but *dhan* is raised, and the fields in which it is sown are so small, ill formed, and to all appearances so badly attended to, that abundant crops are, I suspect, of rare occurrence.'[20] Half a century later, the same prejudice was reasserted by James Taylor, a Settlement Officer, who wrote:

> The Kol is a very poor cultivator compared with the *ryots* of Orissa and other parts of Bengal. The fact is that he has never really outgrown the state of his prehistoric ancestors. He is a hunter who has been forced to agriculture by the contraction of the forest areas and a consequent decrease of game. The Kol's ideal cultivation is *jhuming*, pure and simple, and as he is probably inferior to none in the clearing of forest and in the felling of trees, he stands pre-eminent as a pioneer, but there his value as a cultivator ceases. He will put in some labour in the damming of *nullah* beds and the construction of embankments, but once the field is roughly made, he is careless of keeping it in repair.[21]

Any improvement in cultivation was ascribed to the civilizing influence of British rule. In 1867, the Deputy Commissioner Dr Hayes noted that,

> The people of Colehan still have much to learn by way of

> cultivation; still, looking back a few years we cannot but be struck with the improvement that they have made. Far from being nomadic in their habits, moving from place to place with herds of cattle on which they were assessed, and cultivating patches here and there for one or two crops only, they have gradually become stationary, established themselves in picturesque villages.[22]

Hayes had further suggested that the purpose behind imposing a land revenue settlement on the Hos was to make them 'stationary in their cultivation, to get rid of the dense jungle the district is noted for and to make the Coles good agriculturists'.[23]

In course of colonial rule there occurred a general increase in the extent of cultivation and the intensification of the process of cultivation. This was not, however, backed up by innovations in methods of cultivation. The government laid the blame squarely on the Ho cultivator, who 'does not worry much about improvements'. Tuckey, a Settlement Officer in the early nineteenth century thus argued,

> Most of the rice land in the Kolhan is sown broadcast including much land that is fit for cultivation of transplanted rice...Little attention is paid to changing the seed in different years or procuring seeds from other villages. The ploughs are small and only scratch the ground and the plough cattle are very poor... The harvesting is done in a manner which is very wasteful of the straw.[24]

The government failed to take into account the hard labour that went into constructing the irrigation *bandhs* and ascribed the reluctance of the Ho tenants to undertake the task to their improvidence and inherent idleness. H. McIntosh, a Commissioner of Chota Nagpur thus reported that,

> It is surprising that the experience [i.e., the failure of the early rice crop] has not made the tenantry more willing to construct protective irrigation works. The usual procedure is for Government to pay half the cost and the *raiyats* to give the other half in the shape of labour. In more than one instance where this was proposed, the *raiyats* refused to work at the rate at which payments for labour had been hitherto made. On one occasion a *Manki* explained that he had not made a

> water channel from a *bandh* to some fields where the crops were in a precarious state, because it would be hard work (*mehnat hoga*). It is difficult to know what to do with *raiyats* who take this view.

Yet the British government hardly undertook any measures to bring about an improvement in agrarian techniques and practices. There was little investment in irrigation on part of the government, although successive settlements emphasized its necessity and also recognized that the Ho villagers lacked the capital resources necessary for the purpose.[25] Nevertheless, irrigation was left to the initiative of the villagers and the tenants, who had to expend large amounts of labour and capital on the construction of these irrigation reservoirs. Thus in agrarian policies as in other areas of governance the British increasingly began to assume a policy of non-interference. The initiative for reform was left to the Hos, who were portrayed as idle and improvident. The pious paternalist desire for reform and the agenda for 'civilizing the savage' that Wilkinson had expressed at the time of British annexation in 1837 was quietly forgotten in the programme of the late nineteenth and the twentieth century.

Inventing tradition: socio-cultural movements among Hos in the twentieth century

What needs to be highlighted is that the Ho *adivasis* did not simply react passively to colonial attempts at categorization but actively attempted to forge a new identity for themselves through socio-cultural reform movements. The primary intention behind these attempts on the part of the Hos to reinvent themselves was to gain in self-respect vis-à-vis the non-Hos. These were thus intended to strengthen their tribal identity so that they could better deal with their enemies. Such movements reveal that an ethnic communitarian consciousness, transcending village and kin ties, had developed in course of the twentieth century, as the interaction of the Hos with outsiders groups increased. These also reflected the changing perceptions of the Hos regarding themselves and their enemies. This section will explore four such instances which occurred in the early years of the twentieth century.

Under colonial rule, the traditional village structure of the Hos faced new onslaughts particularly as a result of the influx of alien outsiders. The colonial state proved incapable of providing adequate safeguards to protect the interests of the tribal community. Under these circumstances it became imperative for the tribal people to devise a new social order which would enable them to effectively cope with the new realities. This required a re-evaluation of tradition, particularly of their old religious beliefs, which seemed inadequate in the changed times. Increasingly, since the beginning of the twentieth century new religious reformist movements spread among the Hos which aimed at strengthening the community through reforming their customs. Reforms entailed both a rejection of certain traditional beliefs and practices and borrowing from Hindu cultural life. Yet it would be misleading to characterise such reform movements as assimilation with the Hindu cultural world since only certain aspects of the Hindu traditions were selectively introduced within the belief structure of the tribals.

In 1907, a religious reform movement spread among a section of the Hos. Believed to have been started by one Singrai Ho of Bhuta village in Barkela *pir* (district subdivision), the Satya Dharam or the Punya Dharam movement was looked upon as a 'new religion'[26] by contemporary British officialdom. After the death of the founder the religion was propagated by four gurus or teachers, namely Bamiya Ho of Garahatu, Hari Ho, Dula Ho and Birjo Ho of Guira.[27] The movement aimed at the purification of the Ho religion through reform of some customary practices and the adoption of certain Hindu mores. For instance, they put on sacred threads like the Hindu Brahmins. However, it is not clear whether this signified a claim for a higher ritual status. At the same time many other popular beliefs and practices associated with Hinduism were sought to be challenged. The notable feature of the new religion was that its adherents worshipped only one God, who was omnipotent and invisible and was addressed as *Sat Malik* or True Lord[28]. Denouncing the idolatry of the Hindus, the Satya Dharamis did not have any image or representation of their God. The True Lord was an abstract concept who was to be worshipped through *dhyan* and *jap*, that is meditation and devotion. While this went against the popular Hindu practice, it also reflected the influence of abstract metaphysical Hindu thought.

What was more significant was the break with the Ho tradition. The followers gave up the traditional dancing and other observances of the Hos. They also gave up the drinking of rice beer and became pure vegetarians.[29] Neither of these practices were traditionally opprobrious in Ho society. In fact, rice beer was traditionally associated with Ho religion as the Hos believed that the primeval pair of brother and sister could learn to procreate and thus give birth to the Ho people only after Sing Bonga offered them intoxicating rice beer. However, such customs were commonly looked down upon by the higher caste Hindus. Other articles of food were also proscribed, such as *ghee*, sugar and ordinary salt. Instead, they used oil, *gur* and rock salt. They did not eat sweets or food prepared by men of other religions. They observed many ceremonies and every aspect of their daily lives was governed by fixed rules 'even to the minutest details'. For instance, they bathed daily and if they went out they could not re-enter their houses without taking a bath. They did not vaccinate their children nor did they use any medicine when they fell ill. They believed that prayers to their God would save them from sickness.

The Satya Dharam movement was however limited in scope and was confined to the villages around Chaibasa. Judging from the timing, the space and the programme of religious reform, it may be presumed that the Satya Dharam movement was to an extent influenced by Birsa Munda's movement among the Munda tribe, which also had spread from the town of Chaibasa.

Social reform movement among the Hos

Attempts at reforming customary practices were not confined to the realm of religion alone. Their social customs were also sought to be changed as well. Such attempts at social regeneration were spearheaded by educated Hos who organized meetings at various places in Kolhan which, in the words of a contemporary observer, urged upon the Hos to 'guard up their loins and save their society from rack and ruin.'[30] The agenda of reform reveals the concern of the educated, Hos regarding the image of their community among their Hindu neighbours. Thus many of their traditions, which were immoral or degenerate in the eyes of the Hindus, came under attack. Chief among them were drinking rice beer, dancing and sexual 'licentiousness'.

The reformists argued that excessive drinking of rice beer had told upon the health of the people, as a result of which the men had become weak, lazy and worthless. Thus, it was argued that the burden of both domestic work and the task of earning a livelihood fell largely upon the women, because of which they had become sexually licentious. At a meeting in Lupungutu on 25 March 1924 which was presided over by Dulu *Manki*, the tribal member of the Bihar and Orissa Legislative Council, reformist Hos adopted resolutions against the traditional dances *Dama Duma* and *Sisun* attested by seventy influential members of the Ho community. These customs were held responsible for causing ill health among the people on account of keeping late hours, for serving as an impediment to the progress of students, for being detrimental to the morals of young people who went from village to village to take part in the dances and for generally demoralizing the youth. It was also argued that such dances involved an unnecessary waste of time and energy. The most significant objection that the reformists raised was that the music and dances were looked down upon by 'cultured neighbours' as being 'very low and degrading'[31].

At the same time, there were efforts to reinvigorate certain tribal customs which were facing destruction in the changed socio-economic circumstances of the time. A vital issue confronting Ho society related to growing liaisons between members of the same *killi* or clan group. Traditional Ho society was divided into several exogenous clan groups or *killis*. Members of the same *killi* were believed to have descended from a common ancestor and marriage within the *killi* was strictly proscribed. But gradually the laws governing such taboos became more lax particularly with the growth of industrial centres such as Jamshedpur and the coal mines which provided shelter to the runaway couples. Nonetheless, such conduct was generally considered deviant and the participants at the Lupungutu meeting urged the youth not to indulge in such liaisons and suggested that in case of transgression of tribal norms the offending members should forfeit protection from the society and be disinherited from their ancestral property.

The third major issue discussed at the Lupungutu conference related to the practice of bride price. Among the Hos the bride price that was asked had always been very high. Even in the mid-nineteenth century, E.T. Dalton had noted the high incidence of unmarried girls of marriageable age who were to be found in the Kolhan and attributed this to the high rate of bride price that prospective grooms were expected to pay to the brides' family.[32] In the early twentieth century, the bride price often went up to thirty heads of cattle, forty to fifty silver coins and ornaments worth forty rupees, besides 200 to 300 pots of rice beer[33], which was more than what an ordinary Ho could pay. According to Rev. A. Logsdail who was in charge of the Anglican Mission at Chaibasa, a *Manki* (a leader of a group of villages) in Kolhan had received forty heads of cattle as bride price before delivering his daughter over to her husband.[34] The meeting resolved to introduce a fixed rate of bride price in order to improve the social condition of the Hos. It was decided that for those who possessed land of their own for cultivation, the maximum bride price should not exceed Rs. thirty, two bullocks and a cow, while for those without land, the maximum bride price should not exceed ten rupees.[35] These resolutions were corroborated at a subsequent meeting at Chainpur on 13 April 1924.

The other issues touched upon at this meeting included female labour and sale of goods to *dikus*. With increased sale of goods from Kolhan at the numerous *hats* and *bazaars*, the spread of the Hindu influence became apparent so far as reforms related to female labour were concerned. Traditionally, Ho women did not lead a life of seclusion and they could freely participate in the economic affairs of the village. However, at the meeting it was suggested that employment of female labour was incompatible with their ideal of social reform and it was resolved that in future no Ho women should carry straw, hay or grass to the market. Similarly, the practice of hawking fuel from house to house of the *dikus* had come to be considered demeaning to the dignity and self-respect of the Hos. It was decided that in future people should sit in some place to sell fuel. In case a *diku* required fuel to be carried to his house, an additional fee should be levied for the service.

Finally a resolution was passed condemning the habit that labourers particularly had developed of drinking *diang* or liquor in public godowns and liquor shops, over and above the country-made rice beer. It stated, 'This meeting of the aborigines of Kolhan most emphatically condemns the practice of taking liquors in wine shops and urges upon the Ho labourers in the interests of the society to discontinue the practice'.[36] This insistence on temperance as a measure of self-purification can be partly attributed to the influence of the Gandhian movement in the region. It became more apparent in 1931-32 in course of another religious movement, the Haribaba movement.

Another meeting of reformist Hos was organized on 6 April 1924, again at Lupungutu. The issues addressed were all concerned with the status of women. Because of the high bride price, forcible marrying of young girls by men who could not afford to pay for a regular marriage had become common. The meeting decided to introduce a fine of Rs. fifty for offenders in order to discourage such a practice. In case of default the man was to be excommunicated. Another practice of keeping women of 'low social position' as mistresses by the Hos also came under fire. The phrase 'low social position' indicated Hos who ate beef. The reformists argued that Hos traditionally refused to eat with one who took beef and women who did so were looked down upon and regular marriage with them was normally proscribed. A resolution condemning the practice was passed by the reformists and Hos were called upon to purify their lives by not keeping women of low status as their mistresses.[37] This outlook of the reformists undoubtedly owed its origin to the spread of Hindu influence, reflecting as it did the usual Hindu aversion to the eating of beef. Contemporary anthropological accounts reveal that traditionally Hos did not have any taboos against the consumption of beef. However, it may be argued that though the reformers were influenced by Hindu social norms they did not aim at Hinduization of the tribe through assimilation within the Hindu social structure. Instead their aim was to strengthen Ho identity through effecting the regeneration of their social organization which was based partly on borrowing from Hindu cultural life. To do so they attempted to purge the Ho society of what was perceived by their neighbours as their negative attributes. The reformist Hos shared the belief that the *adivasi* society was less civilized than that of the Hindus. They did not, however, wish to become Hindu, but attempted to gain in self-respect through a programme of reform.

Haribaba Movement

In the early 1930s, there were two major religious reform movements among the Santals and the Hos, the former started by Silu Santal or Tarachand and the latter by Duka Ho, who took the name of Haribaba. Although these were apparently religious movements, they also had political overtones. What is interesting is the merging of the movements of the Hos and the Santals, a fact noted by British officers. R.P. Ward, the Deputy Commissioner, stated that, 'the fact that there is some sort of connection between Silu the Santal and Duka the Ho is rather curious as these two tribes usually keep strictly apart and the Hos have very little use for the Santals.'[38]

In 1930 Silu Santal of Rajabasa in Dhalbhum or Tarachand as he came to be known by his followers claimed to have founded a new religion. Claiming divine inspiration through dreams, he set himself up as a healer with miraculous powers and called upon his people to give up drinking, eating crabs and snails.[39] Tarachand attempted to mobilize followers at Rajabasa by circulating mango leaves through villages in Dhalbhum, Mayurbhanj and south Kolhan with the message that the villages would be visited by an epidemic if they were not passed on. On 15 May 1931, a large number of Santals collected at Rajabasa and proceeded to display their independence by pulling down telegraph wires[40], the symbol of colonial power and authority. Tarachand threatened the local authorities that he would win *swaraj* because he had with him a 'large number of soldiers without uniform, to whom the British guns would cause no injury.'[41] He was arrested but while on bail he next shifted his activites to

Hurangda village in neighbouring Kharsawan. There he collected some 3,000 to 4,000 Kols, Bhumijes and Santals of Kharsawan, Seraikela and Tamar on 18 July 1931 and incited them to cut down timber and other trees from the State Reserved Forest and use them for erecting *mandirs* and other houses.[42]

The Haribaba movement spread at around the same time as Tarachand's movement, i.e. in 1931-32. It started in the northern parts of Singhbhum and from there it gradually spread to the whole of Ranchi district. Duka Ho, or Haribaba, was originally from Siriapos village in Seraikela estate. He set up his *ashram* in the forest at Jamrogara, near Chitpil which was located twelve miles north-west of Chakradharpur. Haribaba's fame spread through popular ceremonies from one village to another and people flocked from as far away as Manoharpur to see him and listen to his teachings. In the initial phase the movement was largely concerned with religious reform as he preached the need to re-establish traditional purity. The programme of purification, which aimed at cleansing the unclean elements from Ho culture, was therefore linked with the assertion of Ho identity. Hence Haribaba also laid stress on racial isolation. His disciples were all *adivasis* and he exhorted them not to have to do anything with the *tantis* or the weaver caste and others whom he designated as inferior people. This anger against the *tantis* may be traced to the rapid change during the colonial period in the role of the latter within the Ho village economy. They could take advantage of the new system to acquire new sources of power in the village. An official report of 1897 stated that 'The village accountants or *tahsildars* and *dakuas* or village watchmen are almost invariably of this caste. A *tanti* is the legal adviser of the villagers, no suit or litigation being entered on without his opinion being taken. Some had also acquired land in the tribal village.'[43] In such circumstances the ire against *tantis* is understandable. The movement also aimed to drive out alien oppressors, particularly the Hindus. A Ho of Kera had informed the Kolhan Inspector that, 'if ... the Hindu tried to oppress the Hos, the Hos could drive them out with bows and arrows.'[44] Haribaba also advised his followers to give up the practice of witchcraft, a practice that was popularized by the village priests as it enhanced their authority.

In terms of purification, the Haribaba movement was essentially an anti *bonga* (spirit) movement. The faith of the people in the *bongas* had been eroded by the latters' inability to assist the Hos in their material concerns during a general time of economic and political instability.[45] This indicated the need for religious reformation. *Bongas* and *bhuts* were believed to hide themselves in the deep recesses of the houses and hence a hectic search for *bongas* was carried out amid deafening sounds of drums and gongs. New disciples would be initiated into the order through an elaborate ceremony to expel *bongas*. Those who wanted to join Haribaba's religion had to discard from his house all *agom tapan* objects, i.e. objects kept as outward signs of some promises to perform sacrifices on receiving favours from certain malevolent spirits. All the implements used for practising black magic kept in their houses, such as the *najams* or objects used for poisoning the enemy, the *chuka* or earthen vessels used for divination, the *padkis* or a measure for two seers of grain used for divination, had to be thrown out. Following the cleansing of the spirits in the houses, other purification rites had to be performed by the disciples. They had to bathe in the local rivers and visit the sacred grove or the jahira of the village.[46]

They also developed certain other customs of their own. Haribaba emphasized the need for absolute cleanliness. The followers of the cult bathed twice a day and women had to bathe before cooking. Old cooking pots and baskets were thrown out. They believed that Singbonga created oxen on Tuesday and so they did not work the oxen on Tuesdays. Similarly, since Lakshmi was created on Thursday and since the Harababites called the cow Lakshmi, they did not use cows for work on Thursdays. Haribaba preached that since they worked with cows and buffaloes, they should not eat them. Although it had traditionally been a common practice to sacrifice a buffalo to Marang Bonga and later partake of the meat, Haribabites gave up eating beef.[47] Vegetarianism was a rule and drinking was prohibited among them. These reforms bear a resemblance to the Gandhian temperance movement. As pointed out earlier it may be argued that these practices were adopted by the *adivasi* reformers as they coincided with their own programme of reform.

Together with the purification of tribal usages and customs certain Hindu customs were also adopted. The Haribabites worshipped the tulsi plant and wore the sacred thread. They worshipped Hanuman and imitating him they danced with bows and arrows in their hand. Haribaba's wife Harima used to sprinkle holy water (*haripani*) on the followers on payment of a nominal amount.[48] Mathew Areeparampil argues that these reforms amounted to an attempt at Sanskritization and emphasized the influence of the model of the Hindu caste system on the Haribabites.[49] However, as B.B. Chaudhuri points out, it is not certain that the emulation of such Hindu cultural traits amounted to the introduction of the caste hierarchy among the Haribabites.[50] Even the official report was not clear as to the implications in terms of any positional change in the caste system. The influence of Hindu cultural traits in the movement is unmistakeable, but this was utilized to strengthen the Ho identity by cleansing it of what was perceived to be evil within it. Similarly, there was no attempt to reject their tribal identity and adopt the traditions of the Hindus. There are no indications to show that the 'purified' Ho tended to be integrated into the Hindu caste system. In fact the movement aimed at strengthening the Hos against the *dikus*, most of whom were Hindus, by reforming and purifying those aspects of Ho society which were considered derogatory by the Hindus.

The Haribaba movement however did not remain confined to religious reformation but gradually developed into a political movement in its second phase.[51] Despite the influence of the freedom struggle, the trends in the Haribaba movement were largely determined by the existing Ho culture. Gandhi's social and cultural programmes only marginally affected the 'purification' movement. On 19 July 1931 Duka Ho or Haribaba visited the Congress headquarters. Prior to this visit the Congress had little connection with the *adivasi* population of the neighbourhood. The few volunteers who did enlist to the Congress included the *tantis* and non-*adivasis*. According to the police report, it was after this visit that Haribaba began to preach the non-payment of rents and the wearing of *khaddar*.[52] It was around this time that Haribaba established links with Tarachand

and his disciple Jaichand or Jai Singh Santal who had set up their abode at Hurungda, about seven miles from Kharsawan. Haribaba visited Tarachand so as to 'exchange ideas' [53]. Haribaba declared to his followers that if they listened to his teachings and carried on the worship according to his instructions, he would arrange for a great meeting on some hill near Jamshedpur which would be attended by Haribaba himself, Tarachand and Gandhi[54] and he promised to restore the same set of things that existed before the coming of the British. Haribaba in fact told his followers that British Raj had come to an end and the reign of Gandhi had begun. The advent of the reign of Gandhi was celebrated with dances and feasts [55] and exuberant disciples danced and shouted *Haribol, Haribaba ki jai, Gandhi ki jai*.[56] As the Haribabites increasingly displayed a 'seditious attitude' the three most influential leaders were arrested. The Kharsawan police arrested Tarachand on 25 July 1931, his disciple Jaichand was arrested on 27 July on the charge of assaulting the police and Haribaba himself was arrested on the evening of 27 July for disturbing peace.

With the arrest of the three leaders, the political phase of the movement gradually came to an end. However, the aspect of spiritual purification persisted for some time. Haribaba's disciples refused to accept the news of his imprisonment. Several miraculous tales were circulated regarding his whereabouts. There were rumours that he had gone out to fight the British[57] and that he lived at an unknown spot on the banks of the Kanchi river, his body had turned to stone chest downwards, but was flesh and blood upwards and through his long hair flowed milk and water which were endowed with supernatural powers.[58] Several lesser 'Haribabas' came up to propagate the new religion. One Jojo Tamaria called himself a disciple of 'god Hari' in Chota Nagpur and preached on the lines of Duka Ho.[59] After Duka Ho's arrest his wife Nani Kui set up her *akhara* at Nandpur near Manoharpur and preached Haribaba's religion. To avoid imprisonment herself she restricted the movement to its purely religious form and took written engagements from her followers that they would not disobey the government. Nonetheless, the local government authorities decided to stop the movement, as they were not certain what it would lead to eventually. Some *Mundas* (headmen) who had been removed from office for their participation in Congress activities in 1924 in Kolhan called upon the people to flout the authority of the *Mankis* and *Mundas* (the traditional leadership) loyal to the British. They were arrested and the Haribaba movement was declared illegal [60]. Although the *Mundas* and *Mankis* were ordered to stop it there were furtive attempts to continue it at Kasira. The Deputy Commissioner of Singhbhum visited six villages in the area on 18 January 1932 and broke up the bamboo fences and huts.[61] A few Hos in Manoharpur instigated the people not to pay the rent and they were arrested as were Hari Ma along with Jojo Tamaria.[62] What is interesting is that even Christian *adivasis* were forced to join the movement, while a missionary records that many Christian *adivasis* willingly joined the movement.[63] However, ultimately the government's repressive measures succeeded in subduing the movement and the new religion of Haribaba gradually subsided.

Pan-tribal identity movement: Sarna Dharam movement

Around the same time as the Haribaba movement there were attempts to forge a distinctive pan-tribal identity for the *adivasis* of Chota Nagpur based on the ancient ritual practices of the *sarna* or the sacred grove, which was associated with almost all the Chota Nagpur tribals. The *sarna*, or the *jahira* as it was known among the Hos, referred to cluster of *sal* trees located at the outskirts of a tribal village in which lived Dessauli or the village deities. Traditionally, there was a strict taboo against cutting trees in the jahira. However, in course of the nineteenth century, as the village community structure weakened because of the new pressures brought about by the colonial government, the communal laws upholding this taboo had also weakened. In the changed circumstances the Hos had come to lose much of their old reverence for their sacred traditions and institutions. Although formerly no Ho would dare to cut even a branch or use the wood for his household and other domestic purposes, a report on Ho society and culture in the second decade of the twentieth century noted that this respect due to the abode of the *bongas* was gradually dying out.[64] This change in the cultural values could be explained partly in terms of economic needs, as was indicated in the report. It stated that during the settlement operations of 1913-1918, 'it was noticed that the trees had been skinned off, so that the trees may die and the villagers be able to appropriate the dry wood without being accused by the local authorities of having felled live trees.'[65]

In the early twentieth century an attempt was made to unite the tribal groups of Chota Nagpur on the basis of the practices centring on the sacred grove. To create a common platform for the *adivasis* a conference was held at Chaibasa in 1932, which was attended by *adivasi* delegates from Bihar, Orissa and Bengal. The conference agreed on a common name, Sarna Dharam, to denote the ancient religion of the tribals of Chota Nagpur. Each of the *adivasi* communities developed its own organization for the propagation of the religion. Thus the Mundas called it Munda Sarna Sangh, the Santals called it Sarna Dharam Semlet and the Oraons called it Sarna Nav Yuvak Sangh.[66] The Hos did not have any organization on the lines of the Sarna Dharam, but they formed an association known as Dupup Samaj which urged its members to follow the Dupup Dharam. While the Hos accepted the tenets of the Sarna Dharam, they did not use the term, preferring use their own nomenclature of Dupup Dharam.[67]

Conclusion

In conclusion, we may make two observations. In the first place, this essay demonstrates that British policies were seldom motivated solely by ideological considerations. This is not to deny the role of ideology in policy-making, but to stress the fact that often ground realities and the exigencies of the time played the determining role. Thus it would not be correct to talk of colonial tribal policies as a well thought-out project as some recent scholars have done. Under colonial rule there existed a multiplicity of opinions regarding tribes, generated either by the colonial power itself or arising out of a process of interaction and adaptation. Thus, several, often contradictory policies towards the indigenous people emerged in course of the nineteenth and twentieth centuries. At a time when a section of colonial administrators glorified the Hos as noble savages, other groups such as the Koravas of South India, the Bhils of Western India and Lodhs of Western Midnapur were classified as 'criminal tribes'. In fact the idea of the criminal tribe germinated and developed over a long period of time, as Stewart Gordon shows with reference to the Bhils of Western India.[68] Secondly, while British rule undoubtedly created categories and policies that impacted in a major way on indigenous identities, we should remember that tribal people were not simply passive participants in the making of their destinies. In fact, they too sought to actively recreate their self-identity in keeping with the socio-economic and political culture of the time. By highlighting the specificities of the issues affecting the Hos of Singhbhum, this essay underlines the complexities in the tribal situation in Chota Nagpur and lays emphasis on the multiplicity of both policies and responses.

Notes and References

1 See Kavita Philip, *Civilising Natures: Race, Resources and Modernity in Colonial South India*, Hyderabad: Orient Longman, 2003.

2 E.T. Dalton, *Descriptive Ethnology of Bengall*, Calcutta, 1872 (Reprint, Delhi, 1974).

3 Ramgarh Magistrate to Bayly, 30 June, 1817, *Govt. of Bengal, Judicial Criminal Proceedings*, no. 39 of 29 July 1817, West Bengal State Archives, hereafter WBSA.

4 Ibid.

5 Dalton, *Descriptive Ethnology of Bengal*, p. 192.

6 At the time of its formation, the Kolhan Government Estate comprised of 620 Ho villages in 26 pirs of Singhbhum and Mayurbhanj. *Govt. of Bengal, Judicial Criminal Proceedings*, no. 15, 6 June 1837, WBSA.

7 S.R. Tickell, 'The Memoir on the Hodesum', *Journal of the Asiatic Society of Bengal* IX, part II (1840), p. 806.

8 Ashis Nandy, *The Intimate Enemy. Loss and Recovery of Self under Colonialism*, Delhi: Oxford University Press, 1983, pp. 11-18.

9 Wilkinson to Tickell, 5 May 1837, paras. 1-2, *Govt. Of Bengal, Judicial Criminal Proceedings*, no. 15, 6 June 1837, WBSA.

10 *Govt. Of Bengal, Judicial Dept. General Letters to the Court of Directors*, GOB 19, no. 8 of 1838, 1 March 1838, para. 4, WBSA.

11 Mangles to Wilkinson, 6 June 1837, para. 5, *Govt. Of Bengal, Judicial Criminal Proceedings*, no. 28, 6 June 1837, WBSA.

12 Ibid.

13 The non-regulation provinces were exempted from the Company's regulations and were especially administered by 'officers from the ranks of the army for their acqauintance with the vernacular tongue and their supposed aptitude for civil business.' J.C. Marshman, 'Bengal as it is', *The Calcutta Review*, January 1845, p. 168.

14 Dalton, *Descriptive Ethnology of Bengal*, p. 10.

15 The rulers of Singhbhum, that is, the Porahat raja, his vassals, the *kumars* of Seraikela and Kharsawan and in the south, the raja of Mayurbhanj

16 Like the Nagbanshi Raj of the neighbouring Chota Nagpur, the state system of the Singhbhum Raj had entrenched itself in the countryside over time and thus had a well-organized bureaucracy which was chiefly associated with collection of tributes and impositions of various kinds. Significantly, the Porahat Raja also claimed military service of the Hos partly through the ritual status they had gained, and partly through promises of booty. Thanks to their serving as the Raja's militia, the Hos came to acquire the popular epithet 'Larka Kol' or the warrior Kol.

17 Dalton, *Descriptive Ethnology of Bengal*.

18 Ibid.

19 Tickell, 'The Memoir on the Hodesum', p. 706.

20 W. Dunbar, 'Some Observations on the Manners, Customs and Religious Opinions of the Lurka Coles', *Journal of the Royal Asiatic Society of Great Britain and Ireland* XVIII (1861), p. 372.

21 James H. Taylor, *Final Report on the Survey and Settlement Operations in the Porahat Estate, District Singhbhum, 1900-03*, Calcutta, 1904, p. 10, paras. 44-45.

22 Hayes to Dalton, 22 February 1867, p. 130, *Govt. of Bengal, Revenue Proceedings*, no. 122 of June 1867, WBSA

23 Hayes to Dalton, 20 June 1864, para. 6, *Govt. of Bengal, Revenue Proceedings*, no. 13 of November 1864, WBSA

24 Ibid., p. 6, para. 16.

25 A.D. Tuckey, *Final Report on the Resettlement of the Kolhan Government Estate in the District of Singhbhum*, 1913-1918, Patna 1920, p. 5, para. 14.

26 D.M. Panna, 'Note on the Hos', in ibid., p. 128.

27 Ibid.

28 Ibid.

29 Ibid.

30 D.N. Majumdar, 'The Cry of Social Reform Among the Aborigines', *Modern Review,* March 1925, p. 287.

31 Ibid., p. 287.

32 Dalton, *Descriptive Ethnology of Bengal*, p. 200.

33 Majumdar, 'The Cry of Social Reform Among the Aborigines', p. 288.

34 Eyre Chatterton, *The Story of Fifty Years' Mission Work in Chota Nagpur*, London, 1901, p. 127.

35 Ibid., p. 288.

36 Translation provided by Majumdar in 'The Cry of Social Reform Among the Aborigines', p. 289.

37 Ibid.

38 Extract from A.D. Tuckey's fortnightly D.O. No 287 TC, 27 July 1931, *Govt. of Bihar & Orissa, Political (Special) Dept.*, File no. 57 , 1931, Bihar State Archives (henceforth BSA).

39 A. Majid to A.D. Tuckey, *Comm., CND*, 27 March 1931, cited in K.S. Singh, 'The Haribaba Movement in Chota Nagpur, 1931-32', *Journal of the Bihar Research Society* XLIX (1963), part 1-4, p. 285.

40 Ibid.

41 Extract from Confidential diary of Superintendant of Police, Singhbhum for the period ending 27 May 1931, cited in ibid.

42 Raja Sriram Chandra Singh Deo, Ruling Chief of Kharswan Feudatory State to the Deputy Commissioner of Singhbhum, 26 July 1931, *Govt. of Bihar & Orissa, Political (Special) Dept.*, File no. 57, 1931, BSA.

43 J.A. Craven, *Final Report on the Settlement of the Kolhan Estate in District Singhbhum in the year 1897*, Calcutta, 1898, p. 21, para. 73.

44 Extract from A.D. Tuckey's fortnightly D.O. No 287 TC, 27 July 1931, *Govt. of Bihar & Orissa, Political (Special) Dept.*, File no. 57, 1931, BSA.

45 R.P. Ward to Tuckey, Confidential D.O. No 132/C, 30 July 1931, para. 8, *Govt. of Bihar & Orissa, Political (Special) Dept.*, File no. 57, 1931, BSA.

46 Ibid., p. 400.

47 Ibid.

48 F.E. A. Taylor, *Final Report on the Revisional Settlement of Porahat Estate, district Singhbhum 1928-32*, Patna, 1938, p. 31.

49 Mathew Areeparampil, 'Socio-Cultural and Religious Movements among the Ho Tribals of Singhbhum District of Bihar', in *Continuity and Change in Tribal Society*, edited by Mrinal Miri, Simla: Institute of Advanced Study, 1993, p. 402.

50 B.B. Chaudhuri, 'Society and Culture of the Tribal World in Colonial Eastern India: Reconsidering the Notion of Hinduisation of Tribes' in *Perspectives on Indian Society and History: A Critique*, edited by Hetukar Jha, Delhi: Manohar, 2002, p. 65.

51 For a detailed discussion, see Singh, 'The Haribaba Movement in Chota Nagpur, 1931-32'.

52 R.P. Ward to Tuckey, para. 4.

53 Ibid., para 5.

54 Extract from A.D. Tuckey's fortnightly D.O. No 287 TC, 27 July 1931.

55 G. Vanhoutta, 'Haribaba', *Chotonagpur Mission Letter*, no 11 (November 1931), pp. 236-239

56 Ibid.

57 W.G. Dickson, 'The Haribaba Movement, what it is', *Chota Nagpur Diocesan Paper No. 40* (New series) cited in Singh, 'The Haribaba Movement in Chota Nagpur', p. 288.

58 Vanhoutta, 'Haribaba', pp. 236-39.

59 Singh, 'The Haribaba Movement in Chota Nagpur, 1931-32', p. 292.

60 Ibid.

61 Ibid., p. 293.

62 Ibid.

63 Vanhoutta, 'Haribaba', pp. 238-39.

64 Dhan Mashi Panna, Assistance Settlement Officer, Kolhan Government Estate, 'Notes on the Hos', Appendix E, p. 128.

65 Ibid.

66 P.C. Hembram, 'Return to the Sacred Grove' in *Tribal Movements in India*, edited by K.S. Singh, Vol. 2, Delhi: Manohar, 1982, p. 87.

67 Ibid.

68 Stewart Gordon, 'Bhils and the Idea of a Criminal Tribe in Nineteenth Century India', in Stewart Gordon, *Marathas, Marauders and State Formation in Eighteenth century India*, New Delhi: Oxford University Press, 1994, pp. 151-62.

Sastric modernity

mediating Sanskrit knowledge in colonial Bengal

Brian A. Hatcher

> There is no longer a transparent society in which the universal can show itself in a direct unmediated way.
>
> Ernesto Laclau[1]

The premise of this essay is that that the key to understanding the experience of modernity in South Asia lies in recognizing that it is best understood as something multiple rather than singular. Furthermore, the key to grasping the multiplicity of South Asian modernities lies in historicizing them. While we may be accustomed to thinking of South Asian modernity as a narrative that commences with Rammohan Roy, runs through Rabindranath Tagore and Mahatma Gandhi, and carries on through Jawaharlal Nehru and the attainment of Indian independence, we are perhaps less accustomed to pausing the narrative at specific junctures to explore the particular ways in which modernity is announced at given times in given places. Were we to do so, we would surely be led to conclude that the modernity of Rammohan is not that of Jawaharlal; we would come to see that the apparent universalisms of modernity have 'no necessary body and no necessary content.' Instead, post-Enlightenment universalisms come to expression only as mediated through a set of 'particularisms'. This is the recognition that motivates my attempt to explore one particular experience of modernity in colonial Bengal. I call this experience 'Sastric Modernity'.

One experience of modernity in colonial India

It goes without saying that it has proven difficult to capture the experience of modernity in any simple formula. Powerful suggestions of the character of modern life can be found in Rousseau's eighteenth-century image of the social 'whirlwind'; in Marx's famous evocation of the sweeping away of 'fast-frozen relations' during the nineteenth century; right down to Weber's twentieth-century image of the 'iron cage' of bureaucracy, legalism, and capitalism.[2] Alternatively, the thematic of modernity can be captured under a number of inter-related headings: capitalism, industrialism, rapid urbanization; the quest for emancipation from traditional norms in the name of reason, individualism, and anti-supernaturalism; liberty, secularism, and democracy; voyages of discovery, conquest, and imperialism. All of these confirm Marshall Berman's observation that while the experience of modernity may appear to be something monolithic and universal, it is in fact 'a unity of disunity'.[3]

Berman's instinct, when discussing the experience of modernity in the West, was to historicize it. He divided modern history into three chronological stages: the first, running from the sixteenth to the nineteenth centuries; the second spanning what is sometimes referred to as the long nineteenth century (i.e. 1789-1914); and the third comprising major developments during the twentieth century. It is a straightforward approach, but insofar as it encourages us to think of modernity as something developing differentially over time, Berman's model has obvious utility.

An even more ambitious attempt to historicize the experience of modernity has been undertaken by Charles Taylor in his *Sources of the Self*. Taylor combines epic chronological scope (from Aristotle to Heidegger, Augustine to Horkheimer) with an attempt to isolate and comment on what he takes to be the central thematics of modernity. He is able to show in fine detail how such modern notions as 'inwardness' and the 'affirmation of worldly life' emerge from the long history of European thought, while simultaneously providing tools for assessing the complex and on-going permutation of such notions. It is a masterful work and, as I have remarked elsewhere, provides a model for the kind of research one might like to see done on the question of South Asian modernity.[5] While I cannot claim even to have begun that task here, my attempt in the present context is to delineate a mode of Sastric Modernity with reference to Taylor's work.

In keeping with the idea of historicizing modernity, Taylor has more recently remarked that no single theory of modernity premised upon Western history will be adequate to the task of comprehending the various ways non-Western cultures have experienced modernity. Instead, he suggests we should be on the lookout for 'multiple modernities'.[6] If Western modernity is grounded in a new social and moral order—a new 'social imaginary'—then our task must be to search for the emergence of new social and moral orders outside the West that may help account for divergent experiences of modernity. In the present essay, I begin the task of exploring the social imaginary of mid-nineteenth-century Bengal in order to see how this might help us make sense of the particular mode of experience I propose to call 'Sastric Modernity'. My suggestions here are meant to be tentative and heuristic. I would like to ask whether this way of proceeding offers any promise of illuminating the nature of sastric-based reform in colonial India. In the spirit of a heuristic, I would like to venture some parallels suggested by Taylor's analysis of modernity in the West. In particular I would like to explore a possible parallel between mid-nineteenth century Bengal and the period of early modernity discussed by Taylor in connection with the likes of John Locke—what would fall roughly under Berman's first chronological phase as noted above. Chronologically speaking the two periods do not coincide, but I think there are important parallels with respect to the articulation of modernity in each.

In discussing Locke's world, Taylor calls attention to the process of transformation that led from a pre-modern 'ontic' moral social order toward a universe of God-ordained, but human-centered moral striving.[7] Unlike the pre-modern universe, this modern imaginary is no longer hierarchical, nor does it emphasize renunciation of ordinary life as a supreme norm (as in medieval monasticism). As Taylor elsewhere puts it, the gradual disenchantment from 'ontic logos' means that fundamental values and ideas are seen to exist within the individual and not in the world as given to us.[8] In Locke, for instance, Taylor sees the emerging norms of 'self-responsible independence', 'recognized particularity', and 'personal commitment', which in turn help support notions of rational industriousness and imaginative creativity.[9] As Taylor sketches it, such transformations stand at the start of a gradual shift toward egalitarianism, expressivism, and the sanctification of ordinary household life—themes that will come to be central within later manifestations of Western modernity.

On the one hand, this account fits with generally-accepted notions of the emergence of reason, individualism, and scientific inquiry in the post-Enlightenment West. But I find Taylor's discussion of Locke to be especially suggestive when thinking about intellectual changes taking place in nineteenth-century Bengal, in particular within the world of an intellectual like Isvaracandra Vidyasagar (1820-91). For all that Locke and Vidyasagar clearly represent very different time periods, cultural contexts, and religious backgrounds, the nature of the moral imaginaries they inhabit and their responses to the worlds in which they live are strikingly similar. This is not to say that Vidyasagar's colonial experience recapitulates the prior experience of Locke in England. I endorse no such simplistic view of modernization. While there may well be important shared socio-structural themes within the experience of modernity, our goal should be to identify the particular ways modernity is articulated in concrete contexts. In this respect, the parallel between Locke and Vidyasagar is advanced to open up the particularity of Vidyasagar's modernity rather than to suggest the paradigmatic quality of Locke's.

The point at which to begin exploring the parallel comes when Taylor says of Locke that he is at one and the same time 'one of the most important articulators of disengaged freedom' and a 'believing Christian'.[10] This tension between Locke's commitment to disengaged reason and his faith in Christianity seems in some sense structurally parallel to Vidyasagar's predicament as we shall see. The nature of that predicament can be seen very clearly when considering Locke's attempt to argue for the 'reasonableness' of Christianity. Taylor cautions that it is wrong to view Locke's attachment to orthodox belief as something 'residual'. Likewise, he says it is wrong to think Locke used his profession of belief as a smoke-screen to hide his unbelief.[11] To understand Locke's experience of modernity—and as I shall suggest to likewise appreciate Vidyasagar's—is to find a more adequate way to interpret their respective responses to this problem of freedom and belief. One thing we must not do is retroject anachronistic understandings of modernity onto either figure.

If we should avoid attributing to Locke a kind of late-modern skepticism, we should not project onto a mid-century brahmin *pandit* like Vidyasagar more radical versions of liberated reason. To be sure, Vidyasagar had internalized Enlightenment-inspired norms of 'disengaged procedural reason';[12] his work as an educational administrator provides ample evidence of his mastery of colonial bureaucratic practice. Yet Vidyasagar also famously undertook a program of social reform predicated on the appeal to religious authority in the form of the Hindu *sastra*.[13] Understanding his commitment to this program requires us to avoid the same kinds of mistakes Taylor warns against when considering Locke's commitment to the reasonableness of Christianity.

Hitherto, it has been customary to view Vidyasagar's dependence upon the Hindu *sastra* as either cynical or naïve. In the former case, we are asked to believe that the reformer invoked proof-texts from the sastric archive merely when they were convenient for advancing his agenda.[14] What is assumed in this case is that no genuinely modern reformer could be committed to scriptural texts or the worldview they represent; if he made use of such texts, it must have been part of a cynical strategy to garner support for his views by playing upon popular religious beliefs. In the latter case, we are asked to believe that the reformer (for all his modernity in other respects) nevertheless remained handcuffed to a naïve belief in the truth of the *sastra*; somehow he trusts in the near-magical truth-force of these scriptures to secure his success.[15]

Both these views are inadequate for understanding the modernity of a figure like Vidyasagar. Lurking within each is the ghost of 'tradition' as a reductive interpretive category. It is reductive because it invokes tradition as something before which the reformer must either dissemble or submit; it offers no way of putting the reformer into an active relationship with tradition. The inadequacy of the category of tradition is in fact revealed in the metaphors it calls forth. In the former case, we think of the reformer as someone who has 'turned his back' on tradition, someone who merely invokes *sastra* for good effect. In the latter case, we think of the reformer as remaining 'mired' in tradition; though we otherwise credit him with a measure of procedural reason, we conclude he is nonetheless unable to emancipate himself fully from tradition. That is, the reformer is either employing smoke-screens or he is tainted by the residue of tradition.

Taylor's discussion of Locke leads me to ask whether it is possible to imagine Vidyasagar's adoption of the *sastra* as in fact an exercise of the modern. Can we see in Vidyasagar's employment of *sastra* evidence of his particular attempt to engage with colonial modernity? What if we began by thinking of Vidyasagar as someone upon whom change impinged with great force but also as someone eager to effect his own changes along lines congruent with his own reasonable vision of the world? Seen from this perspective, the reforming Sanskrit intellectual turns to his work equipped with the tools he knows best, the tools that have served him well thus far. And yet with the passing of the 'ontic logos' of premodern Hinduism (better understood in this case as the hierarchical cosmos of classical Hindu *dharma*), the reformer's attitude toward knowledge and truth has changed as well. He now operates from the premise that values and ideas ultimately reside in him, not in the *sastra* or the sastric-ordained cosmos.[16] Meaning is now sought not in the structure of the world as given in the *sastra*, but within the subject himself. Tradition is neither abandoned nor parodied; rather, the reformer applies his own reason to the materials of tradition.[17]

The man who was Vidyasagar's intellectual forefather in so many ways, Rammohan Roy, seems to anticipate these themes. In introducing his translation of the *Kena Upanisad* he provides a fine example of procedural reason applied to tradition:

> I have often lamented that, in our general researches into theological truth, we are subjected to the conflict of many obstacles. When we look to the traditions of ancient nations, we often find them at variance with each other; and when, discouraged by this circumstance, we appeal to reason as a surer guide, we soon find how incompetent it is, alone, to

> conduct us to the object of our pursuit. We often find that, instead of facilitating our endeavours or clearing up our perplexities, it only serves to generate a universal doubt, incompatible with principles on which our comfort and happiness mainly depend. The best method is perhaps, neither to give ourselves up exclusively to the guidance of the one or the other; but by a proper use of the lights furnished by both, endeavour to improve our intellectual and moral faculties, relying on the goodness of the Almighty Power, which alone enables us to attain to that which we earnestly and diligently week for.[18]

While he was no *pandit strictu sensu*, Rammohan enunciates the attitude of Sastric Modernity. A fervent admirer of the European Enlightenment, Rammohan appreciated the need to break with what Kant had called 'self-incurred immaturity'. Though unaware of Kant, Rammohan responded to the Enlightenment challenge: 'have the courage to use your *own* understanding'.[19] At the same time, Rammohan appreciated the corrosive power of reason. Reason can lead to doubt, uncertainty, loss of bearings. The choice, from Rammohan's perspective—and I would say from Vidyasagar's as well—was not one we can easily capture with our preconceived notions of 'tradition' and 'modernity'. Rather, the choice was between attempting to find a way to read tradition rationally and handing over the interpreter's right to the 'unenlightened'. Taking the former option, Vidyasagar turns to the *sastra* armed with an enlightened—though not necessarily an Enlightenment-hermeneutic, refocusing the Sanskrit tradition upon itself in the interest of pursuing new goals.

I find it helpful here to appeal to the terminology of Hans Frei, who has written of Locke as a 'mediating theologian'.[20] Unlike the more radical Deist, John Toland, who could dispense outright with orthodox belief in the name of a higher reason, Locke seeks to establish that Christianity is in fact reasonable. Like Locke, Rammohan and Vidyasagar are committed to advancing on the basis of reason; but like Locke, they also hope to express their new outlooks by drawing on the continued saliency of their scriptural traditions. In their Bengali writings in particular, we see men like Rammohan and Vidyasagar engaging directly with Sanskrit traditions to demonstrate what Locke would have called the 'beauty, force and reasonableness' of their position.[21] Sastric Modernity, in this respect, is a method driven by the desire to demonstrate the reasonableness of sastric Hinduism.[22]

Sastric Modernity, then, is a useful heuristic category for two reasons. On the one hand, it allows us to identify a particular intellectual stance. That is, by suggesting that the experience of modernity could be articulated in terms of an attempt to find meaning in the *sastra*, the rubric serves to distinguish this hermeneutic from more radical forms of skepticism. Sastric Modernity is neither the skepticism of the Young Bengal faction of the early nineteenth-century nor is it the Comtean positivism of the late nineteenth-century. On the other hand, Sastric Modernity also identifies a particular historical moment, one that runs roughly from the advent of Rammohan to the failure of Vidyasagar's anti-polygamy effort. Our task, following Taylor's lead, is to give an account of the social imaginary of this period that provided the background to such a vision.

The social imaginary of mid-nineteenth century Calcutta

One of the distinctive features of the period from roughly 1820 to 1880 is the guiding assumption that the goals of social reform could be achieved by enlightening the colonial state regarding the need to address certain pressing social issues.[23] As Asok Sen remarked in connection with Vidyasagar's widow marriage campaign, it did not announce change from 'an enclave of enlightenment', but sought to garner 'necessary state and social support for his desired goals'.[24] From the *suttee* controversy to the Age of Consent, reform was predicated on the need for remedy in the form of government legislation. The reformer's goal was to educate the state regarding both the need and the viability of the reform. This explains the prominence during this period of the genres of polemical tract and public petition, both print devices that allowed reformers to connect directly with the public and the state.[25] By the time of Bankimcandra Cattopadhyay, sentiments had begun to change. Thinking about the question of high-caste polygamy, Bankim concluded there was no need to pass a law to suppress it; he trusted the practice would wither away with the increased spread of modern education.[26] Partha Chatterjee explains this attitudinal shift by suggesting how, by the latter quarter of the nineteenth century, reformers had begun to forego appeals for legislative intervention in favour of promoting the nation's ability to 'act for itself'. As Chatterjee puts it, the great reform efforts on behalf of women lost their saliency when 'woman' was enlisted for the task of safeguarding India's unique spiritual realm.[27] Henceforth the *sastra* would have significance primarily in defending the nation's culture, not in bolstering legislation. Seen from this perspective, Sastric Modernity, as I use it here, represents an earlier, pre-nationalist mindset. Within the experience of Sastric Modernity the nation as such is not yet a problem. Clearly, though, the decision by Vidyasagar and others to seek change on the basis of sastric authority would in time unlock a powerful resource for later cultural nationalists.

In order to appreciate something of the mind-set of the sastric reformer during the period from roughly 1820 to 1880, we need to recall the early aspirations of the colonial bourgeois elite. The 1830s, in particular, had seen a great flowering of public sphere activities in debate, journalism, and associational behaviour. Likewise, under the influence of modern education and the spread of European philosophical ideas, the 'ontic' realities of an older Hindu worldview – in which duty and religious belief were given in the dharmic cosmos – gave way to the individual's ability to find meaning on his own. A representative piece of sastric thinking in this regard can be found in the discourses read before the early Tattvabodhini Sabha in 1839-40. These discourses reveal pandits like Vidyasagar and Ramcandra Vidyavagis, working in concert with an array of *bhadralok* intellectuals, to redefine Hindu belief and practice. Their Bengali discourses, peppered with Sanskrit quotations from the *Upanisads, Tantras* and *Manu,* represent another expression of Sastric Modernity.[28] In the case of the Tattvabodhini Sabha, *sastra* (broadly construed) is called upon to articulate a vision of individual spiritual striving and an ethic of this-worldly engagement. Here again, we note the centrality of notions of inwardness and the affirmation of worldly life that are characteristic of an emergent modern outlook.

This is not to suggest that Sastric Modernity is merely another name for a kind of Brahmo modernism. If anything, Sastric Modernity provides a larger framework within which to situate the particular intellectual moves made by men like Rammohan, Ramcandra, and Debendranath Tagore.[29] Beyond the explicitly Brahmo orbit, Sastric Modernity could be used to think about the scriptural thinking that led *pandits* like Madanmohan Tarkalankar to support the idea of female education (finding support in a verse from the *Mahanirvana Tantra*) and to participate actively in efforts to edit, translate, and repackage Sanskrit sources in Bengali, as Vidyasagar successfully pioneered at the Sanskrit Press.[30] Looking at late nineteeth-century Benares, we might wonder if Sastric Modernity is a category that might be applied to Pramadadas Mitra's goal of widening the horizons of Sanskrit learning in the light of Western knowledge, while protecting the authority of the 'traditional' *pandit*.[31] Here, though, we also begin to encounter the limits of Sastric Modernity as a pre-nationalist mode of knowledge, insofar as men like Mitra and Guru Dutt Vidyarthi, were also beginning to articulate a defense of India's cultural norms from perceived challenges by Orientalist knowledge.[32]

Sastric Modernity is thus best seen as an interpretive mode that correlates with a particular period. During this period, elite reformers mustered scriptural materials to support reasonable appeals for social reform or religious transformation. The point is, we can historicize Sastric Modernity, just as we can historicize the position of Locke with respect to later developments in Europe. I say this because, in suggesting this category, I have no desire to use it to generalize toward an over-arching set of claims about how Hindus have modernized. Rather, Sastric Modernity speaks to a local moment and a particular imaginary, and as such, helps us think in terms of 'multiple modernities'.

The goal might then be to use this rubric as a way to begin collecting examples of such intellectual activity during the period from 1820 to 1880. As I have suggested, we might begin by paying attention to Sastric Modernity as evidenced in such developments as the work of groups like the Brahmo Samaj and Tattvabodhini Sabha and the great reform campaigns surrounding widow marriage (*vidhava vivaha*) and polygamy (*bahuvivaha*). Once we have collected a range of such examples, we might then proceed to flesh out in even more detail the social imaginary of high-caste reformers and intellectuals in mid-century colonial Bengal. A more nuanced understanding of this imaginary would in turn assist the effort to explore in greater detail the lives and activities of Sanskrit intellectuals in colonial India, the need for which remains pressing.

Sastric modernity and widow marriage

In the space remaining, I would like to focus on Vidyasagar's widow marriage tracts as one example of how a *pandit* trained in, and in some sense devoted to, the *sastra* made use of them not simply to confront change, but to foster it and justify it. These two tracts were written in what might be called a hybrid Sanskrit and Bengali. Both were issued as printed tracts during 1855 under the same Bengali title, *Vidhava vivaha pracalita haoya ucita ki na etadvishayaka prastava*, or loosely 'A Proposal Concerning the Promotion of Widow Marriage'.[33]

By using these two tracts as an occasion to reflect upon the category of Sastric Modernity, I also hope to refine and supplement what I have said elsewhere about Vidyasagar's approach to sastric-based reform. In *Idioms of Improvement*, I took up the question of how best to understand the relationship between Vidyasagar's appeal to norms of modern rationalism and his use of *sastra* in pursuit of social reform. In thinking about how Vidyasagar seemed to shift between appeals to the universally accessible norms of reason and the particularist authority of the *dharmasastra*, I suggested we view it as an 'unresolved' tension in his thought.[34] That said, I went on to conclude that by carefully attending to nuances in Vidyasagar's use of the language of *dharma* and *sastra* we could also see how he was able to effectively combine these idioms with others he adopted from the realm of modernist theology.[35] I concluded that while there may not have been 'complete harmony', there was clearly a kind of 'convergence'.[36]

Since I offered that interpretation, Sekhar Bandyopadhyay has advanced his own original interpretation of the mid-century widow marriage movement, in which he takes up the issue of this apparent tension. Of Vidyasagar's tracts on widow marriage, Bandyopadhyay writes:

> At the very outset, in his first treatise on widow remarriage, Vidyasagar did not overtly privilege reason as a strategy of presenting his reform agenda, for he believed that people were not amenable to reason and were only governed by *shastra*. So he went on interpreting and reinterpreting the *shastra*, trying to prove that his reform had sanctions within the corpus of traditional religious texts. However, this approach stood at an interesting epistemological intersection between modernity and tradition.[37]

My concern is that Bandyopadhyay reads more disjunction into the picture than is necessary. Two points bear noting: one is Bandyopadhyay's suggestion that Vidyasagar downplayed the saliency of reason for arguing his reformist cause; the other is Bandyopadhyay's suggestive (if ambiguous) remark that Vidyasagar's appeal to *sastra* was 'interesting' insofar as it seemed to waffle on its commitment to modernity. The full import of these observations is made clear in what Bandyopadhyay goes on to say:

> On the one hand, [Vidyasagar] seems to have accepted the colonial stereotype of a rationalist divide in Indian society, with a small rational elite and the masses of unreasonable people governed by the scriptures. But at the back of his mind, there was also a rationalist hope that if he could argue his case with textual evidence from the *shastra*, he would be able to convince his people about the legitimacy of his reform agenda. On the other hand, what he was doing was qualitatively perhaps not very different from what the Nabadwip and Bhatpara pundits did when they issued *vyavastha* on various social issues.[38]

While one has to appreciate Bandyopadhyay's attempt to capture the subtleties of Vidyasagar's approach, one might also wonder whether the psychologism of such an interpretation does not presume to say too much about Vidyasagar's intentions. That Vidyasagar was a Brahmin and a member of the colonial *bhadralok* is indeed worth noting; there certainly is a paternalism to his work as an educator and reformer. Does it therefore follow that Vidyasagar had internalized the colonial stereotype of an irrational Indian populace? Must we conclude he saw his mission as one of liberating this populace from the chains of *sastra*? Perhaps we should recall what Vidyasagar himself says at the outset of his first tract in favour of widow marriage:

> If we rely on reason alone to show that [widow marriage] is a required sacred performance the people of this land will not be persuaded. But if we can establish that it is a required sacred performance according to the *sastras*, they will agree and be able to act accordingly. In this land the *sastras* are the ultimate valid authority in all such matters, and actions in agreement with the *sastras* are everywhere accepted as required sacred performances. Therefore, we must first determine whether or not widow marriage is in accord with the *sastras*.[39]

There is no suggestion here that Vidyasagar considers his countrymen too irrational to see the truth; nor does he invoke an image of blind enslavement to *sastra*. Instead, he states what he takes to be a fact of Hindu culture: in all matters bearing on family, life, religion and ritual, the *sastra* is considered to be the ultimate guide. What this suggests is only that Vidyasagar accepts the fact that people will not be ready to follow his lead if they cannot be convinced, first of all, that reform can be reconciled with the *sastra*. He does not so much turn his back on reason, as Bandyopadhyay seems to suggest, as he considers reason one normative guide to be invoked alongside that of *sastra*.[40] For Vidyasagar the key question is not whether reason and *sastra* can be harmonized. The question is how. The way forward, for him, was to abandon neither *sastra* nor reason, but to work with both in mind.

Seen in this light, an appeal to *sastra* need not mean a concession to *sastra*. Within the mindset of Sastric Modernity, the goal is to read the *sastra* in the light of new epistemological, hermeneutical, historical, and moral insights offered by the discourse of modernity. This brings us to the second aspect of Bandyopadhyay's interpretation, namely the suggestion that by taking up the *sastra* Vidyasagar necessarily waffles on his commitment to modernity. Bandyopadhyay suggests that

Vidyasagar's decision to take up *sastric* exegesis puts him on a par with pre-modern modes of intellectual activity—hinted at here by the mildly disapproving reference to the *pandits* of Bhatpara and Navadwip.[41]

I would argue, by contrast, that while Sastric Modernity addresses the concerns of a Hindu readership attuned to the *sastra,* it does so from a modern perspective. Vidyasagar is not torn between tradition and modernity. His mode of sastric interpretation is modern. If anything is 'interesting' here, it is our reluctance to acknowledge the modernity of what he attempts. And a major determining cause of this reluctance is none other than the bogeyman of *sastra.* Like the word *pandit,* the idea of *sastra* is so freighted with notions of stasis and obscurantism that we have trouble viewing it as a potential source or locus of change.

Hindu law is premised on *dharmasastra.* It is easy to think of the legal tradition of *dharmasastra* as representing a kind of monolithic, unchanging normative order. This view is often adopted by those who wish to suggest there is a fundamental incompatibility between modern legal reasoning and traditional Hindu exegesis. However, C. J. Fuller reminds us that the dichotomy here is overstated. His study of modern Indian legal decisions in the area of religion shows in fact that 'indigenous Hindu ideas of scriptural authority employed in indigenous styles of reasoning can be brought to bear on modern ideas.'[42] Where others find discontinuity, Fuller finds continuity. One way he accounts for this seeming impossibility is by suggesting that 'Hindu scriptural discourse is not and never has been monolithic.' Instead, 'it does perennially generate reinterpretations of itself, influenced by both internal and external factors.'[43]

In other words, there is—and has long been—a dynamic tension between scriptural tradition and change within Hinduism, a tension that derives from such realities as the on-going interplay between scriptural texts and local customs, as well as from the ever-present possibility of exegesis and interpretation. Fuller cites Robert Lingat, who once noted that 'The role of [sastric] interpretation amounts to this: it offers society the means whereby it can rediscover itself in fact.'[44]

More recently, Sudipto Kaviraj has discussed how sastric hermeneutics were able to achieve newness when applied to scriptural texts that otherwise appear to be transcendent and unchanging. Put simply, Kaviraj demonstrates the possibility for change within Sanskrit knowledge systems. Most helpfully, he sketches a dialectic between root text (or *sastra*) and commentary. The central act of commentary is in fact the making new of a pre-existing text. This does not mean, however, that the original text is done away with. If the commentarial supplement calls the original text into question by means of a particular interpretation, the original text also acts as a kind of counter-force to pure innovation. In the end, the interplay of text and commentary leads to what Kaviraj refers to as a 'generative extension'.[45]

Thinking of *sastra* as an ahistorical blueprint that fixes Indian society to unchanging patterns of 'tradition' forces us to adopt the kind of interpretation employed by Bandyopadhyay. However, by historicizing scriptural traditions and attending to the generative processes of commentary – whether pre-modern (as discussed by Kaviraj), or colonial (as in the case of Vidyasagar) or postcolonial (as in the Supreme Court cases addressed by Fuller) – we are able to conceptualize a modernity that can include sastric thinking. By attending to the 'newness within traditions' we open up the possibility of seeing how *sastra* has been able to play a dynamic role throughout Indian history.[46]

Skeptics might respond that while premodern India may provide proof of the generative flexibility of sastric knowledge, especially as interpreters were able to take advantage of the fluid interplay of customary practice and sastric code, colonial India witnessed the loss of such fluidity as orientalists and legal administrators worked to textualize Hinduism. Such attempts to codify Hindu law, it might be objected, closed down avenues for interpretive creativity.[47]

This is a complicated set of developments and one to which others have paid a great deal of attention. What we can do in the present context is to attempt to re-insert the indigenous intellectual into the picture. A great deal of postcolonial scholarship gives one the impression that the emergence of such a scripturalist paradigm took place through the agency of British orientalists and administrators, in the universities of Europe and the law courts of India. The *pandit*'s place in this history is often overlooked; it seems as if *sastra* was scripturalized in spite of the local scholar, who then becomes little more than a victim of the process. Ultimately, colonial hegemony was achieved through the 'expropriation' of indigenous authority by British law;[48] British jurisprudence and orientalist scholarship did eventually work together to write the *pandit* out of the picture, especially after 1865.[49]

These are no small developments and they have rightly been taken to represent the disruptive force of colonial rule in India. This fact notwithstanding, it is important to bear in mind that the *pandit* was not always a passive victim within this process. If anything, he was complicit in it, sometimes scripting his own obsolescence. The modern *pandit* internalized the norms of colonial law and interpretation and often turned these weapons against his own tradition.[50] Nevertheless, the key point is that the modern *pandit* thereby acquired a new set of intellectual tools like the norms of historical study, standards of textual criticism, and procedures for editing, translating, and publishing traditional literature.[51] These he could adopt and adapt for his own purposes. If a reformer like Vidyasagar turned to the *sastra* to advance his argument for reform, it might not have been because he was too blind to see what transformations were taking place; it might have been that he saw all too well the kinds of transformations that were taking place!

A turn to the *sastra* need not indicate a gesture of blindness or denial (though at times it may have been). It could also be a carefully reasoned gesture. In fact, the tools of scientific, historical research made it possible for a *pandit* like Vidyasgar to engage in a more aggressive interaction with the legacy of Hinduism. He may have operated on what appears to have been a scripturalist premise in investigating sastric norms, but we should begin by recognizing that the Hindu scriptures were his métier. It was colonial modernity that provided him with a new set of hermeneutical keys to apply to these scriptures. Herein lies the origin of Sastric Modernity.

It is this modern attitude toward the *sastra* that I want to emphasize, rather than the particular reformist goals to which it was applied. The modernity lies in the mode of intellectual activity as much as, or perhaps more than, it does in the emancipatory vision of reform. After all, the idea of appealing for a sastric ruling on the viability of widow marriage was nothing new. It has been said that the medieval lawmaker Raghunandana Bhattacarya sought to get his widowed daughter remarried.[52] In the mid-eighteenth century Raja Rajvallabha of Vikrampur sought support from *pandits* on the same issue.[53] Similar attempts had been made earlier in the nineteenth century in various parts of India.[54] If nothing else, these examples unsettle the simplistic view that Vidyasagar's reform goals were modern. Such a view is especially problematic if it is paired with the assumption that while the goal was modern, his recourse to the *sastra* was therefore traditional. If anything, he applied a modern reading of the *sastra* to what was clearly something of a perennial issue within the Hindu tradition.

As is well known, Vidyasagar premised his support for the practice of widow marriage on the testimony of the *Parasara-smrti*, a *dharmasastra* from the first half of the first millennium CE.[55] Unlike other major authors on *dharma* such as Yajnavalkya and Manu, Parasara claimed to address the duties that were relevant to the last of the four world ages, the *Kali Yuga*. In a nutshell, Vidyasagar adopted the argument that since we currently live in the *Kali Yuga*, Parasara should be the treatise we follow in this matter. Much of Vidyasagar's argument was devoted to defending his choice of this particular *sastra* against criticisms from other *pandits*.[56]

In *Parasara Samhita*, chapter four, Vidyasagar found his central proof text:

Naste mrte pravrajite klibe ca patite patau
Pancasvapatsu narinam patiranyo vidhiyate

Another husband is ordained for women in five extraordinary situations, namely if her husband is missing, deceased, a celibate renouncer, a eunuch or outcasted.[57] This passage would become the linchpin of Vidyasagar's argument that widow marriage is enjoined (*vihita*), rather than prohibited (*nisiddha*), by the *sastra*.[58]

Vidyasagar begins his second tract by pointing out that since the publication of the first, shorter tract (a half year earlier), numerous individuals had raised objections to his proposal. He acknowledges that each of these objections must be addressed in order for all doubts to be removed. Accordingly, the second tract is composed of 25 chapters, 24 of which each address a separate objection. The final chapter provides Vidyasagar's concluding appeal. The point I wish to make is that he structures the tract around a set of scriptural arguments, often traced to the concerns raised by other contemporary *pandits*. By refuting each objection, he seeks to establish the validity of his own position.

It needs to be noted at this juncture that Vidyasagar's tracts are clearly artifacts of colonial modernity; this is not a traditional sastric ruling, or *vyavastha*. These tracts adopt the conventions of modern print technology and are directed at the existence of an educated Bengali-reading public. Indeed, Vidyasagar went on to great fame as a publisher, capitalizing on his gifts as an author and his sense for the emerging schoolbook market. It was his particular genius to create, publish and print several defining works of early modern Bengali. While his success in this regard was somewhat unique, the general phenomenon was not, as countless native-owned printing presses sprang to life around mid-century.[59] This emerging print culture provided the concrete setting within which Vidyasagar composed his tracts in support of widow marriage.

Earlier I referred to these tracts as being composed in a hybrid Sanskrit and Bengali. I introduce the concept of the 'hybrid' here deliberately, if cautiously. While Vidyasagar himself remarks that he composed the two tracts in the vernacular, or *bhasa*, we should not let his description blind us to the fact that these tracts are in effect composed in two languages. Strictly speaking, Vidyasagar did not compose any original Sanskrit for these tracts; rather, the Sanskrit is culled from a legion of premodern texts (*sastra*, *purana*, *nibandha*, etc). These Sanskrit sources then take their place within the framework of Vidyasagar's Bengali prose. It is in this respect that we can say the tracts are both Sanskrit and Bengali.

I make this point to suggest that we should not read too much into Vidyasagar's comment that he wrote in *bhasa*, lest we be tempted to think that Bengali was chosen at the expense of Sanskrit. Put differently, by overemphasizing the vernacular character of these texts, we might be tempted to conclude that Sanskrit had ceased to play a central role in Vidyasagar's intellectual life?[60] But that really is not the case. Sanskrit actually plays a vital role within these tracts. Viewing them as hybrid Sanskrit-Bengali works encourages us to keep this fact in mind.

Ironically, Vidyasagar's explanation of why he chose to write in Bengali provides compelling evidence of his continued respect for Sanskrit knowledge. He tells us he chose to write in Bengali because most people do not know Sanskrit. As such, they have no way to judge between legitimate and illegitimate interpretations of the *sastra*. If the *sastra* is the standard by which his co-religionists will make their decisions, then people need to be equipped to understand sastric arguments. The saliency of Sanskrit is not in question; it is the public's ability to interpret Sanskrit that is in question.

Compounding the problem is the fact that the people most qualified to adjudicate sastric questions – the *pandits* – are among the most interested parties. Many *pandits* inhabit positions of orthodoxy. Can they be trusted to provide a clear and open analysis of the *sastra*? As Vidyasagar puts it in the opening to the first tract, 'scholars greedy for victory are so eager to ensure their own opinion that they do not even consider investigating the truth of the proposal.'[61] In the opening of the second tract he returns to this theme, remarking that some *pandits* are not averse to taking advantage of the public's general ignorance of Sanskrit in order to promote illegitimate positions; nor are they above using satire and other illegitimate means to defend their position.[62]

Vidyasagar's decision to write in Bengali reflects his attempt to find a way to make the arguments of Sanskrit exegesis available to ordinary readers. What has changed is less the validity of Sanskrit than the context in which sastric questions are debated and resolved. Of central importance here is Vidyasagar's awareness of the modern reading public. If traditionally the *dharmasastra* placed the resolution of legal questions in the hands of *pandits* arguing in the assembly of a king, Vidyasagar knew that in his day the case for or against widow marriage would need to be made before the public, even if legislation would ultimately derive from the British government. The case for widow marriage needed to be tried within the rapidly-developing public sphere of mid-century Calcutta, with its plethora of voluntary associations, periodicals, and public meetings. As the *Hindoo Patriot* reported at the time of the publication of Vidyasagar's first pamphlet:

> One most hopeful sign in our social condition was made apparent by the issue of this pamphlet. It elicited replies from a host of opponents the majority of whom belonged to the priestly and the professionally learned classes. Doctors of Hindoo doctrine and learning, who viewed the printing press with almost the same jealousy that the priests of mediaeval Europe viewed it, resorted to the suspected engine for the marvelous facilities it afforded for publishing one's wisdom and knowledge. The fact was placed beyond a doubt that we are a pamphlet-reading nation, and that is a fact of unspeakable social importance.[63]

Clearly, Vidyasagar's direct engagement with colonial modernity in his role as a professor, and then Principal, of the Government Sanskrit College prepared him to appreciate in full measure the many changes taking place in the areas of education, law, and government administration.[64]

We might say Vidyasagar's decision to publish these Bengali tracts reflects his awareness of the 'published word' as the 'decisive mark' of the public sphere.[65] He notes in particular that the well-to-do reading public of Calcutta (he calls them the *visayi loka*) lacks a sufficient command of Sanskrit to grasp the meaning (*artha*) and purport (*tatparya*) of the *sastra*.[66] By referring so explicitly to the educated and wealthy leaders of Calcutta society, Vidyasagar acknowledges that the dispute over the viability of widow marriage has a special resonance within the socio-political climate of colonial Calcutta. He knew all too well that there were important factions and wealthy patrons (zamindars, merchants, aristocrats) involved on both sides of the issue.[67] These men, in particular, needed to understand the complexity of the issue.

Without the support of Calcutta's indigenous elite, Vidyasagar knew his campaign could have little success.[68]

That said, the debate was still centered on the *sastra* and as such it would be essential to speak directly to *pandits* and other learned individuals. This explains the hybrid character of the tracts. For all that these may be Bengali texts, they operate largely in terms of Sanskrit and sastric argumentation. These are not just Bengali tracts enhanced with Sanskrit passages.[69] Nor is the inclusion of Sanskrit merely a nod to tradition. If anything, there is a kind of 'two-in-one-ness' that speaks to Vidyasagar's desire to think in, with, and through the *sastra*—even as he does so from the vantage point of a modern. I would like to explore this two-in-one-ness by taking up two issues: First, I would like to call attention to the basic structure of the texts; second I would like to focus on Vidyasagar's use of a Bengali idiom shaped by sastric categories.

To appreciate the structure of the text, it helps to think of a work of classical Hindu philosophy such as the *Yoga-sutras* of Patanjali. But not just the root text of Patanjali; rather, we have to picture the *Yoga-sutras* as commented on by Vyasa and glossed by Vacaspati Misra. In the case of the *Yoga-sutras* and its commentaries, the overall structure is something like a cream-filled layer cake, with the *sutra* at its core, layered over by comments from Vyasa and Vacaspati Misra. We can imagine that such a textual model would have been close at hand for Vidyasagar as he set about composing his tracts. However, in the case of these widow marriage tracts, the *sutra* 'core' is occupied by selected Sanskrit passages culled from the *sastra*; to these Vidyasagar adds his own layers of commentary. In a departure from classical works, here the act of commenting also includes an act of translation from Sanskrit to Bengali. The structure is something like:

Commentary – (Bengali)
SASTRA – *(Sanskrit)*
translation – (Bengali)
Commentary – (Bengali)

Within this structure, a crucial role is played by the

intermediary layer, which consists of Vidyasagar's Bengali translations of Sanskrit passages. In a sense, this layer is oriented in two directions—one looking back toward the Sansrkit, the other looking ahead to Vidyasagar's argument. The key structural dynamic is one of mediation.

If one looks at any of the major sections of the second long tract, it is clear how this structure operates. First an objection is raised in Bengali. This amounts to the outermost layer of commentary.[70] From there we shift to the innermost layer, where Vidyasagar quotes the Sanskrit passage that prompts the objection. In the mediating layer of the text, Vidyasagar then translates the Sanskrit passage into Bengali. The translation and the original remain closely juxtaposed, mirroring one another (even if Vidyasagar's Bengali version sometimes truncates or slightly rephrases the Sanskrit). Only then do we shift back to the outermost layer, where Vidyasagar incorporates the Sanskrit texts and Bengali translations within his on-going argument. In looking at this outermost layer of argument/commentary, the reader is struck by how often its content repeats that of the embedded Sanskrit passages and Bengali translations. If anything, all these layers seem needlessly redundant; the reader who is eager to move ahead might be justified in growing impatient. But there is strategy amid the apparent repetition.

Vidyasagar's strategy is to connect sastric teachings with public awareness. If the goal of mediating the *sastra* to the public is to be accomplished, all this material (Sanskrit and Bengali) must be included. Structurally speaking, the tracts keep their dual audiences in mind at all times—*pandit* and public. I would like to argue that it is in this very structure, in this textual performance of mediation, that we discover the key to the tracts on widow marriage. The effort at mediation embodied by these tracts constitutes their modernity. What is central is neither the Bengali nor the Sanskrit *per se*. Rather, by mediating sastric thought to his readers—and by moving between the two linguistic registers—Vidyasagar attends to Rammohan's concern (cited above) that change be pursued in light of both reason and tradition. The search is for a reasonable use of one's tradition, just as it had been for Locke in the early modern West.

My second illustration concerns the Bengali idiom of these tracts, which likewise seeks to keep two audiences in mind, *pandit* and public, and to mediate between them. An educated Bengali reader of the day could easily make his way through the text. At the same time, Vidyasagar adheres closely to conventions of sastric thought, keeping his argument congruent with the methods and criteria of his *pandit* peers. Consider the first chapter of the second tract, which begins with the following statement of the topic:

> Some have determined that the intention of the passage found in Parasara regarding marriage is that upon the disappearance . . . of a bridegroom who has been betrothed to a virgin she can be married to another bridegroom . . . [but that] it was never his intention to say that a married woman who is widowed should marry again . . .

In response, Vidyasagar states: '[We must] consider whether the determination of my respected opponents is valid.'[71] This ushers in a detailed discussion of various sastric sources and received opinions that occupies twelve pages of alternating Sanskrit and Bengali text. Vidyasagar's central concern is to address one of most important commentaries on Parasara composed by Madhavacarya around the fourteenth century.[72] In particular, Madhavacarya had argued that it was Parasara's intention to say that widow marriage was a matter for the other three *Yugas*, but not for the *Kali Yuga*. Vidyasagar felt he must demonstrate that Madhavacarya's opinion was not tenable.

In moving to reject Madhava's opinion, Vidyasagar says we must establish the purpose (*uddesya*), the intention (*abhipraya*), and the purport (*tatparya*) of *Parasara-samhita*. I highlight these terms to indicate that although the framing medium for the entire discussion is Bengali, the terminology and categories of analysis are decidedly Sanskritic and sastric; they are drawn directly from the critical vocabulary of sastric exegesis. Here again we encounter the two-in-oneness of these tracts.

To be sure, Vidyasagar has been faulted for creating a highly Sanskritized Bengali, but the present analysis may at least help us appreciate that his choice of idioms was not merely grounded in the arrogance or prejudices of a *pandit*.[73] Rather, to achieve the goal of mediating the *sastra* he required a language that could look in two directions simultaneously. In this strategy he had been preceded by Rammohan, whose engagement with orthodox opponents required him to work in a similarly Sanskritic Bengali. In this light, it is difficult to accept the verdict that such a choice led Rammohan—and by extension Vidyasagar—to inhabit a contradictory position.[74] To be sure, this is not the prose of the common man, but to say that it represents an alienated and reactionary psyche is to trap authors like Rammohan and Vidyasagar within an interpretive framework that denies them the ability to choose and to innovate. The present perspective allows us to appreciate that their choices were grounded in strategies of innovation.

While space is limited, we can illustrate Vidyasagar's strategic choices by examining how he rejects Madhava's attempt to adduce as proof a Sanskrit passage from the *Adipurana*. On the one hand, Vidyasagar comments that the passage cannot be found in any extant versions of the *Adipurana*. How, he asks, can an unattested passage be considered authoritative? On the other hand, Vidyasagar points out that even if we accept this passage from the *Adipurana*, it would still not constitute a refutation of *Parasara*. He reminds us that *Parasara* is a *smrti* text whereas the Adipurana is a *purana*. In any conflict between a *smrti* and a *purana*, sastric exegesis states that the *smrti* text is more binding. Furthermore, the *Adipurana* can be called a general treatise (*samanya sastra*), whose teachings apply to all times, while *Parasara-samhita* is a special treatise (*visesa sastra*); it applies only to the *Kali Yuga*.[75] The rules of sastric exegesis stipulate that in any dispute between two authorities, a special treatise is always more binding than a general one. For all these reasons, the *Adipurana* cannot be used to contest the authority of *Parasara*.

The goal of all this Sanskritized argumentation is not to preserve the exclusivity of sastric discourse. If anything, the goal is to open up Sanskrit learning for rational discussion. In his role as mediator, Vidyasagar seeks to honour the traditions of classical exegesis while inviting that exegesis out into a new, more public arena.

The choice of sastric modernity

Viewed in this light, these tracts on widow marriage allow us to appreciate more fully the choices made by Vidyasagar in advancing his reform campaign. It becomes easier for us to see that his appeal to the *sastra* was rooted in an awareness of the changing climate of intellectual and political life. His recourse to the *sastra* was neither cynical nor unthinking. Rather, we must see him as someone who, in Michael Dodson's words, acted 'knowingly' with respect to his own Sanskrit intellectual tradition.[76] Thinking about Sanskrit intellectuals in north India at around the same time, Dodson has written of the way such intellectuals chose to engage with Enlightenment modernity in very local ways, linking such universals as 'reason' to localized notions of *tarka*, for instance. I suggest that Vidyasagar's Sastric Modernity arises from just this sort of intellectual choice, a choice that ushers in 'localized particularizations of universal values'.[77]

To get at the particularity of this choice, we could also think of Vidyasagar adopting a mode of legal reflection that Donald Davis has captured by speaking of 'law as rhetoric'. By taking his place, as it were, within Hinduism's 'ongoing rhetorical conversation' on law and duty, Vidyasagar found a strategic vantage point from which he could address both pandit and public.[78] Traditional Hindu legal reflection had always recognized that *pandits* could make use of texts as the platform for advancing new opinions in response to 'new social circumstances'.[79] That Vidyasagar chose to promote widow marriage by a sastric commentary on *Parasara* need not be construed as a misguided appeal to codified texts. It can instead be seen as a choice to work within a local conversational matrix that was still accorded enormous respect. One thinks of the nineteenth-century *pandits* discussed by Dodson, who responded to 'the changing criteria of the Benaresi intellectual landscape' by transforming the 'ritualized argumentation' of the *sastra* into 'a new language'. Like the vantage point achieved by Vidyasagar in these texts, this new language allowed the *pandits* of Benares to 'produce an authoritative space from which to speak to a new series of cultural debates.'[80]

Similarly, other *pandits* in Bengal composed tracts to support or refute Vidyasagar's arguments. The number and range of such works is staggering and it should lead us to conclude that Sastric Modernity need not be applied only to figures like Rammohan and Vidyasagar whom we have come to view as progressive in matters of religion and society.[81] The distinctive thing about Sastric Modernity is the attempt to fashion an authoritative space within an emergent colonial public sphere—a space articulated in direct recognition of the need to bring the *sastra* to bear on contemporary issues.

We may conclude with an illustrative contrast. In the earliest reform tract written by Vidyasagar, he chose as his vantage point the universalist norms of colonial reason. In *Balyavivaher dosa* ('The Evils of Child Marriage') from 1850, a rational, historical, and scientific mode of analysis is offered as the bedrock for making normative decisions about social and ethical life. This short tract was composed in Bengali alone and made no direct appeal to *sastra* or Hindu law. Yet little came of this approach, and the reformist journal in which it appeared soon folded.[82] Within five years Vidyasagar took up the widow marriage campaign, opting for an approach based on the *sastra*. Had he given up? Was his resort to Parasara a gesture of defeat? Or was it indicative of his appreciation that his reformist goals were best served not by abandoning, but by reframing sastric analysis? The present analysis hopes to suggest that it was the latter, that Vidyasagar's Sastric Modernity represents an attempt to reconstruct the 'cultural meaningfulness of Sanskrit and the *sastra*'.[83]

In view of the subsequent history of modern India, the choice in favour of Sastric Modernity may appear to have been too particularist. By seeming to encourage the resolution of social problems by an appeal to the *sastra*, this localized strategy encouraged the proliferation of sastric-based apologies for Hindu customs. These in turn supported the well-documented shift toward Hindu revivalism after 1880.[84] As I have noted briefly elsewhere, one of Vidyasagar's greatest collaborators in the widow marriage movement was Taranatha Tarkavacaspati.[85] One might even say that it was Taranatha who helped bolster the *sastra* in Vidyasagar's early efforts at Sastric Modernity.[86] However, Taranatha did not always agree with Vidyasagar. Indeed he would eventually challenge Vidyasagar over his attempt to show that *Kulin* polygamy (*bahuvivaha*) was not consonant with the *sastra*.

In the *bahuvivaha* campaign, Vidyasagar once again chose to put into play his version of Sastric Modernity. Taranatha met him on the same ground, but argued that the *sastra* clearly supported the practice of polygamy. Tellingly, Taranatha accused Vidyasagar of finding 'modern' (*abhinava*) meanings in the *sastra*. Just as tellingly, Vidyasagar faulted Taranatha for composing his anti-reform tracts in Sanskrit.[87] In the introduction to his second lengthy tract on *bahuvivaha*, Vidyasagar asked what help works like Taranatha's could provide to a reading public uneducated in Sanskrit and sastric discourse.[88] It is rather ironic that many Bengali readers would only come to know of Taranatha's interpretation by reading the Bengali translations Vidyasagar inserted in his own tracts. Taranatha either did not appreciate or did not condone Vidyasagar's method of mediating sastric knowledge to the Bengali-reading public.

Nevertheless, Taranatha's recourse to the *sastra* did have its appeal among groups fearful of the decline of sastric norms in colonial India. Even though the majority of educated Bengalis could not read Taranatha's Sanskrit arguments, his use of *sastra* had another kind of persuasive power. In works like Taranatha's *Bahuvivahavada*, *sastra* takes on the status of a 'scriptural emblem', a powerful symbolic marker capable of creating chains of nostalgia linking the present to a glorified Hindu past. Such scriptural emblems contributed greatly to the revivalist atmosphere of the late nineteenth century, though their hold on the public was premised less on their reasonableness than on their emotive power.[89] It is no coincidence that Taranatha spent the latter part of his career extolling the importance of 'Vaidika Dharma' and encouraging the careful preservation of brahmanical orthopraxy.[90] This sort of appeal to the *sastra* contributed greatly to the strengthening of revivalist visions of Hinduism whose exclusionary legacy remains alive in India to the present day. Insofar as Taranatha's break with Vidyasagar was also a break with Sastric Modernity, it is illustrative of the way local struggles contributed to the articulation of multiple modernities in colonial India.

ACKNOWLEDGEMENTS

Some of the research for this essay was funded by a Fulbright-Hays Senior Research Fellowship during 2006-07. I would like to thank the U.S. Department of Education and the United States Educational Foundation in India for their support. I would also like to thank Michael Dodson and Kari Irwin for helpful comments on an earlier version of the essay. Needless to say, any errors are my own.

NOTES AND REFERENCES

1 Ernesto Laclau, *Emancipation(s)*, New York: Verso, 2007, p. 35.

2 See Marshall Berman, *All that is Solid Melts into Air: the Experience of Modernity*, New Edn., New York: Penguin Books, 1988, pp. 15-27.

3 Ibid., 15.

4 Berman's approach has nonetheless come in for criticism, notably in Perry Anderson's essay, 'Modernity and Revolution' in *New Left Review* 34, no. 1 (1984): pp. 96-113.

5 See Brian A. Hatcher, 'Bourgeois Vedanta: The Colonial Roots of Middle-Class Hinduism', *Journal of the American Academy of Religion* 75, no. 2 (2007): pp. 298-323.

6 Charles Taylor, 'Modern Social Imaginaries,' *Public Culture* 14, no. 1 (2002), p. 91.

7 Ibid., p. 96.

8 Charles Taylor, *Sources of the Self: The Making of the Modern Identity*, Cambridge: MA: Harvard University Press, 1989, pp. 186-87.

9 Ibid., p. 185.

10 Ibid., p. 234.

11 Ibid., p. 235.

12 Ibid., p. 242.

13 On the category of *sastra*, see Sheldon Pollock, 'The Idea of *Sastra* in Traditional India', in Anna Libera Dallapiccola, ed. *Shastric Traditions in Indian Arts*, Stuttgart: Steiner Verlag, 1989: pp. 17-26.

14 This seems to be the tenor of Asok Sen's otherwise insightful reading of Vidyasagar's widow marriage campaign. Sen notes Vidyasagar's arguments had a 'distinct tone of reason' and adds that he 'attempted to tap the root of popular

sentiment' by appealing to the *sastra* (*Vidyasagar and his Elusive Milestones*, Calcutta: Rddhi India, 1977, p. 75). Elsewhere he speaks of the job of finding scriptural sanctions as presenting a 'purely intellectual challenge', suggesting there was little real commitment to the *sastra* (ibid., p. 73). Before accepting Sen's verdict, however, we should note that Bankimcandra Chatterjee, who questioned Vidyasagar's strategy of appealing to the *sastra*, nevertheless was certain Vidyasagar had a firm belief in the *sastra*. See Bankimcandra Cattopadhyaya, *Bankim Racanavali*, Jogescandra Bagal, ed., vol. 2, Calcutta: Sahitya Samsad, 1986, p. 318.

15 On this point, Partha Chatterjee's interpretation is inadequate: 'Vidyasagar, despite his professed disregard for the sanctity or reasonableness of the *sastra*, felt compelled to look for scriptural support for his programmes.' Chatterjee, *Nationalist Thought and the Colonial World: A Derivative Discourse*, reprint edn., Minneapolis: University of Minnesota Press, 1993, p. 25.

16 As I endeavored to show in my earliest work on Vidyasagar, the solution to the apparent ambiguity of his religious worldview does not lie in proving he was either a Hindu or an atheist, but comes to us when we recognize that in Vidyasagar's worldview respect for the transcendent truth of *dharma* converges with the imperatives of reason. See Brian Hatcher, *Idioms of Improvement: Vidyasagar and Colonial Encounter in Bengal*, Delhi: Oxford University Press, 1996, p. 262.

17 Taylor, *Sources of the Self*, p. 188.

18 Rammohun Roy, *The English Works of Raja Rammohun Roy*, Allahabad: Panini Office, 1906, p. 37. Killingley refers to this passage when discussing Rammohan's use of the *sastra* in his interpretation of the Vedanta (Dermot Killingley, *Rammohun Roy in Hindu and Christian Tradition*. Newcastle upon Tyne: Grevatt and Grevatt, 1993, pp. 85-88).

19 Kant as quoted in Taylor, *Sources of the Self*, p. 366; emphasis in original.

20 See Hans Frei, *The Eclipse of Biblical Narrative: A Study in Eighteenth and Nineteenth Century Hermeneutics*, New Haven: Yale University Press, 1978.

21 John Locke, *The Reasonableness of Christianity*, I.T. Ramsey, ed. Stanford, CA: Stanford University Press, 1958, p. 92.

22 One might compare the scriptural interpretation of Bhaktivinod Thakur, a 'modern theologian, mediating the

Vaisnava tradition to the *bhadraloka* of his day'. See Shukavak N. Dasa, *Hindu Encounter with Modernity: Kedarnath Datta Bhaktivinoda, Vaisnava Theologian*, Los Angeles: Sri, 1990, p. 201.

23 See Partha Chatterjee, *The Nation and its Fragments: Colonial and Postcolonial Histories*, Princeton: Princeton University Press, 1993, p. 132. Compare Chatterjee's earlier comment that 'Vidyasagar's own attempts at social reform . . . placed great reliance upon liberal backing by the colonial government' (Chatterjee, *Nationalist Thought and the Colonial World*, p. 25).

24 Sen, *Vidyasagar and his Elusive Milestones*, p. 73.

25 See N. K. Vaidya, *A Collection Containing the Proceedings which led to the passing of Act XV of 1856*, Bombay, 1885.

26 Cattopadhyaya, *Bankim Racanavali*, vol. 2, pp. 318-19.

27 Chatterjee, *The Nation and its Fragments*, p. 132.

28 For a translation of these early discourses, see Brian A. Hatcher, *Bourgeois Hinduism, or the Faith of the Modern Vedantists: Rare Discourses from Early Colonial Bengal*, New York: Oxford University Press, 2008.

29 This is the context in which to consider the new scripture Debendranath created for the Brahmo community; see Debendranath Tagore, *Brahmo Dharmah*, reprint edn., Calcutta: Sadharan Brahmo Samaj, 1975.

30 See Yogendranath Vidyabhusan, *Madanmohana Tarkalankarer Jivanacarita*, Calcutta: New India Press, 1871.

31 Vasudha Dalmia, 'Sanskrit Scholars and Pandits of the Old School: The Benares Sanskrit College and the Constitution of Authority in the Late Nineteenth Century', *Journal of Indian Philosophy* 24 (1996), p. 332.

32 See Michael Ṣ. Dodson, 'Contesting Translations: Orientalism and the Interpretation of the Vedas', *Modern Intellectual History* 4, no. 1 (2007): pp. 43-59.

33 The first, and shortest, tract originally appeared in the Bangla journal *Tattvabodhini Patrika* in 1854 (reprinted in Benoy Ghosh, *Samayik-patre banglar samaj-citra*, part four, no. 1, Calcutta: Papyrus, 1980, p. 145-57). Vidyasagar then reprinted it as a pamphlet in January of 1855. The second, much longer tract, was published in October of 1855. Both tracts are reprinted in Isvarcandra Vidyasagar, *Vidyasagar-Granthavali*, Sunitikumara Cattopadhyaya, Brajendranatha Bandyopadhyaya, and Sajanikanta Das, eds., vol. 2, Calcutta:

Ranjan Publishing, 1939. Vidyasagar created his own English version shortly thereafter, though it omitted many of the more technical issues he had addressed in the original version of the second tract. For more on the English text in relation to the Bangla original, see Hatcher, *Idioms of Improvement*, pp. 254-58.

34 Hatcher, *Idioms of Improvement*, p. 259.

35 Ibid., p. 262.

36 Ibid., p. 259.

37 Sekhar Bandyopadhyay, *Caste, Culture and Hegemony: Social Domination in Colonial Bengal*, New Delhi: Sage, 2004, p. 125.

38 Ibid.

39 Vidyasagar, *Vidyasagar-Granthavali*, vol. 2, p. 24. All translations are my own, unless otherwise noted.

40 That Bandyopadhyay actually sees this to be the case, and that he may be hedging things a bit, is suggested by his comment that 'at the back of his mind' Vidyasagar harbored the hope that a reasonable reading of the *sastra* might convince his countrymen (*Caste, Culture and Hegemony*, p. 125). I merely propose that a phrase like the 'back of the mind' relegates reason to a far lower register in Vidyasagar's intellectual range than he would have himself allowed.

41 A bit later on, Bandyopadhyay speaks of Vidyasagar remaining 'embedded' in the sastric discourse of hierarchy (*Caste, Culture and Hegemony*, p. 126).

42 C. J. Fuller, 'Hinduism and Scriptural Authority in Modern Indian Law', *Comparative Studies in Society and History* 30, no. 2 (1988), p. 247. Fuller addresses in particular the attitude toward modern Indian law expressed by Marc Galanter (see the essays on 'indigenous law' in Marc Galanter, *Law and Society in Modern India*, Rajeev Dhavan, ed. Delhi: Oxford University Press, 1989).

43 Fuller, 'Hinduism and Scriptural Authority in Modern Indian Law', p. 241.

44 Quoted in ibid. On the theme of 'rediscovery' as a mode of sastric interpretation, see Sheldon Pollock, 'The Idea of *Sastra* in Traditional India,' in edited by *Shastric Traditions in Indian Arts*, Anna Libera Dallapiccola, Stuttgart: Steiner Verlag, 1989, p. 20. 17-26.

45 Sudipto Kaviraj, 'The Sudden Death of Sanskrit Knowledge', *Journal of Indian Philosophy* 33 (2005), p. 128. Kaviraj builds

upon Sheldon Pollock's comments on the ability of Sanskrit discourse to generate 'innovations . . . from within the intellectual tradition itself'. See Pollock, 'The New Intellectuals in Seventeenth-Century India.' *Indian Economic and Social History Review* 38, no. 1 (2001), p. 11.

46 Kaviraj, 'The Sudden Death of Sanskrit Knowledge,' p. 124.

47 See Galanter, *Law and Society in Modern India.*

48 Ibid., p. 17.

49 Among a variety of works touching on these themes, see J.D.M. Derrett, 'Sanskrit Legal Treatises compiled at the Instance of the British', *Zeitschrift für vergleichende Rechtswissenschaft* 63 (1961): pp. 72-117; Brian A. Hatcher, 'What's Become of the Pandit? Rethinking the History of Sanskrit Scholars in Colonial Bengal', *Modern Asian Studies* 39, no. 3 (2005): pp. 683-723', and Rocher, 'Henry Thomas Colebrooke and the Marginalization of Indian Pandits', in *Pramanakirti,* edited by B. Kellner et. al., Vienna, 2007: pp. 237-56.

50 See Hatcher, 'What's Become of the Pandit?'

51 On Vidyasagar's use of the modern historical-critical method, see Wilhelm Halbfass, *India and Europe: An Essay in Understanding,* Albany, NY: State University of New York Press, 1988, p. 247. For a fine example of this method in action, see Vidyasagar's discussion of the problem of attributing the *Dattakacandrika* to the ancient author Kubera in *Vidyasagar-Granthavali,* vol. 2, pp. 183n, 121.

52 Vaidya, *A Collection Containing the Proceedings which led to the passing of Act XV of 1856*, pp. 17-18.

53 Sen, *Vidyasagar and his Elusive Milestones*, pp. 54-5.

54 Biharilal Sarkar, *Vidyasagar: Isvaracandra Vidyasagarer Jivani*, 4th edn., Calcutta: Orient Book Co., 1986, p. 177.

55 For background on Parasara, see Robert Lingat, *The Classical Law of India*, J. Duncan and M. Derrett, trans., Berkeley: University of California Press, 1973, p. 103.

56 See *Vidyasagar-Granthavali,* vol. 2, pp. 66-87, and Sarkar, *Vidyasagar*, p. 178.

57 *Vidyasagar-Granthavali*, vol. 2, p. 42.

58 See Krishna Datta, 'A Controversy over a Verse on the Remarriage of Hindu Women,' in *Faces of the Feminine in Ancient, Medieval, and Modern India*, edited by Mandakranta Bose, New York: Oxford University Press, 2000: pp. 7-20.

59 See Tapti Roy, 'Disciplining the Printed Text: Colonial and Nationalist Surveillance of Bengali Literature,' in edited by *Texts of Power: Emerging Disciplines in Colonial Bengal*, Partha Chatterjee, Calcutta: Samya, 1996: pp. 30-62.

60 Sheldon Pollock, 'The Death of Sanskrit', *Comparative Studies in Society and History* 43, no. 2 (2001): pp. 392-426.

61 *Vidyasagar-Granthavali*, vol. 2, p. 23.

62 Ibid., pp. 39-40.

63 Quoted in Indra Mitra, *Karunasagara Vidyasagar*, Calcutta: Ananda Publishers, 2000, p. 253.

64 During the nineteenth century, some pandits in Benares responded in similar fashion by entering 'into the public sphere through publishing, literary societies, and public debate' (Michael S. Dodson, *Orientalism, Empire, and National Culture: India 1770-1880*, New York: Palgrave Macmillan, 2007, p. 183.

65 Jürgen Habermas, *The Structural Transformation of the Public Sphere: An Inquiry into the Category of Bourgeois Society*, Thomas Burger and Frederic Lawrence, trans., Cambridge: MIT Press, 1989, p. 16.

66 *Vidyasagar-Granthavali*, vol. 2, p. 40.

67 When Madhusudana Smrtiratna composed a refutation of Vidyasagar's arguments, he also framed the discussion as taking place between a wealthy individual and a Sanskrit pandit (see the foreword to his *Vidhava vivaha prativada*, Calcutta: Ramayana Press, 1885).

68 On his attempts to gain the support of the Shobabajar Deb family, see Sarkar, *Vidyasagar*, pp. 173-74.

69 Unfortunately Vidyasagar's English translation of the tracts gives this impression, since it looks like a book sprinkled with some Sanskrit passages (see Isvarcandra Vidyasagar, *The Marriage of Hindu Widows*, Calcutta: K. P. Bagchi, 1976).

70 Notice that Vidyasagar employs the *mimamsa* method of argumentation, in which one begins by stating the topic, or *visaya* (a term Vidyasagar uses throughout the tracts). Regarding this topic, some doubt (or *samsaya*) is raised. After this, the two sides of the argument are considered: first the *prima facia* view of the opponent (the purvapaksa) and then its refutation (or *siddhanta*, though Vidyasagar does not use these exact terms). Finally, a determination (*nirnaya*) is made by which the issue is settled. On this method see Kisori Lal Sarkar, *The Mimamsa Rules of Interpretation as applied to Hindu*

Law, Calcutta: Thacker and Spink, 1909, p. 62; and Pashupatinath Shastri, *Introduction to the Purva Mimamsa*, Chaukhambha Oriental Research Series, no. 19, 2nd edn., Delhi: Chaukhambha Orientalia, 1980, pp. 179-222.

71 *Vidyasagar-Granthavali*, vol. 2, p. 42.

72 According to Derrett, the Parasara-Madhaviya, was a text of great authority in British India (J. D. M. Derrett, *History of Indian Law (Dharmasastra)*, Handbuck der Orientalistik, Zweite Abteilung, dritter Band, Leiden: E. J. Brill, 1973, p. 16.

73 On the problem of Vidyasagar's Bangla, see Poromesh Acharya, 'Politics of Primary Education in West Bengal: The Case of "Sahaj Path", *Economic and Political Weekly* 16, no. 24 (1981): pp. 1069-74.

74 See Pradyumna Bhattacharya, 'Rammohun Roy and Bengali Prose,' in *Rammohun Roy and the Process of Modernization in India*, edited by V. C. Joshi, Delhi: Vikas, 1975: pp. 195-223.

75 *Vidyasagar-Granthavali*, vol. 2, pp. 46-7; see also Shyamacharan Sarkar, *Vyavastha-Darpana, a Digest of Hindu Law, as Current in Bengal*, 3rd edn., Calcutta: Stanhope Press, 1883, p. xiv.

76 Dodson, *Orientalism, Empire, and National Culture*, p. 14.

77 Ibid., p. 15.

78 Donald R. jr. Davis, 'Hinduism as a Legal Tradition', *Journal of the American Academy of Religion* 75, no. 2 (2007): p. 257.

79 Richard W. Lariviere, 'Dharma *sastra*, Custom, "Real Law" and "Apocryphal' Smrtis", in *Recht, Staat und Verwaltung im klassischen Indien*, edited by Bernhard Kölver, Munich: R. Oldenbourg, 1997, pp. 107-8.

80 Dodson, *Orientalism, Empire, and National Culture*, p. 182.

81 For some representative examples, see Dharma Sabha, *Vidhava vivaha nisedha visayaka vyavastha*, Calcutta, 1846; Dinabandhu Nyayaratna, *Vidhavavivahavada*, Serampore: Tamohar Press, 1854; and Smritiratna, *Vidhava vivaha prativada*.

82 See Brian A. Hatcher, 'The Evils of Child Marriage: Ishvarcandra Vidyasagar', *Critical Asian Studies* 35, no. 3 (2003): pp. 476-84.

83 Dodson, *Orientalism, Empire, and National Culture*, p. 148.

84 See Amiya Sen, *Hindu Revivalism in Bengal 1872-1905: Some Essays in Interpretation*, Delhi: Oxford University Press, 1993.

85 See Hatcher, 'What's Become of the Pandit?'

86 Taradhana Tarkabhusana, *Taranath Tarkavacaspatir jivana evam sanskrta vidyar unnati*, Calcutta: Brahmo Misssion Press, 1893, p. 47.

87 See Taranatha Tarkavacaspati, *Bahuvivahavada*, Calcutta: Kavyaprakasa Press, 1872.

88 See Iwvarcandra Vidyasagar, *Vidyasagar-racana-samagra*, vol. 2, Gopal Haldar, ed. Calcutta: Saksarata Prakasan, 1972, pp. 248-49.

89 On the idea of 'scriptural emblem' as it relates to theories of collective memory, see Hatcher, 'Remembering Rammohan: An Essay on the (Re-)emergence of Modern Hinduism', *History of Religions* 46, no. 1 (2006): pp. 50-80.

90 See Taranatha Tarkavacaspati, *Gayatriprakaranam*, Calcutta: New Sanskrit Press, 1871.

The 'modern' popular

emergence of a film culture in Bengal

Sharmistha Gooptu

In Bengal, film-going emerged as an important leisure activity in the 1920s and early 1930s, consolidating a nascent film industry and generating cultural contestation around the new medium. It produced a film culture, integrated by a film-going public, an aspiring group of entrepreneurs and a new class of critics/ commentators. This essay examines Bengal's early film culture and the emergence of a discourse on cinema as the 'modern' popular. It unravels the mixed baggage of Bengal's early film culture, and makes the case that, by the end of the 1920s and early 1930s, the range of signifiers of the early cinema had been sifted through by a Bengali discourse, to produce 'bad' and 'good' prototypes, the latter being linked to a Bengali bourgeois interest in the 'modern' art form. Informed by the bourgeois literary ideal of novelistic realism and an elitist self-consciousness of 'world standards', the 'Bengali' prototype of 'good cinema' was pitted against the theatrical mode of early Indian films and corporate structures underlying the stage-cinema complex, setting up the model for a modernist project.

Early film fare

The first cinema shows in Bengal have been dated to the latter half of 1896, not long after the first Indian showing of the Lumiere Brothers' Cinematographe in Bombay earlier that year. These were held in Calcutta, then the capital of British India, and later in Dacca and other provincial towns, and are believed to have generated considerable excitement.[1] During the early years, films were exhibited in make-shift venues by itinerant showmen or featured as part of an evening's program at playhouses. At this time, Calcutta had a thriving professional theatre, mostly patronized by a middle class clientele, and the earliest efforts at filmmaking in Bengal drew upon and reproduced the popular stage. By 1888-9, episodes in popular stage plays were being filmed, the filmed portions often being shown as parts of the same play.[2] This practice may be understood as part of a response to growing contemporary criticisms of the Bengali stage. As discussed by Kironmoy Raha, sets, costumes and make-up were crude, generally poor copies of English models, often constructed from pictures or plain hearsay,[3] and growing criticisms of shoddiness and inconsistencies had propelled sporadic efforts towards regeneration. Of these, the most notable was the successful creation of magical effects, of 'actors vanishing through trapdoors, toy trains trundling across the stage', or 'close combat in chariots',[4] and films were an addition to this repertoire of special effects. As Tom Gunning has shown, in its early years, cinema was itself an attraction,[5] and the earliest film shows in Bengal were largely aimed at boosting the theatre industry. However, with Calcutta emerging as a centre of the film business, and the coming together of an exhibition system in the 1900s and 1910s, the cinema established a more separate presence. By the 1920s, film-going was a familiar leisure activity in Calcutta.

Insertions in contemporary newspapers indicate that by the beginning of the 1920s, 'picture shows' were a part of the regular amusements available in Calcutta.[6] American serial films, chiefly action thrillers, comprised a large chunk of the offerings, though comedies and the Arabian Nights fantasies[7] were frequently advertised. Indian features, mostly mythologicals, were fewer in number. Between 15 January and 3 February 1921, for instance, *Amrita Bazar Patrika*, a leading English daily, carried successive announcements by the Calcutta branch of the American Bioscope Company which was showing 'the sensational serial supreme *Elmo the Mighty*' at 6.00 pm and 9.00 pm everyday in a tent on the open spaces of the Howrah Maidan in Central Calcutta. During the same period, the Phoenix Picture Palace in Chitpur in north Calcutta advertised '*The World's Master Wizard Houdini in Terror Island*-A fascinating romance of sunken treasure, puzzling plots, deadly encounters and escapes, made miraculous by the genius of Houdini',[8] followed by the serial *Mystery of '13'*.[9] Around the same time that *Mystery of '13'* was showing in the Phoenix, the Albion Theatre on 4, Corporation Street, in the heart of the business district in central Calcutta, was showing the 17-part Universal serial *The Great Radium Mystery*.[10] In addition to the regular shows of 6.30 pm and 9.30 pm,[11] the Phoenix had weekend matinee shows, pointing to the currency of cinema as a leisure pursuit.

Among Indian productions advertised during the month was the 'Hindu Mythological Drama *Mahabharat*' to be shown at the Cornwallis Theatre in north Calcutta on Tuesday 4 January 1921 at 6.00 pm and 9.30 pm.[12] On Saturday, 5 February the same venue was to screen a Bombay production, the 5-reel mythological feature *Ahalya-Uddhar*, publicized as a 'splendid Indian film', 'dealing with thrilling episodes in the life of the famous Indian beauty Ahalya. Her sensational marriage with sage Gautama, its after effects and the jealousy caused to Indra'.[13] Two weeks later, on 19 February, the Cornwallis Theatre was showing *Shiva-Ratri*, advertised in *Amrita Bazar Patrika* as the first Hindu mythological film with Bengali actors and actresses and Bengali titles.[14]

One of the earliest genres of the Bengali film that appeared on the heels of the first mythologicals was the comedy, that drew partly on Hollywood's comic genres and partly from the nineteenth century Bengali literary tradition of farce, epitomized by tracts such as Kaliprasanna Sinha's *Hutom Penchar Naksha*, and Madhusudan Dutt's *Sadhabar Ekadashi* and *Buro Saliker Ghare Rno*. Dhirendra Nath Ganguli's 1921 production, *Bilet Pherat* (England Returned) is the earliest known film of the genre which satirized the anglicized Bengali elite. Another trend that was established by the first half of the '20s was the screen adaptation of literary classics as 'socials'. First attempted by the Tajmahal Film Company in their 1922 adaptation of a short story by the best-selling Bengali novelist Sarat Chandra Chattopadhayay (*Andhare Alo*, 1922), this became a formula of sorts for the Bengal market, and was followed by successful adaptations of another literary figure, Bankim Chandra Chattopadhayay. Adaptation of famous writers was a logical choice, given the centrality of literary movements and a literary culture in shaping the Bengali middle class worldview, and was evidently aimed to draw a 'better class' of Bengali audiences to the cinema.

The film-going public

The class composition of early cinema audiences in Bengal remains unexplored. This section documents the same, primarily based on the *Report of the Indian Cinematograph Enquiry Committee,* 1927-1928 (henceforth, Indian Cinematograph Committee, ICC)[15] instituted by the colonial state to enquire into the workings of the Indian film industry. The ICC secured evidence from witnesses representing a cross-section of society, and including industry persons, educationists, health officials and noted public figures to produce the first authoritative report on the Indian film industry. According to ICC Evidence (*ICCE*), a significant proportion of Calcutta's film-going public was comprised of 'clerks' and 'Middle class *Bhadurlokes,* belonging to all walks of life.'[16] Here 'Bhadurloke' or bhadralok is a generic term indicating middle class Bengalis mainly engaged in the professions and services. Estimates by some respondents put 'the educated classes' as comprising between 75 and 85 per cent of the film-going public in Calcutta and Dacca.[17] In the words of a written statement submitted to the committee, 'educated Indians very often frequent to cinema houses (sic). They patronize cinema shows much more than any amusement. The modern educated class mainly youths are fast lovers of films and cinema shows.'[18] According to producer-director Dhirendra Nath Ganguli, Calcutta audiences had the highest proportion of the educated classes, 75 per cent, followed by 50 per cent in Bombay and 40 per cent in Madras.[19] It needs to be qualified, however, that this percentage could substantially vary depending upon the location and profile of movie theatres and the films shown. As noted by S. N. Guha, Director, Bengal Educational Film Co., in his written statement to the Committee, 'it is difficult to give any correct idea of the composition (of cinema audiences), as it varies according to the locality and the quality of picture'.[20] At the same time, 'educated classes' is a rather broad category, and could include a cross-section of the Bengali middle classes, an upper class elite shading off into the most modest segments of the middle class, the latter epitomized by the poor clerk, who's material existence could border on impoverishment. It would also include students, who constituted a sizeable proportion of cinema audiences, according to *ICCE.*[21]

The 'educated and cultured', presumably indicating the more elitist sections of the middle classes were seen as preferring 'the superior class of Western features and social subjects, or adaptations of well-known literary and classical works of fiction.'[22] 'Socials' based on the well-known works of Bankim Chandra Chattopadhayay had been particularly successful. According to ICC respondent S. B. Banerjea, the Indian representative of *The Cinema News*, the attendance of the 'educated classes' also increased 'when a particular film favourite, like Palo or Ford, or Fairbanks, or Lloyd, or Pickford, for instance, is starred.'[23]

The growing popularity of cinema among the 'educated' classes had prompted exhibitors to upgrade and improvise. From the end of the 1920s, Calcutta movie theatres were undertaking renovation and re-structuring projects in an effort to assume greater respectability. Contemporary popular journals frequently carried reports on the opening of new film theatres, often with the details of amenities and associated conveniences, pointing to the cinema's bid for a more up-market clientele. A bit report in *Naachghar* of February 1928 thus informed its readers that the management of the Albion had undertaken to reorder its profile, which had taken a beating as a result of rowdies frequenting the premises, as well as its offerings of mundane serials.[24] According to another report of 21 October 1934, in *Varieties Weekly*, the Purna Theatre in Bhowanipore, in south Calcutta,[25] had assigned a renovations project to the Engineers' Syndicate Ltd., a reputable firm of eastern India. The report concluded, 'Thus in Bengal not only has the whole trend of cinema enthusiasm improved but it has also induced the province to undertake to build respectable show-halls that provide the audience with maximum comfort at minimum cost.'[26]

Cinema and the urban dynamic

For the professional classes, the growing patronage of cinema may be tied to its suitability to the schedules of urban life, with its structured work hours, and equally structured leisure time.[27] An indication of changing leisure preferences among this section of Bengali society is available in the following testimony by a writer in the journal *Naachghar*, possibly a theatre critic who admitted his growing penchant for the cinema:

> Recently, while turning the pages of my old dairy, I was struck by a certain ratio. Comparing the last few years I realized that in 1929 I went to the theatre on 62 occasions and 127 times to the bioscope; in 1930 and 1931 the distribution was 35 and 142 and 40 and 213 respectively. Till date this year, I have been to the playhouse 23 times and have sat in front of the screen 198 times. Since I write for the press, I have had to go for every noteworthy stage performance at least once. Even then, my attendances at the playhouse have not crossed 23. If my visits to the theatre had been according to my own discretion, this number would probably have been 10![28]

Accounting for this changing preference, he declares that though drama was one of the oldest arts and had provided gratification since ancient times, it was becoming outdated in an age of motor-cars and aeroplanes. Likening the ethos of live performances to the tardiness of a bullock-cart, he offers the following reasons for his new preference of the cinema:

> It is possible to go to the cinema for a couple of hours at the end of a day's work at the office, and go home in a happy frame of mind. The custom there is to start the show by the clock and end by the clock. In our playhouses, on the other hand, the show starts a half hour, an hour, or an hour and a half after the announced time. Taking into consideration the intervals during the changing of backdrop, it is another five or six hours before the curtain finally drops. After thus sitting still in one's seat for seven to eight hours, one's annoyance is greater than pleasure when it is time to go home... Many (more) inconsistencies are noticed on stage. A certain gentleman has not been paid on time. So, he does not concentrate on his performance. Someone else has not recovered from his inebriated condition, so he has no idea of what he is saying. Another day the star actress is not available, so someone from among the junior artistes has taken her position. The list is endless. There is no room for such discrepancies in the cinema.[29]

The laid-back and somewhat erratic culture of the stage was understandably falling out of favour with those classes whose lifestyles had generated a preference for a more structured pursuit of leisure, which could neatly be fitted into the daily trek between home and the office. The evening film shows of 6.30 pm were particularly suited to the home-ward moving stream of office goers, and were possibly calculated to draw this outgoing traffic. It also explains why a cluster of movie theatres had sprung up in and around the main business district of Dharmatolla in central Calcutta.[30] Film shows were also better value for money, with the lowest class of film tickets priced at 4 annas[31]. The low priced tickets were particularly popular among the army of clerks who left the Dharmatolla offices every evening.[32]

Cheap access to movie theatres had also made film-going popular among those groups that ICC respondents referred to as the 'uneducated/illiterate classes'. In his statement, Khan Bahadur M. Azizul Haque, member of the Bengal Legislative Council, identified this segment of the film-going public as comprising those who 'serve(d) town life with amenities like hackney and motor-traffic, petty-shopkeepers, middlemen, etc.'[33] According to Khagendra Nath Mitter, lower class audiences were more common in the northern parts of the city, where they comprised nearly two-thirds of the spectators of Indian films.[34] These groups frequented the travelling shows or filled the cheap seats in cinema theatres,[35] and mostly preferred the action packed Western thrillers, comedies and mythologicals.[36]

On the whole, however, the most significant section of Bengal's early cinema audiences seems to have been constituted by the various strata of the middle classes. Cinema theatres were clustered in and around Calcutta and the bigger provincial towns such as Dacca and Mymensingh, where the middle classes were concentrated. The small towns had a limited access to films, mainly catered by travelling shows[37] with their skimpy repertoire of second hand films. As noted by M. Azizul Haque, 'The question of popularity of any particular class of films arises only in Metropolitan towns, as up till now the film business has not spread into mofussil places.'[38]

Given the growing patronage of the cinema by all strata of the 'educated' classes, as indicated by contemporary testimonies or the industry's efforts to upgrade exhibition, it was not long before there emerged a discourse on film aesthetics that was linked to the middle-class' literary ideals. This discourse, which emerged through the pages of a host of contemporary Bengali journals, distinguished between a 'good Bengali' and 'bad' film aesthetics, the 'good cinema' ultimately being linked to the Bengali middle class' ideal of modernity.

A 'Bengali' discourse of 'bad' versus 'good' cinema 'Film as art' and the call for an aesthetic standard

In a stream of writing in the Bengali press of the late 1920s and early 1930s, Madan[39], Bengal's leading entrepreneur in film business, appears as the cutthroat capitalist, who had no sense of the intricacies of the film form and was totally ill-equipped to treat the medium in tune with a refined Bengali sensibility. In 1923, in one of his earliest writings on cinema, the noted intellectual Sourindramohan Mukhopadhayay had laid out these terms of criticism, when he expressed a discomfort with identifying Madan films as Bengal productions. His reason was a spurious depiction of Bengali life in Madan films, which for him was a totally unaesthetic experience. As he put it,

> Films produced by the Madan Company cannot really be called Bengali films. Even though the actors, photographer and even the director may be Bengali, the directives come from the Parsi bosses...they use Parsi costumes and settings in Bengali mythological and social films, making them so unauthentic that viewers are totally dissatisfied.[40]

What seems to have been at stake for an elitist critic like Mukhopadhayay was his investment in a naturalist aesthetic, derived from Western models of taste and beauty, which were integral to the Bengali engagement with Western modernity.

Most of the early Madan productions, such as the 1921 social farce *Tehmuras and Tehmuljee* were filmed versions of Parsi theatre plays, using the staff of their theatre companies.[41] They continued to draw heavily upon what Kaushik Bhaumik calls 'the multi-generic performative world of the Parsi theatre'[42], clearly alienating critics like Mukhopadhayay who approached cinema from their location in a culture of literary realism. Mukhopadhayay displayed a much more sympathetic appraisal of the productions of the Tajmahal Film Company, which marked the film debuts of the leading theatre personalities Sisir Kumar Bhaduri and Nares Mitra. Sisir Bhaduri, the famous Bengali actor-director and playwright was taken to have revolutionized the Bengali stage with his debut *Alamgir* in 1921. Bhaduri had been a professor of English at Calcutta's Vidyasagar College for seven years before he joined the professional theatre. As noted by Kironmoy Raha, 'he had won the acclaim of the learned and the elite, as well as tumultuous praise from the public and the press. He created an excitement among the intelligentsia such as no theatre man had done before or, probably, since.'[43] It was Bhaduri, who first adapted a work of modern Bengali literature for the screen, Saratchandra Chattopadhayay's novel *Aandhare Alo* in Tajmahal's 1922 production of the same name, of which the contemporary Bengali writer Hemendra Kumar Roy had remarked, 'By adapting *Aandhare Alo*, Sisir Bhaduri changed the prevalent practices of the film world.'[44] Sourindramohan Mukhpadhayay, though more qualified in his appreciation of the same film, nonetheless clearly displayed his cultural priorities in the article referred to above, when he noted that the Tajmahal Film Company, in the able hands of the likes of Bhaduri and Naresh Mitra, had been formed to address the problems posed by the Madan brand of cinema.[45]

By the end of the 1920s, Mukhopadhayay's kind of reservation with Madan films, namely, their perceived lack of naturalism and heavily coded ethos derived from the Parsi theatre had meshed with an industry-generated rhetoric against the Madan conglomerate. It had produced a discourse which established a direct correlation between the Madans' economic leverage and their failure to establish cinema as an aesthetic project. Thus Madan productions were routinely criticized for their lack of aesthetic appeal, apparently because they were hastily churned out, simply with an eye for quick profits. A writer in *Bioscope*'s March 1930 issue thus offered the following scathing remarks on Jyotish Banerjee, J F Madan's one-time accountant-turned-director, while commenting on the latest Madan release[46]:

> Thanks to the Madans, we have seen Jyotishbabu's calibre on several occasions in the past, but on this occasion his

> potential seems to have reached its full form. God has deprived him of that entity called the mind. He is not to be blamed; rather, he should be pitied! But we cannot say the same for those at the head of the Madan Company. Then why do they carry on employing such people. *We know that they couldn't care less about the advancement of art; they want money-only money.* But if they carry on in this manner money also will soon stop pouring in (emphasis mine).[47]

Another writer noted sarcastically with reference Madan's adaptations of Bankim Chandra's novels, 'the Madans would have chanced upon one of Bankimbabu's works and realized that they sell well. And then there was no turning back. Not a minute's delay! Any and every work by Bankimbabu needed to be filmed. This is what our film industry basically is!'[48] The same writer dismissed the Madans, declaring, 'Whatever anyone might say, as far as I am concerned, the Madan films are useless. They have made a mess of Bankimbabu, and who knows what they will get their hands on next.'[49] The Madans were also criticized for a low moral content associated with the overt sexuality of their early films. In a piece on early Indian cinema J.B.H. Wadia, a leading Bombay producer of the 1930s and '40s, thus wrote, 'In a film called *Pati Bhakti* (1922) produced by the Madans of Calcutta, the vamp played by a voluptuous Italian actress (Signora Minelli) wore revealing costumes, which were considered indecent later on.'[50]

For these critics, the Madans were breeding the same brand of cheap entertainment that one of them dismissively labelled the 'Khel' of Bombay cinema, literally meaning 'mere play', and implying a mindless popular culture.[51] The reference would be to the stunt-filled adventure-romance genres that were mainly popular with the lower classes, and dominated Bombay's output in the second half of the 1920s. In his work on the Bombay film industry of the period between 1913 and 1939, Kaushik Bhaumik discusses how some Bombay concerns such as Krishna and Sharda Film Company established themselves as stunt-film specialists in the latter half of the 1920s, and produced stunt stars out of body-builders like Nandram and Raja Sandow.[52] In addition, Bhaumik makes the case that many of the early Bombay socials of the 1920s 'were full of stunts and thrills of detection, very much in line with the intrigue atmosphere of stunt films'.[53] The 'excesses' of these action genres, which drew heavily upon the Parsi repertoire, were viewed as antithetical to the aesthetic potential of cinema, a medium most closely associated with modern literary realism by the Bengali intellectual elite.

The anti-Madan rhetoric came out of two larger parallel discourses in the earliest Bengali writings on cinema. One was the call for 'aesthetic' standards that came out of the writings of a leading public intellectual like Mukhopadhayay, the other a call for 'professionalization', that went beyond the simple quest for profit, as alleged in the case of the Madans. Both were part of an emerging Bengali bourgeois discourse on cinema, which developed alongside the middle-class' growing interest in the medium.

The call to 'professionalize' and the 'progressive' entrepreneur

The growing popularity of cinema among the middle classes had been accompanied by the proliferation of journals and magazines devoted to film criticism and reportage. Some of the first Bengal publications to undertake sustained film journalism in the 1920s and early 1930s were *Naachghar*, *Bioscope*, *Filmland*, *Dipali*, *Chitralekha* and *Chitrapanji*. Even the highbrow literary monthlies *Prabasi* and *Bharatvarsa* brought out a string of articles on cinema in the early 1930s. Between August and November 1931, *Bharatvarsa* carried a film series by the poet and novelist Narendra Deb. Titled 'Chayar Maya' ('Screen Magic'), this series appeared in four consignments and was later compiled into a book, published in 1934.[54]

A large chunk of this early writing is exceedingly critical of the apparently poor photography, pathetic acting and bad direction of Indian films, comparing them to international standards, Hollywood being the common referent. Critics wrote about the slapdash nature of rehearsals in the Calcutta studios, which speeded up the production process and generated quick returns but often left imperfections in the final product.[55] In a typical complaint of un-professionalism, the future actor Dhiraj Bhattacharya observed in a *Naachghar* article of October 1924,

> I cannot help mentioning a unique flaw in Bengali films. That is, whether good or bad, what is once shot is never discarded. It seems that it is the apprehension of escalating costs that leads producers to ignore badly shot scenes. In America or other countries, however, an important scene may be shot 4/5 times and still not satisfy the director. The amount of hard work they put in to make a film look natural is truly amazing.[56]

On the other hand, initiatives that carried the prospect of 'professionalism' were eagerly welcomed. Thus, in its issue of 15 February 1930, *Bioscope* carried a bit of 'good news', informing its readers that a foreign company, Associated Sound Film Industries, had agreed to instruct a few educated Indian youth in filmmaking every year in return for being granted permission to shoot tri-color talkies in India.[57] What was gaining ground was an idea of cinema as a specialized field, which needed skilled creative and technical personnel. Some writers were making the case that educated young men should be trained in filmmaking in the same way that they were trained in other professions such as medicine or engineering, that only those people with proper knowledge be employed in scenario writing, that theatre actors be discarded and the rise of a new breed of educated actors and actresses be encouraged. One writer mooted for in-house libraries in the studios and regular evaluation sessions involving all departments of production as a measure of self-improvement.[58] The call to professionalize, and indeed modernize the industry, was inspired by the ideal of a 'world standard' for Indian films, which together with a discourse of 'film as art' produced an idealized 'Bengali' prototype, that of the 'progressive/modern' entrepreneur of the Indian cinema.

In one of the earliest critical essays on cinema in the Bengali language, titled 'The Art of Film', the author, Sourindramohan Mukhopadhayay wrote :

> I became curious about cinema when Bengalis started coming into the film business, around the time Tajmahal Film Company was formed. I wished to know who were the artists employed by the company. Because in the film industry it doesn't matter who signs the check. Any fund is good enough. But if those in regular charge don't have a sense of sense of *rasa*, it is useless to start a film enterprise.

Here I use the term 'sense of *rasa*' in the broader sense.[59]

In this article of 1925, 'rasa' or the Sanskrit theory of aesthetics was invoked to elaborate a concept of film art, although in the Griffithian[60] sense of psychological motivation, continuity and identification with characters, as opposed to the showcasing of 'thrills' or attractions, and it is interesting to note how an 'Indian' classical term was being used to denote standards that were quite evidently imported. Noteworthy here is the distinction between the figure of the financier and creative personnel, with the former as relatively secondary in the larger scheme of things-a position that would undergo significant transformation by the end of the 1920s. Mukhopadhyay was one of the first public intellectuals of the time to take a serious interest in films and wrote extensively on cinema, to the extent that his tenure as co-editor of the Bengali literary monthly *Bharati* (1915-24) was criticized for the promotion of 'light subjects'.[61] He was one of the earliest to make a case in favour of a more psychologically oriented brand of cinema and a non-theatrical acting style, which would be in keeping with novelistic traditions of realism as opposed to myth and fantasy that was the stuff of 'thrills'. [62] It was to a large extent through his writings of the 1920s that a discourse on cinema as a legitimate 'modern' art form first emerged in Bengal.

By the early 1930s, the concept 'film as art' was finding supporters among the Bengali intellectual elite and a personality no less than Abanindranath Tagore[63] greeted the talkie in the following words, drawing a lineage between cinema and Bengal's traditions of performance art:

> Many think that we got the talkie from the west. That is not true, the idea of the talkie was with us for a very long time. Take puppet shows, puppets danced and someone made sounds, sometimes spoke lines and sang songs to go with the movements...Then came jatra...it was like coloured pictures on a white screen...Then came the theatre with its scenarios. But soon people no longer wanted to hear other people talking, they wanted to make images speak...This is human nature, to go to one extreme then come back to the origins. That is what happens, man comes back to the beginnings, once again to shadow play.[64]

Yet there was also an emerging appreciation of cinema as a unique art form, given its modes of production and exhibition, and its mass audience, which required the kind of capital investment that most other arts did not. In a letter of 1929 to Murari Bhaduri, brother of Sisir Kumar Bhaduri, now the doyen of the Bengali stage, Rabindranath Tagore wrote, 'The distinctiveness of art is defined by the distinctiveness of its ingredients...the materials for poetry, painting or music are not dear. Film production needs capital and not just creativity.'[65] This idea of cinema as a balance of art and commerce, initially elaborated in the writings of Sourindramohan Mukhopadhayay, was more widely circulated from the end of the 1920s by a stream of writing in popular journals of the time. What came about was a collapsing of the two discourses of 'professionalism' and 'film as art', to produce the ideal of a progressive entrepreneur who would be capitalist and an inspired cultural leader at the same time. In these writings, the producer is construed as the industry's key presence, whose role had to go beyond the conventional capitalist's who simply invested for profit, in other words, making a departure from Mukhopadhayay's earlier stand on the entrepreneurial figure. A writer in *Bioscope* thus noted with reference to the figure of the producer:

> He who is the life-giver of the film must invest all his energies in this direction if the best results are to be obtained. In our country there are still a lot of film producers *who consider their role to be in the nature of 'job-work'. If the mind is busy in other work half the time, where will one get the time or scope to improve.*[66]

Here, the category of the indifferent entrepreneur was possibly an allusion to the Madans, who were often criticized for delegating their Bengali productions in undeserving hands. On the other hand, a new class of producers were expected to be involved in instituting greater professionalism, which would advance the 'art' of Indian films.

In a critical piece on the topic, Chittaranjan Ghosh, editor of *Filmland,* wrote:

> ...in Bengal particularly, the rich man's involvement in the film industry is a matter of indulgence...The directors in

> Bombay work regularly and finish their assignments on time; once the film is completed on time the producer gets his returns on time, is hopeful of future prospects and continues to invest in the industry. *Art is sustained while the entrepreneur makes an income.* Bengali directors take three months to complete three days' work, or start something unsavoury after a few days of work, and finally complete the assignment anyhow in six months...This is bound to happen if business is seen as the arena for indulgence. So, it must be said that if the proper entrepreneur is not found, the film industry, like any other industry will never do well (emphasis mine).[67]

While Ghosh may be according more credit to Bombay directors than they actually deserved, his words are significant for their drawing out of the economic logic of the cinema, and emphasis on the mutual sustenance of 'art' and industry, as epitomized by the ideal of the 'proper entrepreneur, who was expected to offset industry's lack of professionalism and enhance production values.

It is interesting to note here that while the figure of the producer was also central to the Hollywood studio system, his role was construed quite differently from that being ascribed to the producer in contemporary Bengal. Unlike the Indian producer who was, in most cases, the independent entrepreneur, the producer in the Hollywood was generally a person appointed by corporations to oversee the production process within the studios. This person was frequently considered a hindrance to the director's creativity, for his role in the corporations' growing control over the final product. The conflicts between the corporations, who introduced 'supervisors' or 'producers' in the 1920s, and some of the most famous directors of the time such as Maurice Tourneur and Rex Ingram are part of Hollywood lore.[68] These 'supervisors' or 'snoopervisors', as they were often called, were hated by creative personnel and became stock characters for derision in industry circles. One-liners from the time, such as, 'What's a supervisor? A man who knows what he wants but can't spell it' or 'They're like goldfish. They can swim around with their eyes open and still be asleep'[69], offer a very different picture of the relationship between the business and creative sides of the industry than was being elaborated in Bengal vis-à-vis the model of the progressive entrepreneur. The possibilities being attributed to the figure of the producer in the Bengali press were distinctive in that they drew upon certain entrenched notions of the wealthy as 'cultured' patrons of art, in the tradition of the prominent landholding families of Bengal, who had been at the forefront of elite cultural movements, which made the Bengali modernity.

Cinema: the new Bengali cultural project

This essay has shown the emergence of a prototype for 'legitimate' film culture in Bengal, linked to the idea of 'professionalism' and a paradigm of 'film as art', which may be understood in terms of an upcoming Bengali bourgeois interest in the film industry, and the need to legitimize this interest. The latter half of the 1920s had thrown up a configuration of potential clout in the film industry, comprising figures like Devaki Bose, Pramathes Barua, Birendranath Sircar, Nitin Bose, and Modhu Bose, mostly men from middle class and elite landed and professional families, who would assume a leading role during the transition from silent cinema to sound in the 1930s. They inhabited common cultural ground with elitist critics in the vein of Sourindramohan Mukhopadhayay, who played the leading role in shaping the dominant discourse on cinema. Mukhopadhayay and others calling for an 'aesthetic' project were in the process of delineating a 'legitimate' film culture, in the nature of Bengali cultural movements of the latter half of the nineteenth century, which established the standards of a legitimate aesthetic code, and set up an elitist paradigm of 'cultured Bengaliness'. In his study of elite and popular culture in nineteenth century Bengal, Sumanta Banerjee[70] has shown how this paradigm evolved in contradistinction to the street culture of the urban poor, with its frivolous and overtly sexual content, setting up a cultural politics of difference. A similar politics emerges in the Bengali discourse that rejected the popular, Parsi-theatre-inspired Madan brand of cinema, and established a superior 'Bengali' paradigm, as in the prototype of the 'progressive entrepreneur'. It was this politics that fuelled the Bengali bourgeois practice of cinema in the sound era. From early in the sound era, the 'Bengali' prototype of 'good' cinema was mobilized against Bombay, in the process instituting the key categories of a 'serious' Bengali cinema and a 'commercial' Bombay cinema. The former was coterminous with Bengali modernity.

Notes and References

1 Mirza Tarekul Kader, *Bangladesher Chalachhitra Shilpa* (A History of Bangladesh Cinema), Dhaka: Bangla Academy, 1993, p. 44; Anupam Hayat, *Bangladesher Chalachhitrer Itihaas* (A History of Bangladesh Film), Dhaka: Bangladesh Film Development Corporation, 1987, pp. 1-3.

2 Kironmoy Raha, *Bengali Cinema*, Calcutta: Nandan, West Bengal Film Centre, 1991, pp. 1-2.

3 Kironmoy Raha, 'Calcutta Theatre, 1835-1944', in Sukanata Choudhuri, ed. *Calcutta: The Living City*, Vol. I. New Delhi: OUP, 1990, p. 193.

4 Ibid., 193.

5 Tom Gunning, 'An Aesthetic of Astonishment: Early Film and the (In)Credulous Spectator', in *Film theory and criticism: introductory readings*, edited by Leo Braudy and Marshall Cohen, New York: Oxford University Press, 1999.

6 For instance, on Sunday, 16 January 1921, the 'Amusements' column of *Amrita Bazar Patrika* (hereafter *ABP*) announced shows by Shellar's Royal Circus, plays at the Star and Minerva Theatres, film shows at the Phoenix Picture Palace and by the American Bioscope Co.

7 For instance, on 5 February 1921, *ABP* announced the screening of *Aladin and the Wonderful Lamp* at the opening of Russa Theatre, to be followed by 'a rollicking piece by Charlie Chaplin.'

8 *ABP*, 15 January 1921.

9 *ABP*, 22 January 1921

10 *ABP*, 28 January 1921.

11 *ABP*, 15 January 1921.

12 *ABP*, 4 January 1921.

13 *ABP*, 3 February 1921.

14 *ABP*, 19 February 1921.

15 *Report of the Indian Cinematograph Enquiry Committee*, 1927-1928, Calcutta: Government of India, Central Publication

Branch, 1928.

16 Refer, for instance, written statements of Khagendra Nath Mitter and Mr. Lalit Kumar Mitra, in *Indian Cinematograph Committee Evidence* (hereafter *ICCE*), Vol. IV, pp. 141, 152.

17 Refer, for instance, written statements of Professor R. C. Majumdar, University of Dacca and Mr. Sushil Kumar Dutt, and Replies to the Questionnaire by Mohd. Solaiman, *ICCE*, Vol. IV, pp. 139, 161, 178.

18 *ICCE*, Vol. IV, p. 149.

19 *ICCE*, Vol. II, p. 636.

20 *ICCE*, Vol. II, p. 596.

21 For instance, in his written statement Khagendra Nath Mitter mentioned one-third of cinema audiences to be constituted by school and college students, *ICCE*, Vol. IV, p. 141.

22 *ICCE*, Vol. II, p. 813.

23 ICCE, Vol. IV, p. 130.

24 *Naachghar*, B.S. 19 Magh 1335 (1928).

25 Originally, the Russa Theatre built in 1921; For announcement on the opening of the Russa Theatre, see, *ABP*, 3 February 1921.

26 Jyotsna Nath Chanda, 'Bengal's Cinemamindedness', *Varieties Weekly*, 21 October 1933, Vol. IV No. 3, 6.

27 By the early years of the twentieth century, the bureaucratization of commercial institutions and civic bodies had given birth to a class of white-collar workers, whose leisure pursuits were circumscribed by the structure of salaried employment.

28 'Rangamancher Proyojaniyota Ki Phuriyeche?' ('Has the Theatre Lost its Utility?'). *Naachghar*, no. 38 (1932), p. 5.

29 Ibid., p. 6.

30 These included Calcutta's earliest movie theatres, the Elphinstone Picture Palace, Bijoy Theatre on Lindsay Street, and Picture House on Chowringhee, later renamed Plaza and then Tiger.

31 There were four classes of film tickets, with the highest priced at 2-4 rupees and the lowest at 4 annas, *ICCE*, Vol. IV, p. 173.

32 *ICCE*, Vol. IV, p. 173.

33 *ICCE*, Vol. IV, p. 158.

34 *ICCE*, Vol. IV, p. 141.

35 *ICCE*, Vol. IV, pp. 130, 173.

36 *ICCE*, Vol. II, p. 813.

37 In 1927-28 there were around 10-12 traveling companies in Bengal. *ICCE*, Vol. II, p. 1088.

38 *ICCE*, Vol. IV, p. 158.

39 The organizational foundations of Bengal's film industry were laid by Jamsetji Framji Madan, a Parsi capitalist, originally from Bombay, who set up a giant distribution corporation and studio in Calcutta that controlled exhibition and distribution throughout the sub-continent. In the 1890s, J F Madan bought two leading theatre companies in Bombay, the Elphinstone and the Khatau-Alfred, including their entourage, from then proprietor Seth Cooverji Nazir. Around 1902, he shifted base to Calcutta, founding J F Madan and Sons. It is believed that from around 1905, the Madan Company, as it was popularly known, began showing films in tents set up on the Calcutta Maidan and in the Shyampukur area. In 1907, the Madans moved into full-fledged exhibition and distribution, winning the agency rights for Pathe International. In the same year they opened the first permanent movie theatre in Calcutta, the Elphinstone Picture Palace. They continued building their resources into the 1910s, buying out or leasing theatres located in urban areas, until they had a virtual empire spread over the Indian subcontinent. In 1917, Madan's Far Eastern Films and the Maurice Bandmann Company formed the Excelsior Cinematograph Syndicate, which in addition to importing films, owned the chain of Excelsior and Empire cinemas, and later the Empress. In 1919, Madan Theatres Limited was floated in Calcutta, incorporating the Elphinstone and Excelsior Theatres Company. By the middle of the 1920s, the Madans were counted among the four major importers and distributors of foreign films in the subcontinent, which included, apart from Madan Theatres, Ltd., Universal Pictures Corporation Ltd. and Pathe India, Ltd. in Bombay and Globe Theatres Ltd. in Calcutta. More importantly, the Madan Company, which dominated the Bengal film industry in the '20s and early '30s, embodied Calcutta's competitiveness vis-à-vis Bombay. For details on Madan and his film enterprise, see Nawaz Modi, 'Jamsetji Madan-Pioneer of the Film Industry in India', in Nawaz Modi ed. *The Parsis in Western India: 1818 to 1920*. Bombay: 1998; B D Bharucha, ed. *The Indian Cinematograph Year Book*, 1938, Bombay: 1938, pp. 20-21.

40 Sourindramohan Mukhopadhayay, 'Bangla Bioscope (Bengali films)', *Bharati*, Sravan-Bhadra B.S. 1330 (1923), in *Bangla Bhashae Chalaccitra Charcha 1923-33* (Film Criticism in Bengali Language, 1923-33), edited by Debi Prasad Ghosh, Calcutta: Cine Club of Calcutta, 1990, p. 6.

41 J.B.H. Wadia, 'The Indian Silent Film', in *70 Years of Indian Cinema, (1913-1983)*, edited by T.M. Ramchandran, Bombay: A CINEMA India-International Publication, 1985.

42 Kaushik Bhaumik, 'The Emergence of the Bombay Film Industry, 1913-1936', unpublished D.Phil thesis, University of Oxford, 2001, p. 74.

43 Kironmoy Raha, 'Calcutta Theatre, 1835-1944', in *Calcutta: The Living City*, Vol. II, edited by Sukanta Choudhuri, New Delhi: OUP, 1990, p. 193.

44 Madhuja Mukherjee, 'Stories in Light and Shadow: Comment on New Theatres and its Popular Films', unpublished research project, Pune: National Film Archives of India, 2000, p. 22.

45 Mukhopdhayay, 'Bangla Bioscope', p. 6.

46 This was a film based on Bankim Chandra novel *Radharani*.

47 *Bioscope*, 22 March 1930, p. 13.

48 Ibid., p. 10.

49 *Bioscope*, 9 May 1927, p. 9.

50 Wadia, 'The Indian Silent Film', p. 21.

51 For derogatory reference in this vein see, Basu, 'Deshi Film Sambandhe Du Char Katha', *Bioscope*, no. 27 (1930), pp. 9-10.

52 Bhaumik, 'The Emergence of the Bombay Film Industry', pp. 62-64.

53 Ibid., p. 65.

54 Narendra Deb, *Cinema: Chayar Mayar Bichitra Rahasya* (Mysteries of the Silver Screen), Calcutta: Gurudas Chattopadhyay & Sons., 1934.

55 Sourindramohan Mukhopadhayay, 'Cinemar Rehearsal', *Naachghar*, B.S. 5 Chaitra, 1332 (1925).

56 Dhiraj Bhattacharya, 'Bioscope-er Kotha', *Naachghar*, B.S. 17 Aswin 1331 (1924), p. 18.

57 *Bioscope*, 15 February 1930, p. 2.

58 Santosh Kumar Bandopadhayay, 'Chalachitrer Du Ekta Kotha', *Bioscope*, 19 April 1930, p. 8.

59 Sourindramohan Mukhopadhayay, 'Filmer Art', *Naachghar*, B. S. 21 Kartik, 1331 (1924), in Ghosh ed, *Bangla Bhashay Chalachhitra Charcha 1923-33*, pp. 3-5.

60 D W Griffith is commonly credited for the most comprehensive integration of the elements that produced the classical Hollywood paradigm of narrative cinema.

61 'Purbakatha', in Ghosh, *Bangla Bhashay Chalachhitra Charcha.*

62 Mukhoapdhayay, 'Filmer Art', *Naachghar*, B. S. 21 Kartik 1331 (1924).

63 Regarded as the father of modern Indian art. Born on 7th August 1871, at Jorasanko, the family residence of the Tagores in Calcutta, Abanindranath was the nephew of Rabindranath Tagore. For a discussion of the emergence of the 'nationalist' school of Indian art under Abanindranath, see, Tapati Guha-thakurta, *The making of a new 'Indian' art: artists, aesthetics and nationalism in Bengal, c. 1850-1920*, Cambridge, Cambridge University Press, 1992.

64 Abanindranath Tagore's address at the inauguration of Bengal's first known cinema library on 29 April 1931, reproduced in Ghosh, *Bangla Bhashae Chalacchitra Charcha*, p. 60.

65 Tagore's letter to Murari Bhaduri, 26 November, 1929, cited in, Arunkumar Ray, *Rabindranath o Chalachitra* (Rabindranath and Cinema), Calcutta: Chitralekha, 1986, p. 9. Emphasis mine.

66 Santosh Kumar Bandopadhayay, 'Chalachitrer Du Ekta Kotha', *Bioscope*, 19 April 1930, p. 7. Emphasis mine.

67 Chittaranjan Ghosh, 'Banglar Anna Samasya o Chalachhitra' *Dipali Pujah Special* 1931, p. 25.

68 For an account of Tourneur's departure from Hollywood following his tiff with the 'supervisor' system, refer, Kevin Brownlow, *The Parade's Gone By*, Berkeley: University of California Press, 1976, p. 37.

69 Ibid.

70 Sumanta Banerjee, *The Parlour and the Streets: elite and popular culture in nineteenth century Calcutta*, Calcutta: Seagull Books, 1989.

Confronting Western cultural imperialism

soccer, modernity and nationalism in colonial India

Kausik Bandyopadhyay

Introduction

Sport played a critical role in the transmission of Western imperial and national ideas into Asia from the late nineteenth century onwards. In fact, the cultural diffusion of modern sport throughout the world was associated with an attendant ideology of cultural imperialism. Adoption of Western sport was often seen as a given standard of attaining *modernity* in the colonized world, simply because this fitted in well with the conventional paradigm of Western challenge and Eastern response in a colonial, semi-colonial or even post-colonial setting by erecting a simple dualism between modernity and tradition. But once one admits the autonomy of the borrower, the complexity of responses to the introduction and spread of modern sport – imitation, resistance, nationalism and subversion – becomes evident. On the other hand, the formulation of cultural nationalism around modern sports in a colonial setting is neither simplistic nor linear. Its origin, growth, character and impact need to be analyzed in the context of changing balance of intended imperial designs and their unintended consequences via appropriation. Using soccer as a lens, this chapter will attempt to understand and explore the contestations of imperialism and nationalism in the relational perspectives of modernity and culture in colonial India.

Modern sport, cultural imperialism and colonial response: a conceptual framework of study

In an important collection of essays entitled *Geopolitique du sport*, Claude Hurtebize has argued that the global diffusion of modern sports occurred at the same time as 'the constitution of world markets and colonial empires.'[1] Johan Galtung, in the same vein, notes suggestively that the 'massive export of [modern] sports' from developed to underdeveloped areas followed 'old colonial trade and control lines ... into the last little corner of the world.'[2] The football grounds of Calcutta and Bombay are therefore as much the relics of British rule as much the Victoria Memorial in Calcutta. However, Great Britain's dual success as an imperial power in seizing the lion's share of colonial booty as well as becoming the foremost country in the development of modern sports was not merely a coincidence but a result of what Allen Guttmann calls 'causation'. As he rightly argues, 'modern sports abetted the imperial expansion that carried them to the ends of the earth.'[3] In fact, the imperialists themselves emphasized causal connections. As Reverend J.E.C. Welldon, headmaster of Harrow School from 1881 to 1895, proclaimed: 'In the history of the British Empire, it is written that England has owed her sovereignty to her sports.'[4]

Several scholars have taken the view of Welldon and his like at face value. Peter Rummelt, for instance, has characterized the spread of modern sports throughout Africa as nothing more or less than colonialism at work.[5] Other specialists in sports studies, influenced by the writings of Andre Gunder Frank and Fernando Henrique Cardoso[6] or by those of Immanuel Wallerstein[7], see the global expansion of modern sports as a hitherto neglected aspect of the 'development of dependence' on the periphery of the 'world system'.[8] Still others, equally convinced that the displacement of traditional indigenous pastimes by modern sports has been a cultural disaster, have written in Gramscian terms of the 'hegemony'[9] of Western sports.[10]

In the study of ludic diffusion[11] of modern sport, however, most discussions have referred not to cultural hegemony but rather to cultural imperialism, although both come very closer in understanding the process of diffusion. John Tomlinson usefully defines 'cultural imperialism' as 'a form of domination ... not just in the political and economic spheres but also over those practices by which collectivities make sense of their lives.'[12] The question which arises in the broader perspective of colonial response to the intrusion of modern sports in India is: can the diffusion of modern sports from Europe to the rest of the world be considered a form of cultural imperialism? Since team games like soccer seem to evoke an intense collective psychological identification, this chapter will later endeavour to show that the so-called diffusion of football has met quick acceptance than prolonged resistance in colonial India as it suited indigenous appropriation for nationalist purposes.

One of the chief factors that are commonly held responsible for the rapidity or slowness of ludic diffusion of modern sports from one nation to another is relative political, economic, and cultural power of the nations involved. As Ruud Stoviks argues, the popularity of any given sport in any given country 'depends upon the development of the positions of economic and political power among the nations of the world system.'[13] But both political and economic models of ludic diffusion are not entirely adequate to understand the historical complexity of the process. Political motives mostly dominated by a concept of sport as part of a program of political domination, as 'a useful instrument of imperial purpose'[14] seems to be too unidirectional. One influential economic model of ludic diffusion is drawn from Andre Gunder Frank's theories of the 'development of dependency'. This model, which insists that modernization is impossible unless the 'peripheral' society breaks away from the capitalist 'world system',[15] too, seems rigidly deterministic. However, there can be little doubt that the history of modern sports has conclusively demonstrated the ability of 'satellites' to surpass the 'metropolis'.

Sports, like other fields investigated by scholars committed to 'cultural studies'[16], are contested terrain in theory as well as in practice. It is here that the Gramscian notion of 'cultural hegemony' again resurfaces as a useful formula of understanding. Gramscian theory correctly stresses the fact that the cultural interaction is something more complex than the domination of the totally powerful of the entirely powerless. In other words, it is important to emphasize the individual's capacity for active selection and selective retention. Hence, the ethnocentric assumption that non-Western societies simply accept, without selection or interpretation, whatever explicit or implicit messages the Western sports transmit, has long been discredited. In the analysis of sport as cultural imperialism and the resultant colonial response to it, one should neither credit the colonialists with diabolical powers nor deny all *agency* to the colonized. However, although both cultural imperialism as well as cultural hegemony imply intentionality, in fact those who adopt a sport are often the eager initiators of a transaction of which the 'donors' are scarcely aware.[17]

If we wish to understand, in all of its complexity, the process of cultural diffusion of soccer and colonial response to it, Thorstein Veblen on emulation is as applicable as Gramsci on hegemony. Veblen, of course, wrote ironically of emulation in order to satirize the absurdly, pathetically imitative behaviour of men and women frantic to rise in the hierarchy of social prestige, but Veblen points to an important psychological truth: emulation is a powerful motivator. Allen Guttmann makes the point amply clear:

> Culturally dominated groups have often had sports imposed upon them; but they have also – perhaps just as often – forced their unwelcome way into sports from which the dominant group desired to exclude them. To dismiss this kind of emulation as 'false consciousness' or 'colonization of the mind' is not persuasive.[18]

In Western sports like soccer, more often probably than in any other domain, the initially dominated have turned the tables on their erstwhile dominators. As Guttmann succinctly remarks:

> Once successful emulation has shattered the ludic monopoly, the literal or metaphorical colonials have a splendid opportunity to enhance their self-esteem, for nothing can be more delightful than 'beating them at their own game'. Simultaneously, one signals allegiance ('It's your game!') and superiority ('We're better at it than you are!').[19]

In the Indian context, Mohun Bagan's victory over British regimental teams to win the 1911 Indian Football Association (IFA) Shield has been interpreted in these terms.[20]

Joseph L. Arbena writes of the Cuban experience: 'Even the Cubans, for all their nationalistic and ideological rhetoric, prove the success of their Revolution, if only to themselves, by playing Anglo sport better than the Anglos.'[21] In fact, a turnabout in the balance of ludic power can be the prelude to more significant shifts in political and economic power.[22] Modern sports have sometimes functioned to crystallize anti-colonial sentiments and even to provide an organizational framework for a movement of national liberation. Arbena, surveying the diffusion of European sports throughout Latin America, concludes 'that imported sports had a partially imperialistic impact in that they helped to shape local elites and their values in ways at least initially beneficial to the Europeans,' but he goes on to admit that these same sports became, in time, 'the agent of anti-colonialism and anti-imperialism.'[23] Later sections of this chapter will show how the emancipatory impulses were institutionalized in the Indian soccer clubs in colonial India. This emancipatory potential of modern sports has become a parallel theme to the undeniable role of modern sports as means of social control and imperial rule. It also makes room for the argument that if nations are what Benedict Anderson's influential theory claims them to be, 'imagined communities', then modern sports are an important and popularly accessible aid to this politically indispensable form of imagining, particularly in the colonial setting.[24]

Traditionalists insist, however, that that talk of the possible contribution of sports to nation-building misses one important point. For them, modern sports are a form of cultural domination and ludic diffusion is tantamount to the imperialist or hegemonic destruction of authentic native cultural forms. The traditionalist argument has an initial plausibility, but it is seriously flawed. The notion that the adoption of another culture's sports is *ipso facto* a sign of lost authenticity ignores the fact that cultures are never static. As Joseph Maguire has noted, 'cultures and peoples are responsive and active in the interpretation of the global flow of people, ideas, images and technologies.'[25] Edward Said too has made the same point forcefully: 'the history of all cultures is the history of cultural borrowings.'[26] While it is certainly true that a culture can be annihilated, it is also true that cultures can be resilient, adaptive and transformative – in sports as in every other domain. More important, however, as Jay R. and Joan D. Mandle once pointed out, 'is not where a cultural form originated but what happens to it upon its arrival.'[27] This chapter tries to understand what happened to football when it was adopted and adapted into the fold of Indian culture in the first half of the twentieth century.

Football in India : the beginnings

It is reasonably clear that football came to India with the East India Company. Football's early pioneers were the officers and men of Trading Farms and Regimental Battalions, European professors of educational institutions, and Naval men who used to play at ports of call like Calcutta, Bombay, Madras and Karachi.[28] Tony Mason and Paul Dimeo, following the most overarching and widely popular theory of 'games ethic' popularized by J.A. Mangan, explain football's introduction and organization in Calcutta primarily in terms of public school games-playing ethos[29], learnt by the educated Bengali lower-middle and middle classes at the British-run Anglo-Indian colleges.[30] The concept of 'games ethic' had shared with the notion of 'muscular Christianity'[31], propagated by the moral missionary, a firm belief in sport as an instrument of imperial moral persuasion. The implications of games ethic were more clearly discernible in the efforts of evangelicals like Theodore Leighton Pennell and Cecil Earle Tyndale-Biscoe in the North-West Frontier Provinces and in Kashmir respectively, who used the game as a 'key weapon in the battle to win over local populations and to begin transforming them from their 'uncivilized' and 'heathen' state to one where they might be considered 'civilized' and 'Christian'.'[32] In Bengal, especially in Calcutta, the Anglo-Indian schools certainly integrated sports including football as integral part in their educational curriculum. Soccer, to these early missionaries as well as public school teachers, was a moral tool to inculcate 'a series of moral lessons, regarding hard work and perseverance, about team loyalty and obedience to authority and, indeed, involving concepts of correct physical development and 'manliness'.'[33] However, the early inspirational role of the Indian middle class schools should not be overemphasized, nor yet be incorrectly minimized. Other imperial elements like soldiers, businessmen and administrators also might have had an early influence in the process.[34]

In the fullness of time, despite the important innovatory role of these middle class schools and colleges, the role of the public schools for the introduction and promotion of football in India was minimal. Despite football's inclusion and importance as a form of moral training in the public school curriculum in the leading British educational institutions, football's popularization in India cannot solely be attributed to this process. The attitude and response of the general Indian public towards this mass spectator sport was rather different. Football's appropriation by the general public was a complex and both calculated and incidental process, especially in Bengal.

Importantly enough, the period games ethic meshed with colonial masculinity to produce a fruitful stereotype of Bengali as an effeminate non-military race.[35] Bengali response to this charge of effeminacy was uniquely *cultural*. They reacted to the colonial stereotype by way of the pursuit of a 'neo-traditional physical culture' to efface the 'self-image of effeteness'[36]. In fact, many noted Bengali intellectuals of the age too seemed to have internalized this 'self-image of effeteness' and voiced urgency to overcome this supposed physical degeneration by way of resurgence of traditional Bengali physical culture and indigenous games. The motivation spurred up by middle class cultural nationalists such as Rajnarayan Basu, Bankim Chandra Chatterjee, Krishna Kumar Mitra, Sarala Debi, Nabagopal Mitra and Swami Vivekananda led to the emergence of a physical culture movement in the second half of the nineteenth century. This movement led and popularized in Bengal by Nabagopal Mitra's *Hindu Mela* in the 1860s-70s began to promote the rejuvenation of ancient Hindu principle of physical culture.[37] However, the physical culture movement was marked by a conspicuous lack of competitive dimension that distinguished modern western sports like football, cricket or hockey. Moreover, even if rigorous physical exercise was looked upon as plausible weapon to counter British slur of effeminacy, it did not afford the Bengali the opportunity to compete the British on even terms. Middle class Bengalis quickly realized the ultimate ineffectuality of the physical culture movement and the urgent need to cultivate new way to reassert physical prowess and redeem the hurt masculinity. Western sports, especially football, provided the way out. Dimeo has argued that in taking recourse to modern sports Bengalis followed a 'route of mimicry'.[38] But he fails to admit that they adopted Western sports like football with a conscious design of showing their physical worth by competing the Europeans on equal plane. Football's adaptation was therefore more a cultural ploy than a simplistic mimicry. It was in this particular socio-political context that the early pioneers of football – Nagendra Prasad Sarvadhikari, Manmatha Ganguly, Haridas Seal or Dookhiram Majumdar – came to introduce and popularize football play in Bengal.

In the 1880s and 1890s, football was therefore deemed as a cultural weapon to reassert Bengali/Indian physical prowess and masculinity and as a medium of social intercourse between the ruler and ruled. It was yet to become a cultural weapon to fight and beat the colonial masters in a true nationalist sense. By the end of the nineteenth century the game from being an occasional recreation of military men, a school sport and merely a leisure activity among other Europeans, soon became an arena for competition and conflict between the British and the Indians.[39] To suggest that Indian football clubs of 1880s and 1890s from their very inception began to reflect or represent purely nationalist instinct or ethos on the sports field is perhaps overbold. Football, however, at the turn of the century, may be said to have become a new and unique cultural nationalist force in Indian society although the approach of different clubs to the game was not uniform.

It was Mohun Bagan who rose from the Indian clubs to symbolize the true nationalist response of the injured 'cultural self' of Indians against the British. Originally founded in 1889 by a few idealistic North Calcutta gentlemen at Mohun Bagan villa, it proved, from its very inception, to be more than a club. It was an institution with the avowed objective to not only produce excellent sportsmen, but to impart in them impeccable moral and social values. The ideals that the founders had set before themselves were novel for Indians at that time.[40] The executives of the club saw to it that each member combined the development of the body with that of the mind. They prescribed a high moral code for its members. Little did the pioneers envisage, however, that the club would, through its epic victory over the East York Regiment in the 1911 IFA Shield final, bring about a national reawakening?

Nagendra Prasad Sarvadhikari and the formation of a modern sporting identity[41]

Nagendra Prasad Sarvadhikari, a son of the foremost sporting family of contemporary Bengal, rose to prominence as the so-called 'Father of Indian Football'[42] only at the age of ten. With his indomitable sportsman spirit and unparalleled organizational acumen Nagendra Prasad almost single handedly led the Bengali society into an engaging popular pursuit of modern sporting culture. His sincere efforts at the development of modern sporting activities among Bengali people contributed to the initiation of a unique sporting identity in Bengali society. Nagendra Prasad's lifelong effort to raise the physical/sporting prowess of the Bengali can be placed in the broader perspective of social reform and cultural regeneration in Bengal, which had started since the days of Raja Rammohun Roy. Nagendra Prasad used sports like football as a viable cultural weapon to reassert hurt Bengali masculinity and to retrieve India's sinking national prestige. His attempt to inculcate a spirit of militarism among Bengali students may also be seen as a venture corollary to the same end. That he generated an unprecedented sporting spirit in Bengali urban society and organized sport as a bond of social unity is beyond doubt. The renascent culture of sport he bequeathed as a legacy was later utilized by posterity as a means of national cultural self-expression to a greater effect.

It is often argued that Nagendra Prasad rose to prominence when he kicked the football for the first time, the first such act by an Indian on the Calcutta Maidan, at the age of ten and followed it up by introducing the game among his friends at Hare School. This was followed by his successful attempts to spread the game throughout Bengal by forming a number of clubs including the Boys' Club, the Presidency Club, the Wellington Club and the Sovabazar Club, and finally, in collaboration with European officials, the Indian Football Association. It is not known what was in his mind when Nagendra Prasad first initiated his countrymen to outdoor sports. But in his mature days his sole aim for conversion was to make his young countrymen physically fit so that in the field of competition they were able to hold their own against aggression from any quarter. 'That was the nationalism', writes his biographer, 'which Nagendra Prasad preached and practiced in all his life.'[43] It was in fact a religion to Nagendra Prasad to find ways and means to uplift the physique of his country. For Nagendra Prasad, the spirit of equality and fraternity was in the forefront of every department of sports. He subscribed munificently to the true sporting spirit though, it may be presumed, he at his early age was not quite aware of its implications.

Nagendra Prasad was the first Indian to voice the critique of caste-based discrimination in the area of sports. Although he belonged to an orthodox Hindu family, but while establishing a series of sporting clubs, he chose to ignore all caste prejudices. His staunch position against the discriminatory actions based on caste status is clearest in the incident surrounding the induction of a potter's son into the Wellington Club. The club had a membership of nearly five hundred from all classes of society. Well-to-do and middle class young men of Calcutta felt some amount of pride to belong to the Wellington at that time. And Nagendra Prasad was ever vigilant to keep intact the team spirit. When Nagendra Prasad wanted to induct Moni Das, a confectioner's son[44], the richer members protested vehemently. But Nagendra Prasad refused to buckle before the pressure arguing that a sporting association should be free of any prejudice and decided to dismantle the Wellington Club. He made no secret of the exact situation and in his characteristic gait and demeanour said:

> I know sooner or later the matter will be asked to be put to vote. It will be a mean move on the part of those who call themselves sportsman. I can not allow myself to be party of it.[45]

Greatly irked by the intrigues carried on behind his back, Nagendra Prasad dissolved the Wellington Club and by combining the various sporting clubs he had earlier established – the Boys Sporting Club, Friends Club, Presidency Club, the erstwhile Wellington Club – founded the Sovabazar Club in 1887. Moni Das, whose proposed induction was the cause behind the decimation of the Wellington Club, was one of the first members of the Sovabazar Club. He later distinguished himself as one of the best cricketers of the Mohun Bagan Club. 'This attempt by Nagendra Prasad to free sports of all caste prejudices in the 1880s was the first of its kind in India.'[46]

Nagendra Prasad's ingrained sportsman spirit led him to a conscious utilization of sports as a platform of social equality in late nineteenth century Bengal. That he made a very spirited attempt to establish the credibility of indigenous pursuit of the modern sports is quite obvious. But more importantly, he fought against heavy odds to initiate and concretize the formation of a sporting identity among Bengali youths irrespective of caste, class, community, religion or such social affiliations at a critical sociopolitical context. In that sense, he had the spirit of a true social reformist. The Renaissance in Bengal sent its ripples to every spheres of life, albeit at different times. In sports it came through the ability of Nagendra Prasad.

However, Nagendra Prasad's sportsman spirit must be analyzed in the context of social contours of contemporary colonial culture in India. The limitations of the modern sporting identity he intended to initiate and foster in Bengal, therefore, are quite obvious. At that stage, i.e. in the 1880s and 1890s, football was deemed as a *modern* cultural tool to reassert Bengali physical prowess and masculinity and as a medium of social intercourse with the British. It was yet to become a cultural weapon to fight and beat the colonial masters in a true nationalist sense. Hence, Nagendra Prasad's efforts may be situated in the transition of Indian pursuit of modern sports from imitation to competition. Considering his good and friendly relations with the European officialdom and his professional career as an attorney in British Indian judiciary, it may be argued that ideas of 'subversion' and 'resistance'[47] in the arena of sports did not find favour with him.

Soccer as cultural nationalism : the context of colonial India

British imperialism in India was not merely a political or economic venture; it was more so a social and cultural one; and it remains a psychological hang over. The relational complexities of mind, body and society under imperial rule have had far more interesting and lasting repercussions on Indian life than the ongoing socio-political movements of the period. Colonizing the polity, economy and society under imperial rule went hand in hand with colonizing the body and the mind through cultural idioms. Sport furnishes a cultural domain where both body and mind interacted and reciprocated to colonize or indigenise each other. Anti-colonial Indian nationalism, too, in the same vein, was not simply political in origin or character. Rather, socio-cultural nationalism may be said to have predated its political variety.[48] An atypical representation of such unconventional cultural nationalism[49] was reflected through the Indian pursuit of football as a daily cultural activity in first three decades of the twentieth century India, especially in Bengal. In the early twentieth century, football became the rallying point of Indian anti-colonial consciousness and an instrument by which to establish indigenous oriental superiority over the occidental imperialist. Thus the Indian cultural battle against the British on the *maidan* (football ground) in the cultural phenomenon of football went hand in hand with confrontational political nationalism against the colonial government. Each victory of an Indian team over a European military team was celebrated as a triumph of the noble spirit of nationalism over the ignoble spirit of colonialism. Such football victories and their psycho-nationalistic impact played a vital role in infusing confidence into the Indian hearts by demolishing the myth of invincibility of the Raj.

In summary, football in late colonial India came to be looked upon as an apolitical avenue for expression of the colonized against the colonialist. It leapt from its sporting boundaries to become a cultural weapon to fight the imperialist. Playing and watching the game cut across the affiliations of indigenous caste, class or community in Indian society and provided a social bond for the nationalist-minded Indians. Football as a cultural weapon to fight and defeat the British added a new dimension to the anti-British national consciousness of the Indians particularly in Bengal. Thus, parallel to the political struggle against an oppressive colonial power, there began a social struggle of national liberation over a specific cultural component. The success of Indian footballers playing for an Indian team against a European team representative of the colonial rulers led to a nationalization of the their mind. In that context, the football maidan as a *modern* cultural territory began to reflect an Indian nationalist impulse that found heroic expression in the effort of the footballers.

In the aftermath of Mohun Bagan success of 1911, football as an outlet for aggression gradually came to reflect the 'pent-up nationalism' of Bengali professionals and students. A large section of the Bengali community were affluent, educated, practical and decent, but were hesitant to actively take part in the freedom struggle. They considered the football field an ideal place to confront the British. Similarly, the political events of the first decade of the twentieth century had a stirring effect on the Bengali youth. Nevertheless, many of them were reluctant to participate in politics of direct confrontation. Hence football came to be a potent nationalist gesture and beating the British produced a sort of immense emotional satisfaction for them. The urban and suburban middle class Bengalis, who served the British as officials, clerks or professionals, could not show their anti-British resentment in public, and the working class people, who were not drawn into the fold of nationalist politics until the late 1920s, could express their nationalism freely only at the maidan. The 'pent-up' nationalism of the Bengali middle and working classes thus found prolific expression only through emotional outbursts during playing or watching a match when a Bengali team got the better of a British side. Moreover, on the football field it was considered to be an act of great courage to shove an elbow or a fist into the face of a Sahib or a soldier, or kick him under the guise of tackling. Those who could get away with it were respected as great players. Footballers like Gostho Paul, Abhilash Ghosh and Balai Chatterjee earned glamour and fame in Bengali society for their reputation to execute successfully this 'reverse hit' or *palta mar*. Subhas Chandra Bose noted in his autobiography:

> In conflicts of an inter-racial character the law was if no avail to Indians. The result was that after some time Indians, failing to secure any other remedy, began to *hit back*. On the streets, in the tramcars, in the railway trains, Indians would no longer take things lying down. ... The effect was instantaneous. Everywhere the Indian began to be treated with consideration. Then the word went around that the

> Englishman understands and respects physical force and nothing else.[50]

In sporting encounters, it is also said, some Bengali spectators would deliberately pick quarrels with the 'superior' British. Sometimes these encounters would turn violent and afford the Bengalis the opportunity of giving the *gora* Sahibs a 'sound beating'.

Thus what the nationalist politicians and native representatives in the British Indian administration could not do, the footballers were expected to do. They were required to be ideal cultural nationalists and in this role freedom fighters, who would get the success that eluded others in politics and economy, the more crucial spheres of national life. Football heroes like the Bhaduris and Abhilash Ghosh[51], became, for the disorientated Bengalis, the ultimate remedy for all the failures - moral, economic and political - of the country. If India, according to these sporting Bengalis, was constantly losing to its imperial rulers in politics and economics, football was to ameliorate the nation's feelings of inefficacy and emasculation.[52]

Football as a novel instrument of cultural nationalism established a distinctive domain free from colonial interference in early twentieth century Bengal. Spirit of nationalism affected the patterns of spectator culture and fan sub-cultures in colonial Indian football to a great extent. It was an age neither of great stadia nor of radio or televised sport. Hence 'being in the maidan' was the soul of spectatorship. The nationalist element of the Bengali football culture was most obvious in maidan-spectatorship. Spontaneous effusion of nationalist feeling found prolific expression in specific forms of behaviours— pitch-side language, jokes and doggerels, erratic vocal outbursts, peculiar physical gestures, skying umbrellas, tearing shirts, throwing sandals and stones into the ground, torching papers and clothes— and spectator-violence. In this process of the nationalization of a football culture, the 'subconscious' played a very important part. These forms of nationalist spectator culture may be said to have their concrete beginnings in the 1911 Shield finals. A pen picture of the spectators' behaviour at the maidan on 29 July 1911, i.e. the day of final, was vividly depicted two years later by the correspondent of a renowned Bengali periodical[53]. The most commonplace forms of nationalist spectator culture at Calcutta maidan in the 1920s and 1930s are brilliantly delineated in Achintya Kumar Sengupta's autobiographical *Kallol Yug*.[54]

The articulation of this footballing nationalism in its entire vicissitudes was visible in the football maidan of late colonial Bengal. As I have argued elsewhere[55], by 1911 the game may be said to have introduced a new and unique means of 'cultural self-expression'[56] into Bengali society. The massification of Bengal football and the sub-cultures that grew out of it gradually came to be intertwined with the rising tide of nationalism. In other words, nationalism was an important reason why Bengalis/Indians took up football so enthusiastically. By 1947, the year India won independence, football was not only the most popular of Indian sports but also an inescapable part of Indian popular culture.

Subversion and resistance in colonial Indian football

John Plamenatz, in one of his most interesting articles, has considered nationalism as 'primarily a cultural phenomenon'.[57] In his discussion of the two types of nationalism, 'Western' and 'Eastern', Plamenatz stresses the importance of a common set of standards to measure the state of development of a particular national culture. For him, as for Benedict Anderson[58], it was the West that provided this common set of standards to the Eastern nations. However, he finds an inherent contradiction in the attempt of the 'Eastern' type of nationalism to 're-equip' the nation culturally for transforming it. As he goes on to suggest: 'It is both imitative and hostile to the models it imitates …' Partha Chatterjee clarifies the first projection neatly: 'It is imitative in that it accepts the value of the standards set by the alien culture.'[59] But it is the hostility to that model involving two ambivalent rejections, which seems to attract larger attention: 'rejection of the alien intruder and dominator who is nevertheless to be imitated and surpassed by his own standards, and rejection of ancestral ways which are seen as obstacles to progress and yet also cherished as marks of identity.'[60]

Plamenatz's conceptual model of 'Eastern' cultural

nationalism is useful in understanding the character of footballing nationalism in late colonial India. Football field provided a cultural space where the Indian adopted the British game and then tried to beat the master at their own standard. This of course necessitated and in fact resulted in downplaying (if not complete rejection) of traditional Indian games while football was indigenised especially through an essentially Indian style of play without wearing boots. For European scholars like Mason and Dimeo, Indian victory over its colonial master on the football field was nothing but a success story of British cultural imperialism.[61] They read in such football victories Indians' unwitting admiration for, acceptance of and submission to such cultural imperialism. Richard Cashman raised a pertinent question as to whether we can analyze the spread of colonial sports solely in terms of the ideology of colonialism and games ethic or not.[62] For him, the indigenous appropriation (domestication) of modern sport (cricket in his case) calls for more logical explanation.[63]

There are two major differences of interpretation and approach in this regard. First, there are those, Mangan, in part, and Mason and Dimeo in particular, who stress the power of football and its associated ideology to indoctrinate colonial subjects. In the words of Cashman, 'Because it was wrapped up in the garb of a compelling and fascinating game, it was a very powerful imperial weapon.'[64] However, for those who look at football and colonialism more 'from below', or from the perspective of the recipients of the game's ideology, there are significant problems with the perspective which concentrates exclusively on the proselytizer. As Cashman brilliantly argued in the context of colonial Indian cricket:

> Where does the promoting hand of the colonial master stop and where does the adapting and assimilating indigenous tradition start? Is it merely adaptation and domestication or does it go beyond that to constitute resistance and even subversion? And how far can the colonial acceptance of cricket be seen as superior colonial salesmanship or a successful exercise of social control using the highly developed ideology of games and colonialism? Or was it that many colonial subjects chose to pursue a game, because of the ideology, or even in spite of it, because it suited them to

take up cricket for their own reasons? Or was the ideology of colonialism the starting point for the adoption of cricket but once the game was launched other factors came to bear which led to its spread and consolidation?[65]

Cashman's conclusion, too, sounds historically cogent: 'while games are an effective vehicle for proselytization in some circumstances, they can be subverted in others.'[66] The appropriation of football in colonial Bengal for nationalist purposes, as this chapter has shown, is definitely proof to a colonial reformulation of the imperial model of games ethic. It points to football's transformed role as an instrument of reaction, resistance and subversion.

Among European scholars, J.A. Mangan has hinted at the complexity of interpreting indigenous responses to imperial projects of games ethic. That he is unsure of the reality and character of indigenous response is evident when he says, 'the legacy of the game in the region (Kashmir) hints at a more complex story once the game has been adapted and adopted by Indian groups.'[67] Boria Majumdar also has emphasized this potential of indigenization and subversion of a colonial sport in course of time, and on its 'becoming' of 'an area for the articulation of an indigenous brand of nationalism.'[68] He rightly remarks, 'Inverting the colonial ideology on its head, resistance and subversion were often dominant in the second phase of the histories of these games in the colonies.'[69]

In fact, what most of the European scholars miss out completely in analyzing the relational complexities of football, imperialism and nationalism in colonial India is the conscious indigenous attempt to overturn the imperial ideology to suit an overtly nationalist purpose of shattering the so-called British cultural/racial/masculine superiority. Nothing could provide greater satisfaction to the masses than the fact that the allegedly inferior natives would defeat the racially proud imperialists in direct physical/masculine confrontation. Ashis Nandy's analysis comes very closer to deciphering the psychological underpinnings of this cultural nationalism in a colonized society. He talks about the victim's construction of the West, a West that would make sense to the non-West in terms of the non-West's experience of suffering. 'However jejune such a concept may seem to the sophisticated scholar', says Nandy, 'it is a reality for the millions who have learnt the hard way to live with the West during the last two centuries.'[70] This 'Non-West' of Nandy constantly invites one to be Western and to defeat the West on the strength of one's acquired Western ness. Beating the West at its own game is the preferred means of handling the feelings of self-hatred in the modernized non-West.[71]

Thus footballing nationalism in colonial India was not only a subversion of colonial games ethic or cultural imperialism. But, arguably, it informed a more serious subversion of colonial masculinity. And here also Nandy's construction about the psychology of the colonized for an entirely different context is succinctly applicable[72]:

> They (*Indian footballers and spectators*) sought to redeem the Indians' masculinity by defeating the British, often fighting against hopeless odds, to free the former once and for all from the historical memory of their own humiliating defeat in violent power-play and 'tough politics'. This gave a second-order legitimacy to what in the dominant culture of the colony had already become the final differentiae of manliness: aggression, achievement, control, competition and power.[73]

Nandy's construction, as applied to footballing nationalism in colonial India, also resembles Amitear Cabral's espousal of *culture* as a harbinger of protest:

> The study of the history of liberation struggles shows that in general, they are preceded by an increase in cultural phenomena which progressively crystallize into an attempt, successful or not, to assert the cultural personality of the oppressed people in an act of *rejection* of that of the oppressor. Whatever may be the state of subjection of a nation to foreign rule and the influence of economic, political, and social factors in the furtherance of this domination, it is generally in culture that the seeds of protest, leading to the emergence and development of the liberation movement, is found.[74]

The wider perspective into which anti-colonial nationalism around the masculine game of football needs to be contextualized concerns the processes by which the promotion, acceptance, and incorporation of the game occurred. As Brian Stoddart has rightly suggested:

> For the most part, however, the real power of sport did not come from being laid out formally by colonial masters to be studied by colonial subjects. Instead, it perhaps belonged more in the realm of what the Annales school of historiography has identified as *mentalites*, a set of beliefs acquired subconsciously. ... It was largely this subconscious element, outside the bounds of formal policy making, which rendered sport so powerful a factor in the maintenance of and *reaction* to British control throughout the empire.[75]

Football in colonial India certainly provided the ideal space for *reaction* to British control. This constituted one immediate problem for the imperial power. 'Having encouraged the measurement of social progress by comparing colonial against British achievements in sport, there would always come the day of a colonial victory that might be interpreted as symbolic of general parity.'[76] And when such colonial victory came at a time of intense political unrest, as it did happen in colonial Bengal, 'the victory was widely regarded as a sign of Indian development, equality, and even superiority.'[77]

Conclusion

In the colonized world, the process of modernization of sport began with Western cultural intrusion into traditional sports, and consequent to it, formal codification and colonial administration of modern sports. Behind this apparently simple model of the 'modernization' of sport, noted Richard Holt, 'there lie a whole a series of subtle influences and interesting problems.'[78] The present essay has sought to address the dichotomy within such influences and problems in the setting of football and culture in colonial India. If the introduction, adoption, adaptation and consolidation of modern sports like football, in very general terms, ushered the Indian sports world into a broader project of colonial modernity, many amongst the Indian practitioners of such sports were keen to appropriate that modernity to serve entirely different purposes, thereby creating space for an alternative modernity in their *own* terms. Thus while the overt imperial mission of games ethic in introducing the Indians to modern

Western sports was wrought with the embedded notion of cultural imperialism, the Indian appreciation of that imperial purpose in adopting and adapting a particular sport (football in this case) ranged from emulation to appropriation, resistance and even subversion for nationalist purposes. In other words, one standard of Western modernity - namely sport - was appropriated to surpass and discredit that very West. The Indian answer to British cultural imperialism on the football field was therefore *Indian* cultural nationalism. And the growing political tension around nationalist movement in early twentieth century India made sure that the contestation between the two did not remain overtly cultural only, but at times assumed significant political connotations. Thus, even in the arena of sport, the contemplation of modernity clearly points to a subtle notional dichotomy and ambivalence, apparent in the clash between intended designs of the imperialists and their unintended consequences on the colonized in the realm of sport, thereby creating yet another layer of alternative modernity.

Acknowledgements

For the theoretical formulation of this chapter, I am indebted to Prof. Allen Guttmann.

Notes and References

1 Claude Hurtebize, 'Geopolitique de la genese, de la diffusion et des interactions culturelles dans la culture corporelle et le sport', in *Geopolitique du sport*, edited by Borhane Errais, Daniel Mathieu, and Jean Praicheux, Besancon: Universite de Franche-Comte, 1990, p. 87, cited in Allen Guttmann, *Games and Empires: Modern Sports and Cultural Imperialism*, New York: Columbia University Press, 1994, p. 4.

2 Johan Galtung, 'The Sport System as a Metaphor for the World System', in *Sport: The Third Millennium*, edited by Fernand Landry, Marc Landry and Magdeleine Yerles, Sainte-Foye: Presses de l'Universite Laval, 1991, p. 150, quoted in Guttmann, *Modern Sports and Cultural Imperialism*, p. 4.

3 Guttmann, *Games and Empires*, p. 5.

4 J.E.C. Welldon, 'The Imperial Purpose of Education' in *Proceedings of the Royal Colonial Institute* XXVI (1894-95), p. 823,

quoted in J.A. Mangan, *The Games Ethic and Imperialism: Aspects of the Diffusion of an Ideal*, London: Frank Cass, 1998, p. 36.

5 Guttmann, *Games and Empires*, p. 5.

6 Andre Gunder Frank, *Capitalism and Underdevelopment in Latin America*, New York: Monthly Review Press, 1967; Fernando Henqique Cardoso and Enzo Faletto, *Dependency and Development in Latin America*, trans. Marjory Mattingly Urquidi, 1971, Berkeley University of California Press, 1979; James D. Cockcroft, Andre Gunder Frank and Dale L. Johnson, eds. *Dependence and Underdevelopment*, Garden City: Doubleday-Anchor Books, 1972.

7 Immanuel Wallerstein, *The Modern World System*, 3 vols. New York: Academic Press, 1974-89.

8 Alan Klein, 'Baseball as Underdevelopment: The Political Economy of Sport in the Dominican Republic', *Sociology of Sport Journal* 6, no.2 (June 1989): pp. 95-112.

9 For details on Gramscian notion of 'hegemony', see Antonio Gramsci, *Selection from the Prison Notebooks*, trans. and ed. by Quinton Hoare and Geoffrey Nowell Smith, New York: International Publishers, 1971.

10 Borhane Errais, 'La planete sportive', *Sport: The Third Millennium*, p. 582, cited in Guttmann, *Games and Empires*, p. 5; Minseok An and George H. Sage, 'The Golf Boom in South Korea: Serving Hegemonic Interests', *Sociology of Sport Journal*.9, no.4 (December 1992): pp. 372-84.

11 In the present context, 'ludic diffusion' refers to a process of spontaneous transmission or dissemination of modern sports from Britain to the colonized countries of Asia and Africa more or less concurrently.

12 John Tomlinson, *Cultural Imperialism*, Baltimore: Johns Hopkins University Press, 1991, p. 7.

13 Quoted in Guttmann, *Games and Empires*, p. 175

14 J. A. Mangan, *The Games Ethic and Imperialism: Aspects of the Diffusion of an Ideal*, Reprint, London: Frank Cass, 1998, p. 18.

15 Gunder Frank, *Capitalism and Underdevelopment in Latin America*, p. 3, 11. Not all the theorists of 'dependency' are as dogmatic as Frank about the utter impossibility of development within the capitalist system; see Cardoso and Faletto, *Dependency and Development in Latin America*, 185-86.

16 For the relevance to sports studies of Stuart Hall and the Birmingham Center for Contemporary Cultural Studies, see Richard Gruneau, 'The Critique of Sport in Modernity', in

edited by *The Sports Process*, Eric G. Dunning, Joseph A. Maguire, and Robert E. Pearton, Champaign: Human Kinetics, 1993: pp. 85-109; David L. Andrews and John W. Loy, 'British Cultural Studies and Sport', *Quest* 45, no.2 (May 1993): pp. 255-76.

17 Guttmann, *Games and Empires*, p. 179.

18 Quoted in Guttmann, *Games and Empires*, p. 179.

19 Ibid.

20 For a detailed discussion on the historical significance of this event, see Kausik Bandyopadhyay, *Playing for Freedom: A Historic Sports Victory*, New Delhi: Standard, 2008; Dwaipayan Sen, 'Wiping the Stain Off the Field of Plassey: Mohun Bagan in 1911', *Soccer and Society* 7, no. 2-3 (2006): pp.208-32; Soumen Mitra, 'Babu at Play: Sporting Nationalism in Bengal: A Study of Football in Bengal, 1880-1911' in *Bengal: Yesterday and Today*, edited by Nisith Roy and Ranjit Roy, Calcutta: Papyrus, 1991, pp. 45-61; Tony Mason, 'Football on the Maidan: Cultural Imperialism in Calcutta' in *The Cultural Bond: Sport, Empire, Society*, edited by J. A. Mangan, London: Frank Cass, 1992: pp. 142-153; Paul Dimeo, 'Football and Politics in Bengal: Colonialism, Nationalism, Communalism' in *Soccer in South Asia: Empire, Nation, Diaspora*, edited by Paul Dimeo and James Mills, London: Frank Cass, 2001: pp. 57-74; Boria Majumdar, 'The Vernacular in Sports History', *Economic and Political Weekly* XXXVII, no. 29 (20 July 2002): pp. 3069-3075.

21 Joseph L. Arbena, 'Sport, Development and Mexican Nationalism, 1920-70', *Journal of Sport History* 18, no. 3 (Winter 1991), p. 362; also see Joseph L. Arbena, 'Sport and Revolution: The Continuing Cuban Experience', *Studies in Latin American Popular Culture* 9 (1990), p. 325.

22 This is suggested in Harold Perkin, 'Teaching the Nations How to Play: Sport and Society in the British Empire and Commonwealth', *International Journal of the History of Sport* 6, no.2 (Sept. 1989): pp. 145-55.

23 Joseph L. Arbena, 'The Diffusion of Modern European Sport in Latin America: A Case Study of Cultural Imperialism', *South Eastern Latin Americanist* 33, no.4 (March 1990), p. 6.

24 Benedict Anderson, *Imagined Communities: Reflections on the Origin and Spread of Nationalism*, rev. ed., New York: Verso, 1991.

25 Joseph Maguire, 'Globalization, Sport and National Identities: 'The Empire Strikes Back'', *Loisir et Societe* 16, no. 2 (Autumn 1993), pp. 310-11, cited in Guttmann, *Games and*

Empires, p. 185.

26 Edward W. Said, *Culture and Imperialism*, New York: Knopf, 1993, p. 217.

27 Jay R. and Joan D. Mandle, *Grass Roots Commitment: Basketball and Society in Trinidad and Tobago*, Parkersburg, lowa: Caribbean Books, 1988, pp. 19-20.

28 For a brief discussion on the beginnings of football in India, see Bandyopadhyay, 'Race, Nation and Sport', pp. 1-4.

29 The accepted definitive study of public school games as moral training is J.A. Mangan's *Athleticism in Victorian and Edwardian Public School*, Cambridge: Cambridge University Press, 1981 and London: Frank Cass, 2000 (with a new introduction).

30 Mason, 'Football on the Maidan', p. 144; Dimeo, 'Football and Politics in Bengal', p. 62.

31 For a reflective discussion on this theme in Asian context, see Mangan, 'Imperial Origins, Christian Manliness, Moral Imperatives and Pre-Srilankan Playing Fields – 'Beginnings' and 'Consolidation'', in *Sport in Asian Society: Past and Present*, edited by J.A. Mangan and Fan Hong, London: Frank Cass, 2003, pp. 1-49.

32 J.A. Mangan, 'Soccer as Moral Training: Missionary Intentions and Imperial Legacies', in Dimeo and Mills, *Soccer in South Asia*, p. 41.

33 Ibid.

34 An excellent example of the impact of the imperial administrator's enthusiasm for association football is to be found in *Burma and Beyond* by Sir J. George Scott which deals inter alia with his introduction of the game to Burma in the late nineteenth century. The account of his years in Burma was published in London by Grayson and Grayson in 1932. Scott was a serious and sympathetic student of the Burmese cultural panorama in its various elements and took great pains to understand and record it in the clear knowledge that modernization would restore much of it. To catch merely a flavour of his admiration of the country and its people, see his *Burma: From the Earliest Times to the Present Day*, London: Fischer Unwin, 1924. The opening to his Preface encapsulates the approach: 'The country of Burma and the Burmese people are as attractive as any in the world...' (v).

35 In fact, throughout the nineteenth century, British imperialists, perhaps out of their deep dislike for the climate, topography and inhabitants of Bengal, made the Bengali a

butt of satiric criticisms for his supposed physical effeteness - a stereotype that ran all through the period of Imperial rule. This colonial construction of 'effeminate Bengali' could be found in everyday British attitude toward commonplace Bengalis, in their various speeches and most prolifically in their writings, viz. contemporary Anglo-Indian literature.

36 For an in-depth study of this concept, see John Rosselli, 'The Self-Image of Effeteness: Physical Education and Nationalism in Nineteenth-Century Bengal', *Past and Present* 86 (1980), pp. 121-148.

37 For a detailed history of this movement, see Jogesh Chandra Bagal, *Hindu Melar Itibritta*, Calcutta: Maitrayee, 1945.

38 Dimeo, 'Colonial Bodies, Colonial Sport: 'Martial' Punjabis, 'Effeminate' Bengalis and the Development of Indian Football', *The International Journal of the History of Sport* 19, no.1 (March 2002), p. 84.

39 This transformation of football's social dimension has been elaborately discussed by Soumen Mitra in his recent work *In Search of an Identity: History of Football in Colonial Calcutta*, Kolkata: Dasgupta & Co., 2006, chapter 3.

40 *Mohun Bagan Club Platinum Jubilee Souvenir*, Calcutta: Mohun Bagan A. C., 1964, pp. 1-5.

41 For a detailed discussion on Nagendra Prasad's contributions to the growth of modern sports in Bengal, see Kausik Bandyopadhyay, 'The Legend of the 'Father of Indian Football': Sport, Culture, Modernity in Late Colonial Bengal', *Asia Annual 2006*, pp. 427-53.

42 Both of Nagendra Prasad's biographers as well as majority of Bengali sports writers attribute this epithet to him for his pioneering contributions towards the growth and popularization of the game among the Indians. These are: P.L. Dutt, *Memoir of Father of Indian Football Nagendra Prasad Sarvadhikari*, Calcutta: Nagendra Prasad Sarvadhikari Memorial Committee, 1944 (hereafter *Memoir*); and Saurindra Kumar Ghosh, *Krida Samrat Nagendra Prasad Sarvadhikari*, Calcutta: Nagendra Prasad Sarvadhikari Memorial Committee, 1963.

43 *Memoir*, p. 1.

44 There is a controversy over Moni Das's actual caste identity. While P.L. Dutt mentions Das as a confectioner's son (*Memoir*, p. 17), Saurindra Kumar Ghosh, on the other hand, describes him as a smith's son (Ghosh, *Krida Samrat Nagendra Prasad Sarvadhikari*. pp. 118-19). Be that as it may, that Moni Das was

from a low caste family is beyond doubt.

45 *Memoir*, p. 18.

46 Boria Majumdar and Kausik Bandyopadhyay, *Goalless: The Story of a Unique Footballing Nation,* New Delhi: Penguin/ Viking, 2006, p. 22-3.

47 For a brief but instructive analysis of these ideas in the context of colonial Calcutta football, see Majumdar, 'The Vernacular in Sports History'.

48 The former found expression in certain specific domains of society: language, literature, education, art, science, family and women's position, theatre, music, dance, sport and perhaps even cinema.

49 In this chapter nationalism has been considered primarily as a cultural phenomenon.

50 Subhas Chandra Bose, *An Indian Pilgrim: An Unfinished Autobiography and Collected Letters, 1897-1921*, ed. Netaji Research Bureau, London: Asia Publishing House, 1965, pp. 65-6. Emphass added.

51 Sibdas Bhaduri and Abhilas Ghosh were the goal scorers for Mohun Bagan in the 1911 Shield final.

52 I have taken this particular construction from Ashis Nandy, who elaborates on similar role cricket might have played in the last few decades in post colonial India, though in a different context. See Ashis Nandy, *The Tao of Cricket: On Games of Destiny and the Destiny of Games*, New Delhi: Oxford India Paperbacks, 2000, Preface, p.xix.

53 Nagendra Nath Gupta, 'Football Final', *Bharatbarsha* 1, no.4 (1913).

54 Achintya Kumar Sengupta, *Kallol Yug*, Calcutta: M.C. Sarkar & Sons, 1950, pp. 66-72.

55 Bandyopadhyay, '1911 in Retrospect'.

56 Ashis Nandy used this particular term for cricket to denote same meaning and implication in late twentieth century Indian society. Nandy, *The Tao of Cricket*, p. 2.

57 John Plamenatz, 'Two Types of Nationalism' in *Nationalism: The Nature and Evolution of an Idea,* edited by Eugene Kamenka, London: Edward Arnold, 1976, pp. 23-36, cited in Partha Chatterjee, *Nationalist Thought and the Colonial World: A Derivative Discourse?* London: Zed Books, 1986, p. 1.

58 Anderson, in his seminal work *Imagined Communities: Reflections on the Origin and Spread of Nationalism*, London: Verso, 1983, too, talks about a set of 'modular forms'

provided by the historical experience of nationalism in the West and in Russia for the nationalist elites of Asia and Africa to choose and adopt.

59 Chatterjee, *Nationalist Thought and the Colonial World*, p. 2.

60 Plamenatz, 'Two Types of Nationalism', quoted in Chatterjee, *Nationalist Thought and the Colonial World*, p. 2.

61 Mason, 'Football on the Maidan', pp. 150-51; Dimeo, 'Football and Politics', p. 71.

62 Richard Cashman, 'Cricket and Colonialism: Colonial Hegemony and Indigenous Subversion' in *Pleasure, Profit, Proselytism: British Culture and Sport at Home and Abroad, 1700-1914*, edited by J.A. Mangan, London: Frank Cass, 1988, pp. 259-60.

63 Ibid.

64 Ibid.

65 Ibid., p. 261.

66 Ibid.

67 Mangan, 'Soccer as Moral Training', pp. 49, 54.

68 Majumdar, 'The Vernacular', p. 3071.

69 Ibid.

70 Ashis Nandy, *The Intimate Enemy: Loss and Recovery of Self under Colonialism*, Oxford: Oxford University Press, 1983, pp. xiii.

71 Ibid.

72 Nandy specifically referred to 'many pre-Gandhian protest movements' in that context.

73 Ashis Nandy, *The Intimate Enemy*, p. 9.

74 Amilcar Cabral, 'National Liberation and Culture', *Transition*, no. 45 (1974), p. 13; emphasis added. In case of football as a cultural instrument of national liberation in colonial Bengal, the rejection is conceived in terms of *that* of the so-called superiority of the oppressor alias colonizer.

75 Brian Stoddart, 'Sport, Cultural Imperialism and Colonial Response in the British Empire', *Comparative Studies in Society and History* 30, no. 4 (1988), pp. 660-61. First emphasis in original, second emphasis added.

76 Ibid., p. 667.

77 Ibid.

78 Richard Holt, *Sport and the British: A modern History*, Oxford: Oxford University Press, 1990, p. 3.

Modernization
The abiding metaphor of India

Rakhee Bhattacharya

Changing phases

Development, the core tangible component of modernity, can be perceived as a process of change and transition that takes place along a continuum of ever-changing historical, socio-political and economic ideas and ethos in the life of a nation or society. Chasing for a better living in a better world compared to the past, which can transform the quality of life, can be a way to define development *vis-à-vis* modernization and progress. So conceiving modernity 'as the state of being modern', its economic perspective can connote transition in material progress along with tangible growth in a country's economy, which creates opportunities to an individual to acquire modern identity through professional attainment and outlet. Hagos has categorized modernity as 'a period in Western history that includes both nineteenth and twentieth Centuries. It is a period characterized by drastic change or transformation and replacement of aristocratic governments and mercantile economic systems by democratic forms of government and industrial (capitalist) economic system with global expansion'.[1]

The economic structure of modern world can therefore be understood from development theories that have evolved in the Western set-up. Starting from the early school of such theories, modernization can be equated to the conventional Western ideas of 'development' in a functional relationship between output growth and industrialization. More interestingly, economic development can be seen in the 'stage theory', which was actually brought in focus by Alexander Gerschenkron[2] and, more crudely by, W. W. Rostow[3]. The stage theorists are of the opinion that every *nation* passes through the same historical stages of economic development and that contemporary underdeveloped countries are merely at an earlier stage in this linear historical progress while the First World Nations are at a later stage. So economists translate modernity in terms of development and underdevelopment, which are quantifiable in cardinal scale of measurability. Considering development through output growth, economists have equated various indicators to measure its growth. Thus Ragnar Nurkse[4] identified capital formation as the crucial component to accelerate development. Sir W. Arthur Lewis[5], in his celebrated early work on the 'dual economy', precisely emphasized the role of savings in development. Early Keynesians, such as Kaldor[6] and Robinson[7] have taken another vital indicator i.e., income and its distribution as determinant of savings and growth. Robert Solow[8] had generalized the relationship among labour, capital, technology and output in his 'neoclassical production function', which was extensively used as a popular growth model in several research studies over time. Gunnar Myrdal[9], in his 'cumulative causation' theory, argued that a balanced growth can be achieved by strong government intervention - by planning, socio-economic engineering or effective demand and supply management. This reduces imbalanced growth and development. There are economists, who in conformity with the classical doctrine of Adam Smith, have equated growth and progress with international trade by extending market, raising profits and ultimately by increasing capital formation.

These predominant Western ideas of development like income growth and capital formation persisted for decades together, till the time thinkers have realized that this growth process *per se* has not really diffused across the different strata of the society. Rather this growth process has made the lives of only one section better, leaving the rest in utter misery. Only the empowered nations with strong political economy could gain from this development. So the other set of economic theories have emerged to provide the potential explanations to the facet of disparity due to economic development, and its adverse consequence across the nations in the world. In this context, Marx's notion of modernity needs to be understood by looking at his essential arguments on the elemental features of the modern social world.[10] It is important to reexamine Marx's analysis of value, commodity fetishism and capital accumulation and to what extent they go with contemporary analyses of modernity. Also, Marx was a critic of such capitalism, which counters mass welfare and destroys egalitarian society. According to the more recent popular approach of development-disparity theory, conceived in the paradigm of the convergence hypothesis, and propounded by Robert Barro and Sala-i-Martin[11], regional economies with low initial incomes tend to grow faster than those with high initial income, after controlling the rates of savings and population growth. Thus, in the long run, poorer regions will get closer to their richer counterparts, and convergence becomes a general outcome of development. These authors have developed the two tests of convergence viz., σ and β convergence.

So the process of economic development within Western capitalist framework over time has been tested as *necessary condition* but not *sufficient condition* for transforming a society to a better space by minimizing malaise and discrimination across its citizens. Thus social dimension of economic modelling has gained importance to replace the sole Western concept of productivity. Economic growth *per se* cannot simply cater to the needs of human needs and development in general; hence this development remains partial. For example, only capital formation in physical terms is too narrow a concept to deal with inclusive growth and its effects across the society. Gradually the term 'capital formation' for development started getting wider in its perspective and it was T.W. Schultz[12], who emphasized the need of 'human capital formation' by creating skilled people, through education, health, security and other basic needs. This, to a large extent, can be self-sustainable in modernity paradigm, with better societal ethics and values. It is therefore important to understand that economic development should be conceived within a socio-cultural context and modern world cannot simply be determined by sheer economic growth. A society can claim to achieve modernization only when it can eliminate poverty, hunger, all forms of social deprivation, discrimination, insecurity and economic inequality. Myrdal[13] has also emphasized the need for such achievements and more recently economists like Mahbub ul Haq[14] and Amartya Sen[15] have been very vocal about the quality of life index and human development index (HDI), which they feel are the prerequisites for development. Today, almost every country has started compiling HDI with indicators like education, health and income. This is a quantifiable index for human resource and its capability index, improvement of which can significantly raise the overall productivity of a nation. Thus human development index and economic prosperity index should necessarily be positively correlated. The other intrinsic concept that has evolved along with human development is called 'Gross National Happiness' (introduced in a small Asian Nation, Bhutan). This has emerged as the recent but urgent phenomenon for development and prosperity. Stefan Priesner gives us a decent understanding of the concept:

> 'Gross National Happiness', which was introduced by the king of Bhutan in the late1980s and has rapidly evolved into the accepted label for the distinct Bhutanese development concept. In spite of its seemingly recent origin, the term is really a popularization of the distinct Bhutanese perception of the fundamental purpose of development, which can be traced throughout the period of development. Already in the late 1960s, a period during which Bhutan's development policy is generally considered to have followed conventional patterns of rapid modernisation, Late King Jigme Dorji Wangchuck expressed his view on the goal of development as making 'the people prosperous and happy.' Similarly, the prominence of 'prosperity and happiness' is highlighted in the king's address on the occasion of Bhutan's admission to the UN in 1971, one of the most important events in the country's recent history. This vision, first articulated by the late king was elaborated by the present king, Jigme Singye Wangchuck, who declared in the first years of his reign that, 'our country's policy is to consolidate our sovereignty to achieve economic self-reliance, prosperity and happiness for our country and people.' While the emphasis is placed on both, prosperity and happiness, the latter is considered of more significance. For Bhutan 'Gross National Happiness is more important than Gross National Product'.[16]

The index of Gross National Happiness encompasses the components like self-reliance, human development, cultural and environmental preservations at the operational level, which can ensure a sustainable and flexible development and can reach everybody. Thus metamorphosis of development has remained time, place, space and context specific and juxtaposed with both occidental and oriental transformation of ideas and its experimentation. Only Western ideas of hard-core economic gains from *industrialization, urbanization* and *commercialization* cannot therefore provide 'inclusive modernization'. A Nation's prosperity is intimately related to its people's happiness through a capability index to maintain peace and stability. Today, structural issues such as dualism, population growth, inequality, urbanization, agricultural transformation, education, health and unemployment - all have begun to be reviewed on their own merits, and not merely as appendages to an underlying growth thesis. More importantly, in view of several non-traditional threats that have emerged due to different dimensions of modernization, one can recall E.F. Schumacher's view[17] in *Small is Beautiful*, where he argued against the desirability of industrialization and extolled the merits of handicrafts economies. As the world environmental crisis became evident in the 1980s, this debate took a new twist and the very sustainability of economic development was questioned. It has now become clear that the desirability of development needs to be reconsidered, given the depth and dimension of its skewedness and polarity. To re-examine development, one can follow Hagos[18], who has emphasized rightly that it is appropriate to make some distinctions between concepts of civilization, modernization, and Westernization. He has argued that where Westernization is successfully applied to a community with strong and ancient civilization, the result is modernization, a kind of a synthesis. Whereas, when Westernization is forced on a community with rudimentary 'civilization' or on a community at primitive developmental stage, wholesale Westernization takes place there. The result reflects disparity, conflicts and an utter confusion in the society.

India being a land of vast society with a strong civilization and culture, which has evolved over long historical phases of invasions and, then, integrations, has inevitably achieved development at one point of time through Western synthesis.

Recent remarkable achievements in economic development have given India a global identity. But this economic achievement also simultaneously has brought in a crisis of its moral economy – a challenge is alarmingly posed in the arena of inequalities of wealth and power, authority and obedience, reciprocities and loyalties of social relations, might and misery, aspiration and attitudes, vigour and voicelessness, potentialities and preventions. The following sections of this essay will look into the strengths and weaknesses of modernization of Indian economy.

Climax : Indian scenario

Though development is exposed to various hard-core tests by social scientists, but one cannot ignore the need and urgency of its achievements. For example, the modern world could not have benefited from the revolutionary achievement of world-wide communication network through computer, if material and scientific progress were halted. Prosperity, which the world has seen today through globalization (a password of economic development) along its power of inter-country connectivity by trade, commerce, exchange of ideas, culture and human resource is undeniable. The boons of modernization have undoubtedly changed the lives of millions like a 'Midas Touch'. In the words of Shankar Acharya:

> In the long sweep of the world history, modern economic growth is a fairly recent phenomenon. Between 1000 AD and 1800AD there was not much change in the world GDP per capita. With the spread of the industrial revolution in the 19th century, average world income increased by over 200 per cent. In the recently concluded 20th century, global GDP per capita went up by nearly 900 per cent.[19]

India, which, even with its magnificent size and population, had been suffering from vicious circle of slow economic growth trap till late 1980s, has today turned out to be the primary mover of Asian economy. Compared to its economy in the 1980s, today's India has developed enormously in several arenas. But it is essential to look at those determinants of development, which are sustainable and reachable to all in the society. In this context, Alan Richards made some valuable observations:

> A crude view would hold that 'modernity' is the endpoint of a process called 'modernization'. Such a perspective arises from the, often refuted, yet still vigorous discourse of 'modernization theory'. Such a term has as many definitions as it has proponents, with 'modernity' measured by such things as 'urbanization', 'industrialization', 'literacy', and so on. Ever since Daniel Lerner (or Max Weber), the 'image of the modern' has been one of 'literate people living in cities making a living by manufacturing'. Such a crude perspective provokes (at least) four objections. First, why are these specific 'markers' of 'modernity' (e.g., urbanization, literacy, industrial output) particularly privileged? Second, what, exactly, is being measured? For example, if 'industry' is the critical category, what percentage of output must be 'industrial' for a society to be counted as 'modern'? What constitutes 'industrial' production these days? Are transgenetic crops 'agricultural' or 'industrial'? Does a large 'industrial' sector always matter? What about 'services'? Does 'urban' mean 'an agglomeration of settlements with more than 100,000 people'? Why that number? And so on. Third, particularly when the modernization theorist uses not just one indicator but a set of them, what is the justification for any particular 'weighting schema'? If 'modernity' means some combination of urbanization, literacy and industrial production, what weight is assigned to each of these three variables in constructing an index of 'modernity'? What is the theoretical justification for such weighting? Finally, and perhaps most tellingly, many of us object that the entire concept reeks of teleology: history is here conceived as an ineluctable process, a 'progress' toward a predetermined goal. All societies, in this view, move inexorably toward an 'end-point' of 'modernity', which, mirabile dictu, very closely resembles the current society of the United States or Western Europe. All humanity marches toward the same shining goal, the End of History.[20]

Richards's arguments need to be seriously contemplated, but the undeniable fact remains that till today the image of modernization to a large extent is reflected by these common indicators like *urbanization, industrialization and literacy,* which have indeed changed the face of the world in this century. The push from small-scale, agrarian, village and town community economies to large-scale, industrialized economies encompassing nations and regions has immensely affected the economic, social, political, environmental, even moral, aspects of human life. Looking at Asia in general and India in particular, one can very well trace the path of development, which its Western counterparts pursued earlier. One must ask here the question: where exactly does this path lead to? Following Partha Chatterjee's view, one can argue that majority of Indian society lives outside the consciousness of 'civil society' (in Western liberal sense). Chatterjee also insists that this 'is not to say that the majority of the population is outside modernity. It is targeted by welfare policies of the modernizing state and it is mobilized by political formations to express popular demands on the developmental state.'[21] And to assess the developmental states, the cardinal measurability can be the best option for a developmental economist. Independent India has made a sojourn of merely sixty years after it was free from British colonialism, which lasted for around 200 years. According to Robert W. Stern, India's introduction to 'economic modernity' under British Raj, which was not a 'national government', had reflected the inherent structural weakness of imperialism as a system for economic development of its colonies. The British government of India was not able to pursue any vigorous industrialization strategy in India, as that contradicted their sectoral interests 'at home'.[22] He therefore feels that, India industrialized in bits and pieces in 'enclaves' of industrialization in an unindustrialized subcontinent without mass mobilization. The concept of development in terms of the introduction of infrastructure and education had started with the British advent, which was actually done to facilitate the trade and extraction of Indian resources by the British people. This British initiative had transformed Indian society and created an ambience of urban-elite-English-educated class in Indian pockets, leaving aside the miseries of masses in rural sector. So the actual challenge of development started only when the British was forced to leave this country leaving behind the millions in abject poverty, social disorder, political chaos, cultural conflict and economic imbalance. But the gradual transformation of India through various developmental efforts, policies and reforms over the past six decades has made people to think differently. In the words of John Williamson:

> The rise of the Indian economy is one of the most important economic developments of our day. To put it in context, one needs to start by considering how India gained independence. The year was 1947, and it was the culmination of a long struggle between the British government and the Indian independence movement. The movement was led by Gandhi, and his most important lieutenant was Nehru. The two had very different views on a number of questions, and in particular on economic issues. Gandhi believed in a very simple life, while Nehru had absorbed the doctrines of British socialism. The British socialist movement at that time aimed to build up a modern economy as rapidly as possible.[23]

Going by the crude indicator of measurability, one can say that India during the time of independence suffered from a very low per capita income, a common Third World syndrome. There was a manufacturing sector, but it didn't cover many industries. There was even a steel industry and a relatively strong textile industry, but these were limited. It was predominantly a subsistent and more of a traditional agricultural economy. Most of the villages at that time did not even have road connections and were not a part of the market economy. But now India has emerged as a shinning economy with multiple future prospects. This journey began when India had its so called 'Hindu Growth Rate' of 3.5 per cent in the 'slow growth decades' of 1950-80, which was more than four times greater than 0.8 percent per year estimated for the final half century of British rule.[24] Coming to its per capita growth, India has witnessed three times increase from 1.5 percent in 1950-80 to 4.5 percent in 1991-2006. This remarkable increase in growth rates in India, according to Shankar Acharya, is due to the policy reforms carried out slowly in the 1980s and more comprehensively in the 1990s.[25] Apart from India's macro economic policy reforms and structural changes, one should also recognize the path-breaking visionary contributions made by some very prominent Indian citizens, whose works have not only transformed India's image in the modern world but have transformed the Indian mindset and provided livelihood to a huge number of people in the home front. Thus such persons as Dhirubhai Ambani and his Reliance Industry have played a key role to transform India's image of modernization. Dhirubhai founded the company, which stood largest in terms of sale, asset and profits and now it ranks within top 200 in the world in terms of profits. Dhirubhai has thus become one of the glaring icons of Indian economic modernization. Similar is the example with Ratan Tata. These individual efforts and their tremendous contributions to Indian economy have undoubtedly added immense value to India's development, which need to be acknowledged in the paradigm of Indian modernity.

Coming back to the measurable indicators, some of them are discussed below to justify the progress made by India as an independent nation.

Table 1 : Economic Growth in Post-Independence India

Years	Annual Growth Rates of GNP (current prices)	Annual Growth Rates of Per Capita GNP (current prices)
1951-52	5.7	3.6
1961-62	5.4	2.6
1971-72	6.4	3.6
1981-82	16.5	14.0
1991-92	15.0	12.0
2001-02	9.3	6.9
2005-06	13.8	12.1

Source: Economic Survey, 2006-07, GOI

One finds in Table 1 that from 1951-52 (5.7%), just after India's independence, the annual growth rate of gross national product has grown several times higher and, in 2005-06, it has reached the level of 13.8%. Similarly, for per capita gross national product, the annual growth rates have gone remarkably high from 3.6% in 1951-52 to 12.1% in 2005-06. One can see that, from 1980s onwards, India has seen the growth of its economy, which is primarily due to the structural change. Opening up the economic fronts through liberalization and then through globalization has mainly contributed to its economy. Growth path of its national output has risen sharply due to a rise in the sister indicators of modernization i.e., industrialization, urbanization and literacy rates.

Table 2: Modernization Indicators in Post-Independence India

Years	Industrialization	Urbanization	Literacy Rates
1951-52	13.57	17.29	18.33
1961-62	53.25	17.97	28.30
1971-72	46.83	19.91	34.45
1981-82	41.72	23.34	43.57
1991-92	34.09	25.71	52.21
2001-02	26.20	27.78	64.84

Source: Census India Reports, 2001, GOI, Economic Survey, 2006-07, GOI. Industrialization represents here manufacturing, construction + others as the percentage of gross domestic products.

Table 2 shows that industrialization in India was very fast during the period between 1951-52 and 1961-62, registering an increase from 13.57% to 53.25%. But since then, the share of industrial contribution to India's GDP has gone down and this is again due to structural shift in service sector. The urbanization process is also comparatively slow, with an overall increase of 27.78% in 2001-02 from 17.29% in 1951-52. On the other hand, although the literacy rate has gone remarkably high from only 18% in 1951-52 to 65% in 2001-02, still 35% of the population, quite a high proportion, remains outside its orbit. So the basic indicators of modernization in independent India have shown an improvement and progress, and one can find a link between urbanization, industrialization and literacy on the one hand and economic growth on the other. This is an empirical truth and one can hardly find a wealthy, modern country that is not urbanized and has not seen industrial progress and educational advancement. But this urban-centric development becomes a success when it can spill over to its rural masses.

Coming to another fundamental component of modernization i.e., the capital formation, one can see from table 3 that India is surely on the path of modernization so far as the increase in capital formation is concerned. Both its gross domestic capital formation and gross domestic fixed capital formation have gone high.

Table 3: Gross Domestic Capital Formation (% of GDP at constant 1999-00 prices) in India

Year	Gross Domestic Capital Formation	Gross Domestic Fixed Capital Formation
1999-00	25.9	23.4
2000-01	23.9	22.5
2001-02	22.2	22.4
2002-03	25.0	23.5
2003-04	27.4	24.5
2004-05	30.2	25.3
2005-06	32.2	26.7

Source: Economic Survey, 2006-07, GOI

In the recent decades, India has developed immensely its service sector due to information technology and knowledge economy. This has actually transformed its image to the modern world. This sector has provided India with a sizable skilled young population, who can afford to lead a 'modern life' in terms of a luxurious life style with a very high economic remuneration and purchasing power. But with little alertness, it can be easily seen that there lives an 'other India', which is far aside from these concepts of modernization. Development, that we speak today in India, is largely confined, centralized and metropolitized, which has failed miserably to cater to the needs of its rural and peripheral masses. Consumerism amongst the urban elite due to high purchasing power is 'not merely iniquitous but also detrimental to real development involving poor.'[26] This has actually created a crisis in India's economic development. Widened disparity, especially in the post-globalized era, has created an alarming situation, which needs serious attention from the perspective of development.

Crisis: Indian scenario

Amartya Sen sums up the crisis of modernization in the following way:

> The world is both spectacularly rich and distressingly impoverished. There is unprecedented opulence in

> contemporary living, and the massive command over resources, knowledge and technology that we now take for granted would have been hard for our ancestors to imagine. But ours is also a world of dreadful poverty and appalling deprivation. An astounding number of children are ill fed, ill clad, ill treated, and also illiterate and needlessly ill. Millions perish every week from diseases that could be completely eliminated, or at least prevented from killing with abandon. Depending on where they are born, children can have the means and facilities for great prosperity or face the likelihood of desperately deprived lives.[27]

This distressful scenario Sen has narrated above can easily provoke one to conclude that modernization is a 'failure'. The historical evidences of class conflicts due to uneven wealth distribution and Marx's appeal for class struggle could never be erased through modernization. Rather wealth distribution pattern perpetually remained skewed to the potential beneficiaries in this so-called modern urban-centric and industrially developed state. The Indian scenario, in such contexts, can best be understood in the way Sugata Marjit and Nirmala Banerjee have analyzed it: 'in the years immediately after Independence, interpersonal disparities, which should perhaps have had top priority in the design for economic planning, were, on the whole, ignored by economic planners.' [28] They further assert:

> Thanks to the growing protests from groups of those deprived population, several widening differences have come to be politically significant: those between the rich and poor, between men and women and especially between the losers and the gainers of the development process. Policy makers have now accepted that development has to bring about a change in the hierarchies among its beneficiaries. Perpetuation of past imbalances points towards a failure of progress in general, particularly because sharp polarities within a democratic country like India can give rise to problems of many dimensions.[29]

Thus these development-deficiencies have actually posed a threat and eventually a challenge to contemporary India. Looking at sheer human development index in India, which is 126th out of 177 countries (2005, UNDP), one can conceptualize the depth of faulty development that has taken place in the country. It is therefore time to revisit the entire development paradigm and find the flaws that are surfacing simultaneously in the Indian society along with this image of modernization. Some such indicators are discussed below.

An immediate look at the global position of Indian human and gender development indices, as shown in table 5, indicates a very alarming scenario for the country. Thus it is the inclusive development-deficiency, which actually needs to be investigated to find a solution for this scenario.

Table 5 : Global Position of India in Human and Gender Development

Country	Human Development Index (HDI)		HDI Rank		Gender Development Index (GDI)		GDI Rank	
	2000	2004	2000	2004	2000	2004	2000	2004
Norway	0.956	0.965	1	1	0.941	0.962	3	1
Australia	0.947	0.957	5	3	0.956	0.956	1.	3
Sri Lanka	0.747	0.755	89	93	0.737	0.749	70	68
China	0.730	0.768	96	81	0.699	0.765	77	64
Indonesia	0.682	0.711	110	108	0.678	0.704	91	81
India	0.577	0.611	124	126	0.560	0.591	105	96
Pakistan	0.511	0.539	138	134	0.468	0.513	120	105
Bangladesh	0.510	0.530	145	137	0.468	0.524	121	102

Source: Economic Survey, 2006-07, GOI

Coming to economic inequality, with a proxy variable representative of income/expenditure inequality, one can see a huge disparity in India in its shares between rich and poor. Gini Index (a standard measure of inequality) is very high (32.5), showing a high tendency of inequality. The poorest 10% has the opportunity to share only 4% of country's income and the richest 10% has the advantage of sharing 43% of nation's income. Thus though the GDP growth rate is high in India but this *per se* is not finding any mechanism to reach the poor; rather it tends to show a positive correlation between growth and inequality. Thus modernity is meaningful for only a section of skilled and privileged people, who can measure it in terms of economic gains. This has become prevalent in all spheres, even in the sphere of popular culture, from sports to music. The concept of sponsorship and the advent of satellite television have brought in another typical dimension of modernity, where creativity is commercialized and to the extreme, creative personality gets 'sold off', as happened recently with Indian cricketers. Thus money induction is becoming highly concentrated, which is detrimental to the society.

Table 6 : Income/Expenditure Inequality: India's Position in 2006

Indicators	India	China	Denmark	Lesotho
Poorest 10%	3.9	1.8	2.6	0.5
Poorest 20%	8.9	4.7	18.3	1.5
Richest 10%	43.3	50.0	35.8	66.5
Richest 20%	28.5	33.1	21.3	48.3
Richest 10% to Poorest 10%	7.3	18.4	8.1	105.0
Richest 20% to Poorest 20%	4.9	10.7	4.3	44.2
Gini Index	32.5	44.7	24.7	63.2

Source: *Human Development Report, 2006 UNDP*

Looking at the other conventional indicator of modernization, i.e., urbanization and its growth, one can say that though India's masses are migrating into cities faster than the rest of the world for better opportunities, this urban growth is haphazard, unsafe and unhealthy. As noted in one newspaper report: 'The condition of slum dwellers is even worse than poor villagers. Over 90% of slum dwellers are in the developing countries, with China and India accounting for 37% of them.'[30] According to a survey result conducted by the Maharashtra Home Department, 'amongst the mega cities in India, the national capital, New Delhi is the most unsafe city in India, followed by the financial capital, Mumbai. The country's IT capital Bangalore comes next. And Kolkata – still considered India's cultural capital – is at bottom of the crime chart.'[31] This uncontrolled and unplanned urbanization and the growth of mega cities have accentuated the problems of energy, water, sanitation, housing and space.

Table 7: Crime Scenario in Indian Mega Cities : 2005

	Delhi		Mumbai		Bangalore		Chennai		Kolkata	
Indicators	I	R	I	R	I	R	I	R	I	R
Murder	369	2.9	212	1.3	22	4.3	123	1.9	43	0.3
Decoity	23	0.2	47	0.3	35	0.6	5	0.1	17	0.1
Robbery	451	2.1	362	2.2	594	10.4	59	0.9	55	0.4
Theft	16897	132.1	11903	72.7	9617	169.1	3063	47.7	2639	20.0
Rape	562	4.4	201	1.2	38	0.7	43	0.7	13	0.1

Source: *NCRB, 2005. I-incidents R-Ratio: Rate per lakh population*

Table 7 shows that incidents like murders, theft and rape are highest in Delhi. Growth of urbanization is blind towards the safety and security of the citizens. Rather it becomes clear that, due to income disparity within the cities, crime rates, social unrest and insecurity are on rise. They are surely the banes of unplanned economic development in India. This development has also utterly neglected the societal aspect of development.

Industrialization, the other indicator of modernization, too, has proved to widen vertical inequality in India. Recently, the introduction of Special Economic Zones, which aims to boost industry and export, has created hue and cry, as it tends to remain unfavourable to the farming lands. As Bhaduri has rightly argued:

> in the name of high growth, industrialization works ruthlessly against the poor majority.... A spectre of despair and popular anger is striking in all corners of the country. Farmers are committing suicides in hundreds, especially in Andhra Pradesh and Maharashtra.... Land being the largest primary source of livelihood in the agrarian economy becomes the most obvious case of forcible transfer of resources from ordinary people to private corporations, destroying livelihood and displacing people.[32]

This trend and transition towards development is dangerous when almost two third of the Indian workforce is still in agriculture. This land-grab scenario can also lead to a crisis in agrarian land, which in turn will make its marginal productivity negative and lead to a vicious circle of macro imbalances, since foodgrains and agricultural products are both basic necessities of life and for development.

The social sector is even more depressing in modernization perspective. For example, taking an indicator like safe drinking water, one can find, 'for some 1.1 billion people, sufficient, safe, acceptable, accessible and affordable water for life is a hope for the future, not a reality for the present.'[33] The United Nations Committee on Economic, Social and Cultural Rights declared 'the human right to water entitles everyone to sufficient, safe, acceptable, physically accessible and affordable water for personal and domestic use.' In India, it is amazing to see from table 8 that the inter-state disparity is very high in terms of accessing safe drinking water. Thus, in 1981, the maximum people that were having access to safe drinking water was in Delhi (93%) and the minimum people that had access to it was in Mizoram (4.9%). But the situation has improved in the year 2001, with Punjab having maximum people accessing safe drinking water (98%) and Kerala with minimum people i.e., 23.4%. The rural-urban disparity is also tremendous, which was 27% and 75% respectively in 1981 and eventually has improved to 73% and 90% in 2001.

Table 8 : Access to Safe Drinking Water in Households in India (%)

States	1981			1991			2001		
	Total	Rural	Urban	Total	Rural	Urban	Total	Rural	Urban
Max	Delhi (93.0)	Punjab (81.8)	Delhi (94.9)	Delhi (95.8)	Punjab (92.1)	Delhi (96.2)	Punjab (97.6)	Punjab (96.9)	Punjab (98.9)
Min	Mizo (4.9)	Mizo (3.6)	Mizo (8.8)	Mizo (16.2)	Kerala (12.2)	Kerala (38.7)	Kerala (23.4)	Mizo (23.8)	Naga (42.3)
India	38.2	26.5	75.1	62.3	55.5	81.4	77.9	73.2	90.0

Source: *Economic Survey, 2006-07, GOI*

Till today, 'out of 26 million babies born in India, 1.2 million die before completing the first four weeks of life. This amounts to 30 percent of the 3.9 million neonatal deaths worldwide.'[34] India is reported to be the home of highest number of both births and neonatal deaths. Looking at the other indicators like sex ratio (from 2001 Census), Kerala tops the states with 1058 females per thousand males and Haryana is at the bottoms with 861 females per thousand males. Declining sex ratio, especially its declining juvenile sex ratio in an economically prosperous state like Haryana has become a cause of concern. The poverty ratio in 1999-2000, as per Planning Commission, GOI, was highest in Orissa (47.15%) and lowest in Kerala (12.72%). A report brought out by National Commission for Enterprises in the Unorganized Sector (NCEUS, 2007) shows even a worse scenario: a staggering 394.9 million workers, or 86% of India's working population are absorbed in India's unorganized sector, without having any social security. And nearly 80% of these workers are among those, who live on less than Rs 20 per day, no matter how many Indian citizens have added themselves to the billionaire club.

So looking at such dismal scenario, it can argued that India is probably still at the crossroad of many challenges of modernization, given, most importantly, its glaring gap between haves and have-nots. It is unfortunate that even today, for such a large number of population, the basic necessities are still a distant dream, leaving apart their other unmet needs and demands on securities and happiness. Thus talking of modernity is utterly a useless concept for this 'India'. A survey by the UK-based Legatum Institute for Global Development says that India in the happiness index ranks 46th amongst 50 nations.

> According to a new global prosperity index, India ranks as poor as 46 on the list of 50 countries surveyed. The survey, which has US, Norway and Sweden sharing the top spots, has taken into consideration both material wealth indicators and life satisfaction drivers like freedom of choice, good health, equality of opportunity, religious faith, high levels of income, low employment rates and low divorce rates.[35]

A contrast scenario in human development indicators (table 9) is focused with the state Kerala topping the list. For example, literacy rate in Kerala is 91%, where as Bihar bottoms the list, with 47%. Infant mortality rate in Kerala is 14 and in Madhya Pradesh, it is 76! These glaring sites of disparity in development across India leave one in utter confusion about the concept of modernity and compel one to reexamine the viability of its component of economic development and its underlying indicators.

Table 9: Human Development Indicators in India

States	Life Expectancy at Birth 1999-2003			Infant Mortality Rate: 2005			Birth Rate 2005	Death Rate 2005	Literacy Rate 2001
	Male	Female	Total	Male	Female	Total			
Max	Kerala (70.9)	Kerala (76.0)	Kerala (73.6)	Orissa (74)	Madhya Pradesh (79)	Madhya Pradesh (76)	30.4	9.5	Kerala (90.86)
Min	Assam (57.8)	Madhya Pradesh (56.9)	Madhya Pradesh (57.1)	Kerala (14)	Kerala (15)	Kerala (14)	15.0	6.4	Bihar (47.00)
All India	67.8	63.5	62.7	56	61	58	23.8	7.6	64.84

Source: *Economic Survey, 2006-07, GOI*

The findings therefore justify that in India, especially in the initial years of independence, the basic necessities of life needed for a descent standard of living remained out of reach for a large section of population in its transition process from tradition to modernity. However, in recent years, inclusive development with emphasis on social sector is attempting to improve the scenario, which can be seen in the results of the convergence model tested below. It shows that human development index across major Indian states has improved in the present decade. Due to the lack of available data, some peripheral regions like Northeast India could not be incorporated in the model.

Convergence: Indian scenario

The convergence in economic growth and human development amongst Indian states have been tested by σ and β convergence. This econometric test is done basically to show whether economic growth has dispersed across the regions during the period from 1991 to 2001, when India entered the phase of development with its reforms and globalization. The simplest way to test the σ convergence is to estimate the coefficient of variation (CV) of per capita income (PCI) and human development index (HDI) independently for the Indian states. Table 10 shows that within ten years time, from 1991 to 2001, the values of CV for PCI in Indian states increased whereas for HDI, the ratio declined. This indicates that income distribution became more skewed and more unequal, although, for HDI, the disparity amongst the states declined. So human development as a composite index actually showed a sign of improvement across states during those ten years.

Table 10 : σ convergence in Economic Growth and Human Development in Indian States

States	PCI		HDI	
	1991	2001	1991	2001
Andhra Pradesh	2060	3069	0.377	0.416
Assam	1544	1670	0.348	0.386
Bihar	1197	1225	0.308	0.367
Gujrat	2641	4257	0.431	0.479
Haryana	3509	4485	0.443	0.509
Karnataka	2039	3590	0.412	0.478
Kerala	1815	2778	0.591	0.638
Mahdya Pradesh	1693	2084	0.328	0.394
Maharashtra	3483	5283	0.452	0.523
Orissa	1383	1917	0.345	0.404
Punjab	3730	4897	0.475	0.537
Rajasthan	1942	2412	0.347	0.424
Tamil nadu	2237	3643	0.466	0.531
Uttaer Pradesh	1652	1552	0.314	0.388
West Bengal	2145	3745	0.404	0.472
India	2223	3234	0.381	0.472
CV (%)	36.00	40.38	19.02	16.30

Source: *PCI and HDI data is taken from National Human Development Report 2001, GOI and CSO, GOI. CV is the estimated coefficient of variation among Indian States representing ó convergence.*

To confirm σ convergence, both absolute and conditional β

convergences are being tested below for Indian economic growth (EG) and human development (HD) for the same period.

Absolute β Convergence[36]

1. $[\ln(PCI_{i,t}) - \ln(PCI_{i,t-\Gamma})]/T = \alpha_1 + \beta_1 \ln(PCI_{i,t-\Gamma}) + \mu_{1i,t}$

2. $[\ln(HDI_{i,t}) - \ln(HDI_{i,t-\Gamma})]/T = \alpha_2 + \beta_2 \ln(HDI_{i,t-\Gamma}) + \mu_{2i,t}$

$[\ln(PCI_{i,t}) - \ln(PCI_{i,t-\Gamma})]/T$ is the annual average growth rate of per capita income of the ith state for the period t and t–Γ. $\ln(PCI_{i,t})$ and $\ln(PCI_{i,t-\Gamma})$ are the natural logarithms of PCI at time t and t–Γ respectively. T is the total time length. Similarly, for HDI Convergence, equations are estimated here with 10 years lag due to non-availability of time series data for HDI, though for PCI the data is available. The β convergence equations are estimated with OLS methods taking cross-section data for 15 major Indian states. If the estimated regression coefficient $\beta<0$, there exists absolute β convergence, signifying that economically weaker states have improved the most to catch up with the rest.

The estimated absolute convergence type regression for per capita income and human development index derived for the period 1991-2001 is as follows :

$$[\ln(PCI_t) - \ln(PCI_{t-\Gamma})]/T = \underset{(-1.258)}{-0.124} + \underset{(1.585)}{0.020^{***}} \ln(PCI_{t-\Gamma}) + \mu_t$$

$R^2 = 0.162$ $F = 2.513$ $N = 15$

$$[\ln(HDI_t) - \ln(HDI_{t-\Gamma})]/T = \underset{(0.171)}{0.0008} - \underset{(-3.506)}{0.0148^{*}} \ln(HDI_{t-\Gamma}) + \mu_t$$

$R^2 = 0.486$ $F = 12.293$ $N = 15$

It can be seen that for PCI, β convergence results confirm σ convergence, as $\beta>0$ with 0.020, showing a sharp tendency of divergence across Indian states. Whereas, for HDI, $\beta<0$, the convergence has taken place proving a reduction in disparity. So though the disparity across Indian states in human development is still persistent but the degree of such differentials has shown a tendency to come down. Let us look at the results of conditional convergence type regression as follows.

Conditional β convergence[37]

1. $[\ln(PCI_{i,t}) - \ln(PCI_{i,t-\Gamma})]/T = \alpha_1 + \beta_1 \ln(PCI_{i,t-\Gamma}) + \gamma_1 \ln(UR_{i,t-\Gamma}) + \lambda_1 \ln(IR_{i,t-\Gamma}) + \eta_1 \ln(LR_{i,t-\Gamma}) + \phi_1(ESE_{i,t-\Gamma}) + \mu_{1i,t}$
2. $[\ln(HDI_{i,t}) - \ln(HDI_{i,t-\Gamma})]/T = \alpha_2 + \beta_2 \ln(HDI_{i,t-\Gamma}) + \gamma_2 \ln(LR_{i,t-\Gamma}) + \lambda_2 \ln(ELB_{i,t-\Gamma}) + \eta_2 \ln(SD_{i,t-\Gamma}) + \phi_2 \ln(SSE_{i,t-\Gamma}) + \mu_{2\,i,t}$

UR, IR and LR are the urbanization, industrialization and literacy rates of the Indian states for the year 1991. ELB, SD are expectation of life at birth and safe drinking water, SSE and ESE are social sector expenditure and economic sector expenditure in the year 1991. These independent variables are taken for both PCI and HDI as conditional variables to see their impact in regional convergence in Indian development process.

The estimated conditional convergence type regression for per capita income and human development index derived for the period 1991-2001 is as follows

$$[\ln(PCI_t) - \ln(PCI_{t-\Gamma})]/T = \underset{(0.466)}{0.0774} - \underset{(-1.897)}{0.02668^{**}} \ln(PCI_{t-\Gamma}) + \underset{(2.831)}{0.040^{**}} \ln(UR_{t-\Gamma})$$

$$+ \underset{(1.238)}{0.0146^{***}} \ln(IR_{t-\Gamma}) + \underset{(0.463)}{0.0109^{***}} \ln(LR_{t-\Gamma}) - \underset{(-0.665)}{0.0183^{***}} (ESE_{t-\Gamma}) + \mu_t$$

$R^2 = 0.609 \quad F = 5.354$

$$[\ln(HDI_t) - \ln(HDI_{t-\Gamma})]/T = \underset{(-0.280)}{-0.0637} - \underset{(-0.734)}{0.0186^{***}} \ln(HDI_{t-\Gamma}) - \underset{(-0.080)}{0.001^{***}} \ln(LR_{t-\Gamma})$$

$$+ \underset{(0.409)}{0.0165^{***}} \ln(ELB_{t-\Gamma}) + \underset{(0.552)}{0.0015^{***}} \ln(SD_{t-\Gamma}) - \underset{(-0.367)}{0.00273^{***}} \ln(SSE_{t-\Gamma}) + \mu_{,t}$$

$R^2 = 0.318 \quad F = 2.303$

(*, **, *** denote 1, 5 and 10 per cent levels of significance. Figures in the parenthesis are t-statistics. N is the number of observation).

It is interesting to see that inclusion of UR, LR, IR have made conditional coefficient $\beta<0$ in case of convergence in PCI across major Indian States. Also in case of HDI, the rate of convergence has gone high marginally from 1.48% to 1.86%, with the inclusion of variables like ELB, SD, though LR has not made any positive impact. Also the policy variables like SSE and ESE in both the equation have no significant impact on convergence.

Link between EG and HD: 1991-2001

While examining the two way link between EG and HD, it is needless to say that both are complementary to each other. The results of the following regressions justify this link.

1. $\text{In (PCI)}_{t-5} = 10.049 + 2.183 \text{ In (HDI)t} + 0.327 \text{ In (ESE)}_t + \mu_{1t}$

   $(10.54) \quad (4.704) \quad (1.188)$

   $R^2 = 0.683 \quad F=12.96 \quad N=15$

2. $\text{In (HDI)}_t = -3.629 + 0.294 \text{ In (PCI)}_{t-5} + 0.039 \text{ In (SSE)t} + \mu_{2t}$

   $(-3.030) \quad (4.068) \quad (0.180)$

   $R^2 = 0.604 \quad F = 9.161 \quad N= 15$

So the regression estimations have confirmed that, by providing social infrastructure to the nook and corner of the country, the weaker regions will be able to create the base for economic resurgence and are most likely to catch up and converge with the advanced regions in a country like India. Here comes the role of a very strong visionary democratic approach and good governance along with enormous public investment in social sector, which, to a substantial extent, can ease out such degrees of inegalitarianism and the cumulated dissatisfaction that evolves in such society during such transition phase.

Dissatisfied society: vision for a possible world

Feher and Heller conceptualized modernity as 'the dissatisfied society'.[38] By using the word 'dissatisfaction', Grumley[39] connotes the specificity of modernity from the standpoint of human needs. One can see that in a country like India, modernity is yet to fulfill such human needs. Rather a faulty development has widened and deepened the disparity between its different income strata, which has in its turn impacted its society with more malaises, more crimes, more threats of terrorism and more social unrest. The different strata of the society are dissatisfied due to opportunism, cultural degeneration, corrupt political vision and unfulfilled economic promises, whose depth and degree cannot be measured cardinally. Thus the road to modernization in India has been and is still a rocky one and sheer numbers may not be truely reflective of the society's level of dissatisfaction. Time therefore has come to make a conscious effort to redefine the image of a modern world not only through economic development but through an integrated humanitarian approach. This image of modern world probably can take into consideration the following:

- The cultural plethora of the country as a whole with a synthesis of regional/traditional/ethnic perception
- Individual consciousness and spiritual efforts to maintain happiness, peace and stability, which can extend tolerance in the society
- Development around the people and not people around development
- Development defined and practiced in an inclusive growth model and in the humanistic paradigm

If the vision for a possible world incorporates these components, modernity becomes meaningful to the extent that the level of dissatisfaction can be reduced by wiping out the three main Cs, viz., chaos, conflict and consumerism.

Notes and References

1 Tecola W. Hagos, 'Paradigm of poverty and humanism: Undoing Ethiopia's modernity' (2003), available at http:\\www.tecolahagos.com\poverty.htm.

2 A. Gerschenkron, *Economic Backwardness in Historical Perspective*, Harvard: Harvard University Press, 1962.

3 W. W. Rostow, *The Stages of Economic Growth: A Non-Communist Manifesto*, Cambridge: Cambridge University Press, 1960.

4 R. Nurkse, *Problems of Capital Accumulation in Underdeveloped Countries*, Oxford: Oxford University Press, 1953.

5 W. A. Lewis, 'Economic Development with Unlimited Supplies of labour', *Manchester School of Economics and Social Studies* 22 (1954): pp. 139-91.

6 N. Kaldor, 'A Model of Economic Growth', *The Economic Journal* 67, no. 268 (1957): pp. 591-624

7 J. Robinson, 'Notes on the Theory of Economic Development', *Quarterly Journal of Economics* 70, no. 1 (1956): pp. 65-94.

8 R. Solow, 'A Contribution to the Theory of Economic Growth', *Quarterly Journal of Economics* 70, no.1 (1956).

9 G. Myrdal, *Asian Drama: An Inquiry into the Poverty of Nations*, New York: Pantheon, 1968.

10 See Robert J. Antonio, ed. *Marx and Modernity: Key Readings and Commentary*, Malden, MA: Blackwell Publishing, 2003.

11 R. J. Barro and X. Sala-i-Martin, *Economic Growth*, New York: McGraw Hills, 1995.

12 T. W. Schultz, *Human Resource, Human Capital: Policy Issue and Research Opportunities*, New York: National Bureau of Economic Research, 1972.

13 Myrdal, *Asian Drama*.

14 M. Haq, *Reflection on Human Development*, New Delhi: Oxford University Press, 1995.

15 Amartya Sen, *Development as Freedom*, New Delhi: Oxford University Press, 1999.

16 Stefan Priesner, 'Gross National Happiness – Bhutan's Vision of Development and its Challenges' (1999) available at http:\\www.bhutanstudies.org.bt\publications\gnh\GNH_Ch3_Priesner.pdf.

17 E. F. Schumacher, *Small is Beautiful*, London: Blond and Briggs Ltd., 1973.

18 Hagos, 'Paradigm of poverty and humanism'.

19 Shankar Acharya, 'Economic Growth: Some Reflections', *Economic and Political Weekly*, 4 November 2006, pp. 4573-4577.

20 A. Richards, 'Modernity and Economic Development: The "New" American Messianism', *Middle East Policy Council* X, no. 3 (2003).

21 Partha Chatterjee, *Nationalist Thought and the Colonial World: A Derivative Discourse*, London: Zed Press, 1986, cited by David Washbrook in 'The Global History of Modernity: A Response to a Reply', *Journal of Economic and Social History of the Orient* 41, no. 3 (1998): pp 295-311.

22 Robert W. Stern, *Changing India: Bourgeois Revolution on the Subcontinent*, Second Edition, Cambridge: Cambridge University Press, 2003.

23 John Williamson, 'The Rise of the Indian Economy', *American Diplomacy.org* (2006), available at http:\\www.unc.edu\

depts\diplomat\item\2006\0406\will\williamson_india.html.

24 S. Sivasubramonian, *The National Income of India in the Twentieth Century*, New Delhi Oxford University Press, 2000, cited by Acharya, in 'Economic Growth'.

25 Acharya, 'Economic Growth'.

26 A. Bhaduri, 'Alternatives in Industrialisation', *Economic and Political Weekly* XLII, no. 18 (2007), pp. 1597-1601.

27 Amartya Sen, *Identity and Violence: The Illusion of Destiny*, New Delhi: Penguin Books, 2006, p. 120.

28 N. Banerjee and Sugata Marjit, eds. *Development, Displacement and Disparity: India in the last Quarter of the Twentieth Century*, New Delhi Orient Longman, 2005, p. 2.

29 Ibid.

30 *Hindustan Times*, 28 June 2007.

31 *The Times of India*, 26 July 2007.

32 Bhaduri, 'Alternatives in Industrialisation', pp.1597-1601.

33 Human Development Report, 2006, UNDP.

34 *Hindustan Times*, 27 February 2007.

35 *The Times of India*, 4 July 2007.

36 M. Ghosh, 'Economic Growth and Human Development in Indian States', *Economic and Political Weekly* XLI, no. 30 (2006): pp. 3321-3329.

37 Ibid

38 Agnes Heller and F. Feher, *The Post-Modern Political Condition*, Cambridge: Polity Press (1988).

39 J. Grumley, 'Dissatisfied Society', *New German Critique*, no. 58 (Winter, 1993): pp. 153-178.

Index